THE AFGHAN WAR AND ITS GEOPOLITICAL IMPLICTIONS FOR INDIA

The Afghan War and its Geopolitical Implications for India

Edited by

SALMAN HAIDAR

ACADEMY OF THIRD WORLD STUDIES
JAMIA MILLIA ISLAMIA

MANOHAR
2004

First published 2004

ISBN 81-7304-558-5

Published by
Ajay Kumar Jain for
Manohar Publishers & Distributors
4753/23 Ansari Road, Daryaganj
New Delhi 110 002

Typeset by
Kohli Print
Delhi 110 051

Printed at
Lordson Publishers Pvt. Ltd.
New Delhi 110 007

Contents

Introduction

SALMAN HAIDAR

Afghanistan remains near the top of the international agenda. The US-led attack brought that country into an unfortunate prominence, and several of the issues that raised concern about Afghanistan continue to demand attention. True, the Taliban regime was routed in short order, Al Qaeda was scattered, a civilian government installed, and a fair amount achieved through local effort and international assistance. But there are repeated reminders that matters remain fraught in Afghanistan, a country long renowned for the independent and unruly spirit of its people. The warlords who had plagued the land are back, having been given new life as auxiliaries in the anti-Taliban campaign. Central authority is tenuous. Development work is slow, as most donors—with honourable exceptions—have forgotten the promises they made in the immediate aftermath of the campaign. Disturbing, too, is the re-emergence of groups of Taliban, not to mention the Al Qaeda cadres who have also re-surfaced here and there. Osama bin Laden remains at large, and thus a major goal of the anti-terror campaign remains unachieved. The Afghan war is over but its longer term impact is far from clear.

It is against this background that a few months ago the Academy of Third World Studies of the Jamia Millia held a seminar on 'The Geo-Political and Socio-Economic Implications of USA's Involvement in Afghanistan'. A number of leading scholars and experts were requested to take part in the seminar, and this volume is a collection of the papers they submitted on the occasion. Major issues relevant to Afghanistan are examined here: strategic questions, oil and gas, transit issues, matters of internal cohesion and stability, fundamentalism, the terrorist threat. The impact on India and Indo–Pak relations is closely scrutinized, and also a possible role for India in Afghanistan. The effect of Afghan developments on wider regional relationships is also looked at, with special attention being given to Central Asia. Important policy projections flow from this examination of issues, which is not of academic interest alone but gives many pointers to policy makers and diplomats.

The keynote address was delivered by *J.N. Dixit*. He sets present-day developments in a historical perspective, leading up to what came to be known as the Saur Revolution, through which the local Communist party seized power in Kabul. Intense factional strife within the party soon led to the entry of Soviet forces in a bid to stabilize the situation, but instead it provoked a huge international reaction that brought prolonged struggle and destruction. Nor was there any end to it when eventually the Soviet forces were compelled to depart, for rival leaders remained engaged in an ever fiercer and more destructive fight for personal and group ascendancy. In these circumstances, the Taliban were able to seize power, and the forces of religious intolerance and extremism came to dominate the country. It was the climactic events of 11 September 2001 that sealed the fate of the Taliban regime as they brought overwhelming American force to bear on Afghanistan in order to scatter the extremists and, eventually, start the process of rebuilding the country.

The contrasting roles of America and the other countries in the international coalition, the UK prominent among them, are described by Dixit. America, as he sees it, has assumed a broader strategic task, linked to its long-term plans to combat international terrorism and extremism, while the others are principally concerned with internal peacekeeping, especially in providing security to Kabul. The US military presence in Afghanistan is part of its enlarged presence throughout the region, with implications for India and Pakistan as well as for major powers like Russia and China. For the present, dissent from the emerging scheme for a new US-led order is muted. In the longer run, Afghanistan's future can only be determined by its own leadership, aided by an outside world that seeks stability and order in that country.

The Afghan war and US policy towards India and Pakistan is the theme of the paper by *Kanti Bajpai*. He observes that as the USA geared up for war, it found in Pakistan a liability that could become an asset, in contrast to India, which was an asset that could become a liability. Pakistan was by far the most useful launch pad for military operations, but its dubious association with the Taliban and with religious extremists in general led to questions being raised about its reliability. India, by contrast, was a reliable ally and an alternative launch pad in case of need, but could create serious problems if it tried to profit from the crisis by itself mounting a direct assault upon Pakistan. US policy thus had to steer carefully between the two. Pakistan was given no option but to support the war wholeheartedly, for which it received substantial political and economic benefits, while India's forbearance was encouraged by promises that cross border terrorism would be the next target and by encouraging its hope of a larger future role as a regional partner of America, commensurate with its status as an emerging power.

The successful attack on the Taliban and Al Qaeda was beneficial for Pakistan, itself under pressure from these sources. However, terrorist violence in India grew and became more audacious. Pakistan did nothing to restrain the terrorist groups, despite its assurances, and eventually India felt obliged to respond with coercive diplomacy. Armies were moved into forward positions amidst preparations for war. America was seriously alarmed and undertook a strenuous diplomatic course to prevent an outbreak that could have had a nuclear dimension. While the crisis has wound down, relations between India and Pakistan have never been worse. The author argues that America has not been as successful in managing regional affairs as it was in the war, and seems to have run out of ideas on what to do next.

In his survey of Afghanistan, *Jagat Mehta* contends that the tragedy of that country came about as a result of unwarranted attitudes associated with the Cold War. By the 1970s, Afghanistan had evolved a pattern of coexistence with the two superpowers of the time that was threatening to neither. The replacement of the Daud regime by a government of the Afghan Communist party did not affect this reality, and even the entry of Soviet troops in 1979 was for internal damage control, not to mount a threat to America. India was ill advised to side with the USSR at that time, for that was a departure from the non-aligned principle of non-aggression; for the first time, India found itself out of step with neighbours and friends.

Mehta bemoans the lost opportunities in Indo–Pak relations where patient diplomacy could have headed off the increasing Islamic radicalization of the region. Even today, despite the heavy odds against it, he advocates a joint Indo–Pak regional initiative that could inter alia help Afghanistan. That country has always belonged to South Asia, and instability there affects Pakistan, also, indirectly, India. It is in the long term interest of both countries, and of the entire region, that they should develop beneficial functional cooperation that could mature into a wider regionalism.

Iran has been profoundly affected by two US-led wars on its flanks and *Gulshan Dietl* looks at Iranian perceptions of the Gulf War of 1991 and the Afghan war a decade later. Still licking its wounds from its own long war with Iraq, Iran did not conceal its delight when the invasion of Kuwait brought US-led retribution upon Saddam Hussein. There was a subsequent easing of its relations with USA but this did not eventually reach very far: Iran continued to be seen by America as a threat to order in the region. However, Iran's relations with the Gulf States improved considerably. The Afghan war once again brought Iran and USA into rough alignment, for Iran had long been the most unyielding foe of the Taliban. It had been drawn into the intra-Afghan struggle, with more than one of the Afghan warlords looking to Iran for support, and large numbers of Afghan refugees on its soil. With the ouster of the Taliban, problems between Iran and Afghanistan were eased and Iran began providing help for Afghan reconstruction. Yet a considerable rivalry between the two countries remains, one reason being that each would like to provide transit facilities for Central Asian oil and gas. Theirs is thus a complicated relationship.

The expectation that US-Iran ties might improve subsequent to the Afghan war has not materialized: on the contrary, Iran has been clubbed with Iraq and North Korea in the 'axis of evil'. The hostile American attitude has strengthened hardliners within Iran, at the expense of the reformists. Iran will be gratified by the American assault on Saddam Hussein, though its role will be limited to watching from the sidelines, and no early repairing of its ties with America can be expected.

US policy towards South Asia is placed in a global context by *Achin Vanaik*, who sees domination of the world economy and geo-strategic dominion over the Eurasian landmass as America's overweening goals. Neo-liberal economic globalization promotes the purposes of the American state as does the eastward expansion of NATO, which keeps Russia marginalized and precludes any new European security initiative that could in time challenge American ascendancy. The first Gulf War of 1991 saw America pursuing its strategic aim of controlling oil production and of keeping all rivals out of the region. The Oslo Peace Accords of 1993 are to be viewed as part of a global realignment that greatly favours USA and Israel, and though the Palestine leadership has acquiesced in it, the Palestinian people have strongly resisted.

Turning to South Asia and the various moves to upgrade Indo–US ties, Vanaik concludes that despite the talk of a new era, there is little to show on the ground. America pursues unilateral nuclear and anti-terrorism policies, and in the 'fateful triangle' of US, India, and Pakistan, the two South Asian nations compete in wooing American favour against the other. On its part, America has distinct and separate long term geo-strategic interests in each of the two. It should not be assumed that its greater involvement in the region, and in the Kashmir issue, will take it in the direction India seeks: other options for America could be under consideration. Meanwhile, those who want a better and more humane world order must struggle against 'American imperialism'.

The Indian response to US involvement in Afghanistan is examined by *V.P. Dutt*. He refers to the genuine shock and horror felt in India at the events of 11 September, and the immediate offer of all logistic help, even before any request was received from USA. India's own prolonged struggle against terrorism was a factor in this prompt response, as was the expectation that now finally the Pakistan-based terrorism assailing India could be scotched. Geo-political realities are such that America needed Pakistan more than India for its Afghan campaign, and this was bound to affect its approach to the two countries. Pakistan was compelled to do a U-turn in its policy of supporting the Taliban and to provide a launch pad for the military operations, for which it received generous financial consideration. Dutt states that this may not be a short-term revival of US–Pakistan ties, notwithstanding private assurances to India that Pak-based terrorism would be challenged in the second phase of the anti-terror campaign.

The Afghan operations drove top Taliban and Al Qaeda leaders to seek refuge in Pakistan, apparently with the complicity of some Pakistani authorities, though this was officially denied. USA adopted a dual-track approach to South Asia, reflecting its strengthening interests in each of the two contending states. For India, the bane of continued terrorist attacks constrained it to mobilize its army against Pakistan, which was a strategy that worked up to a point. However, some Indians drew the fallacious conclusion that India was now free to follow the Israeli and American lead and mount an armed attack, which was emphatically not on the cards. The author concludes that these events have made both parties totally dependent on American initiative in the region, including Kashmir.

The part played by Russia and Central Asia in the anti-terrorist campaign is *Anuradha Chenoy's* topic. She describes the main features of the Central Asian oil and gas deposits, their extent, American interest in obtaining access to them and the problems of getting them to the global market. After 11 September, America has moved purposefully to develop its ties with the Central Asian States (CAS), which became crucial to its war effort against the Taliban and Al Qaeda. The CAS, too, had much to gain from the American presence. US interests extend beyond the CAS to Trans Caucasia, where it is promoting a new pipeline for Central Asian oil and gas. This will bypass existing pipelines through Russia, which is steadily losing its regional dominance. American companies with very high political support are aggressively pushing their way in. Russia may now be constrained to seek a junior partner's role in the US-led oil-related schemes for the future. As for the CAS, they have to maintain a delicate balance in their dealings with Russia, whose embrace they may shun but whose support they continue to need. US involvement gives them more elbow room. Chenoy concludes that the unfolding of hegemonic politics will be the theme of the future for the region.

USA and Central Asia is also the subject of *Nimmi Kurian's* paper. She sees the quest for energy security as the main focus of American interest in the region, underpinned by appropriate strategic and military policies. The US need for energy imports is set to grow, for which it will continue to look to the Gulf but will also seek to diversify its sources of supply. The Caspian basin is an important alternative. Being landlocked, its oil and gas must move to the market through a network of pipelines, whose alignment cannot disregard political and security considerations. US companies have been very active in the area, with strong official support in consideration of the country's political and strategic interest. The dominance of Russia in the region stands reduced, even while it is seen as a useful source of oil supply.

The military imperatives for the USA are clearly discerned. It pursues geo-political dominance and maintains its military buildup even in the post-Afghanistan phase. It erroneously confronts Islamic fundamentalism by military means and sees Islam as the new enemy of the West. Taking on a global burden as USA has done is replete with risk and could stoke instability. The adjacent regional powers are uneasy and the prospects are uncertain.

After surveying several US interventions in foreign lands during the twentieth century, *Shri Prakash* describes Afghanistan's non-aligned policy and its even-handed approach to the superpowers. Some high level visits and substantial aid helped America maintain a steady relationship with that country. Matters changed drastically when Soviet troops entered Afghanistan at the end of the 1970s: America reacted strongly and provided massive arms and logistics support for anti-Soviet Afghan groups, for which Pakistan became the conduit. India under Mrs Gandhi consistently came out in favour of an independent, non-aligned and democratic Afghanistan. The eventual Soviet withdrawal was followed by intense internecine fighting, which facilitated the rise of the Taliban, in which Pakistan's ISI had a hidden role. The draconian fundamentalist laws they enacted were widely resented, so that there was support within the region for the American attack after 11 September. Pakistan was forced to cooperate with USA, although its continued backing for terrorism in Kashmir showed its double standards.

For the future, there are many problems before the weak and impoverished Kabul administration. Differences between various ethnic groups persist. There is need for a national army and police, and for extensive development measures beginning with the restoration of agriculture. Elections by themselves are not enough to solve the country's problems.

The final piece comes from *Hari Vasudevan* who provides an account of the calculations that have shaped succeeding phases of Russian policy in Central and South-West Asia. Presently, even though the Ministry of Foreign Affairs has its own importance, policy formulation is firmly in the control of President Putin. Notwithstanding a lingering desire on the part of some of his advisers for an independent Russian role, Putin came out in favour of cooperation with the US and NATO, and solidarity with the anti-Taliban alliance. Differences with the USA on strategic issues were relegated to the background and Putin closely involved himself in the Afghan campaign. Significantly, he turned away from the neo-isolationism that some Russians preferred. One reason for this was his steadily decreasing interest in the CIS states, involvement with which offered little direct benefit to Russia. He might have concluded that a substantial presence in Central Asia was not worth the effort, a lesson that must have been noted by Indian and other observers.

In sum, the articles presented here look closely at Afghanistan and, in a broad sweep, examine how Afghan events have affected the region all around. The role of India and the fallout on Indo–Pak relations receive particular attention. So too does the American policy towards the region and what looks like its intention of a long term stay. Central Asia, no less than Afghanistan, has come into new focus, as the repository of important energy resources and as the setting for economic and strategic rivalry between major nations. The contributors to this volume are specialists in their respective areas and the issues they have highlighted are those that will continue to draw global attention and will need to be addressed in the shaping of future policy.

Nation-building Process in Afghanistan After 1970

J.N. DIXIT

The early 1970s were the watershed in Afghanistan's history, beginning with the overthrow of King Zahir Shah by his cousin Mohammed Daud in a bloodless military coup in 1973. Trauma and violence became an integral part of the experience of the Afghan people and State, culminating in the present developments in that country.

If one were to deliberately compartmentalize trends of international politics and Afghanistan's foreign relations separately from the socio-economic and political developments in the country, one would not be wrong in concluding that its history, since the middle of the nineteenth century, has been chequered and there have been continuing attempts at nation-building, especially against external forces interested in Afghanistan due to geo-strategic considerations. While attempting to understand the country, however, some fundamental, even elemental, factors about the emergence of Afghanistan as a nation state must be kept in mind.

Afghanistan emerged as a unified nation state when the Persian and Mughal empires declined in the mid-eighteenth century. The Afghans flourished under Pushtoon domination and Afghanistan acquired its current territorial identity under the rule of Ahmed Shah Abdali. Territories that were previously under the jurisdiction of the Persian empire, the Mughal empire, and later the Khanats to the north, from roughly the fifteenth century, began to merge into a single geo-political unit under the Durrani empire. Before this first phase of national consolidation could be completed, the advent of European colonial powers in Central Asia, South Asia and the Gulf impinged on Afghanistan.

The competition between Russia and Britain for strategic domination and economic objectives in the Central and South Asian regions from the mid-nineteenth century onwards is well known and does not need detailed exposition. Suffice it to say that what is known as the Great Game was nothing 'Great' as far as the Afghan people were concerned. The acquisitive confrontation between the imperial colonial powers disrupted the tenuous process of the consolidation of the new multi-ethnic, multilingual and pluralistic Afghan State. Despite this disruption and the feudal and monarchical power structure of Afghanistan from the times of Emir Dost Mohammed and King Amanullah to King Zahir Shah, efforts at creating a composite national identity continued. The exercise, however, remained asymmetrical with the Pushtoons remaining a dominant factor.

The most radical and vibrant phase of national consolidation in Afghan history during the twentieth century was the political, social, and economic reforms undertaken by King Amanullah (1919–29). Amanullah tried unsuccessfully to resolve the internal contradictions between the forces of modernization and those of orthodox Islam and tribalism by initiating extensive reforms in the spheres of education, women's literacy, abolition of purdah, land reforms, etc. He failed because he could not carry the Afghan people with him—his vision was far ahead of the political orientations and social mores of Afghanistan. Amanullah faced tribal opposition, which evolved into military conflict and ultimately resulted in his exile to Italy. History repeated itself forty-four years later with King Zahir Shah too going into exile in Italy,

Zahir Shah's Regime

Zahir Shah was perhaps the most practical and rational leader of the Afghans in the twentieth century. Learning from King Amanullah's experience, he did not rush and moved gradually into modernizing Afghanistan and consolidating its identity, transcending ethnic and tribal components of Afghan civil society. Realizing that he did not have the resources or the power to exclude external influences on Afghanistan politics and economy, he allocated different parts of his kingdom to the major powers desiring a foothold in his country as areas of political influence and economic activity.

The northern half of Afghanistan was 'allowed' to be under the primary influence and activities of the former Soviet Union and the socialist camp. The southern areas were the arena of influence of the Western powers. Zahir Shah adopted an approach of non-involvement and neutrality throughout his 40-year regime, even during major upheavals like World War II and the subsequent Cold War. It is this insistence on social and economic minimalism that ultimately resulted in his overthrow—he did not anticipate the challenge that he was about to face from the interplay between rivalry for power in his family and the incremental political modernization of an emerging middle class of professionals and military officers trained abroad. Daud Khan exploited this to overthrow Zahir Shah, promising political modernization and socio-economic reforms in Afghanistan.

This brings us to the 1970s, the point of time earlier mentioned as the basic term of reference for examining current developments in Afghanistan.

Mohammed Daud

When Daud captured power in 1973, he inherited an atmosphere of bitterness and economic confusion. Parliamentary elections, which were due in August–September 1973, ran into difficulties because of the difference of opinion between the judiciary and the cabinet on the Supreme Court's role as the watchdog of parliamentary elections. While the judiciary felt that the job belonged to a separate and independent body, the executive, as well as several legal experts, felt that the Supreme Court fitted the role best. A joint committee of representatives of the Cabinet and the Supreme Court could not come to any agreed conclusion. The elections were delayed, finally happening much later.

Though Afghanistan's export performance during Zahir Shah's reign improved, many West-sponsored banking and industrial projects got stuck in procedural wrangles. An increase in foreign loans to Afghanistan during 1969–73 had greatly increased Afghanistan's total foreign indebtedness. The situation was compounded by the lack of infrastructural institutions in the country to manage finances or the emerging industrialization. The armed forces and the small urbanized middle class were getting impatient with the role of the feudal and royal power structure and the very gradual approach to modernization, spread of education. Daud was expected to restructure the Afghan polity with the following objectives:

- Making the elected Parliament a centre of the power structure.
- Ensuring that the Executive had greater representation from the media, academia, and the middle class; removal of members of the royal family and related feudal order from the Cabinet and senior positions in the government.
- Moving away from the pro-Western tilt in foreign and economic policies which had characterized the last years of the Zahir Shah regime, so that a more balanced relationship with the Soviet Union

and Iran could be revived. Daud was also expected to keep the Pushtoonistan claim alive.

Daud, however, failed to meet any of these expectations. He failed to manage the economy well and he was not inclined to assert Afghan nationalism and nationalistic positions vis-à-vis the immediate neighbours and important powers interested in Afghanistan. The biggest mistake he made was to exclude the officers of the armed forces and intellectuals of the Parcham and Khalq movements from power sharing when he consolidated his position by 1973–6.

From the middle of 1976 onwards, the alienation between Daud and his earlier supporters was more or less complete. This ultimately resulted in the army-led coup in 1978. Daud and members of his family were killed in the basement of the Royal Palace in downtown Kabul. The attack on the presidential residence was led by a young armoured corps officer of the Afghanistan army, Khan Aslam Watanjar. The rule of Afghanistan's royal family of Durrani descent ended with Mr Taraqi and the People's Democratic Party of Afghanistan (PDPA) coming to power in 1978.

The PDPA and Soviet Union

The objective of this prologue is not to give a chronologically detailed description of the events that led to the Soviet intrusion into Afghanistan in support of the PDPA rule, or the Saur Revolution as it was called, but to describe the broad trends and events that led to this event towards the end of 1979.

The Taraqi regime that came to power had leftist ideological orientations. Throughout the year that Taraqi ruled Afghanistan, the country's relations with Pakistan and Iran deteriorated. The Taraqi regime also did not maintain an equal foreign policy with USA and the Soviet Union. Policies were initiated that could only have expanded the Soviet economic, technological, and military presence in Afghanistan.

Compared to the modernization and gradualness that characterized the Afghan regime from 1933 to 1978, the PDPA regime decided to launch radical programmes of literacy, women's education, and rapid modernization of the economy, and infrastructural facilities of transport and communications. The Taraqi regime also moved to create government institutions with representation from the various tribal and ethnic groups which constituted the Afghan nation. The domination of Pushtoons in Afghan politics was questioned and sought to be modified. The role of the orthodox clergy was also challenged under the new scheme of things.

The government by now was manned by an increasing number of PDPA cadres, mostly trained in the Soviet Union and East Europe. These cadres replaced a majority of the public servants of the old school. Vested interests in the traditional Afghan power structure were challenged and destroyed in the short span of a few months. Those from the old Afghan elite who could afford to left the country for North America and Europe. Others started migrating to Pakistan, India, and the Gulf. These vested interests with linkages in Pakistan and Iran (the Iranian revolution was still a year away and took place in 1979) generated apprehensions about the likely results of the anti-Daud coup and the PDPA 'revolution'.

The simple argument of Taraqi's detractors was that Afghanistan, a non-aligned Muslim country, was being forcibly turned communist. The other point of worry was that the Soviet Union would find a permanent foothold in Afghanistan, which would be a challenge to American, Pakistani, and Iranian interests, as well as the interests of the countries of the Gulf.

President Daud's pro-Western tilt from the end of 1975 onwards had resulted in Soviet resentment against his regime. When the Afghan army, which was considerably dependent on Soviet supplies and training, conducted a coup against Daud, it had covert Soviet backing. Once Taraqi took over, Soviet advisers started working in different departments of the Afghan government. Both the PDPA and the government patterned themselves on the Soviet Communist Party and governmental systems. The royal family, the Muslim clergy, and the old elite stood excluded from the new arrangements. This gave these elements an opportunity to argue that the Taraqi regime supported by the Soviet Union was challenging the traditional Afghan national identity, and, more importantly, was hurting the religious feelings and the collective Islamic faith of the people of Afghanistan.

Taraqi was in power for a little less than one year. His hold over the government remained tenuous. The major problem he faced was to keep PDPA united, given the intense rivarly and undercurrent of antagonism between the Pushtoon-dominated Khalq faction and non-Pushtoon cadres belonging to the Parcham faction of the PDPA.

One is conscious that this can be seen as an oversimplification of the Afghan situation. However, these are the broad paradigms within which events developed in the country in 1978–9.

1979–1989

The period between 1979 and 1989 was in a sense a sort of Great Leap Forward aimed at national consolidation and modernization. The Soviet-backed Saur Revolution had three purposes—(a) to dismantle permanently the feudal and tribal elite power structure of Afghanistan, (b) to restructure Afghanistan into a modern, secular nation state, and (c) to balance off the traditional Pushtoon ethnic domination of Afghan politics through constitutional and political means aimed at giving due representation to other major ethnic groups of Afghanistan, namely, the Tajiks, the Hazaras, Uzbeks, and other smaller ethnic communities.

The Saur Revolution failed due to various reasons:

- The programme of modernization and reforms, and the move towards the creation of a secular state, did not have the support of the Afghan people.
- The opposition to these programmes was not limited to Pushtoons. Most of the population belonging to all ethnic groups felt threatened and were suspicious of the reforms.
- The conflict between Pushtoons and non-Pushtoons (Khalq and Parcham) in the PDPA prevented unity within the ruling party.
- The Saur Revolution lost credibility because it was perceived as a 'Soviet' revolution forcefully foisted on the Afghans despite the legitimacy or necessity of the objectives of the revolution.
- The major Western powers perceived the revolution as a strategic threat to their interests in the Gulf, and as an instrument in Soviet strategic expansion beyond Central Asia to South Asia and the Gulf.
- Equally important were the apprehensions of the governments of the Muslim countries neighbouring Afghanistan that the ideological fallout of the Afghan revolution, following soon after the Iranian revolution, would threaten their stability and security. This is apart from members of the old power structure at the feudal and tribal levels, seeing the Saur Revolution as dangerous to their vested interests.
- Finally, the last effort at national consolidation also failed, not only because of the contradictions in the internal politics of Afghanistan but also because of direct tangible external intrusive involvement. This

> phenomenon took the form of an international problem and there was a subsequent political campaign against the Afghan revolution and the systematic and full-scale organization of military resistance to Afghan and Soviet troops backing it.

Agreements signed in Saudi Arabia and in Geneva marked the end of this phase with the withdrawal of Soviet forces. Then began a number of unsuccessful attempts at establishing a new government by the various Mujahideen groups and the remnants of the PDPA.

Instead of the establishment of a stable national government, the Soviet withdrawal resulted in a civil war situation during the period 1990–6. Mujadiddi and Rabbani formed tenuous governments, after Najib stepped down. The conflict between Hekmatyar and Masood, and later General Dostum, created levels of conflict and political instability where no meaningful efforts could be undertaken for the stabilization of the country or national consolidation. It is this anarchic situation that led to the creation of the Taliban and its gradual hold over most of Afghanistan.

It is worthwhile noting that the US and other powers withdrew support from the various Mujahideen groups when they felt that these groups were not capable of establishing a government in Afghanistan. Afghanistan was left to its own devices during 1992–6, Pakistan, Saudi Arabia, and Iran being the only countries actively interested in Afghanistan developments. Their purpose was to establish a stable Islamic government in Afghanistan that would not succumb to any form of Soviet (and later Russian) influences. The Shia–Sunni divide manifested itself in the undercurrents of competition and confrontation in Afghanistan between Iran on the one hand and Pakistan, Turkey, and Saudi Arabia on the other. The fact should not be ignored that the latter three are close allies of the United States.

The Taliban

The Taliban came to power and consolidated their position in Afghanistan between 1996–9, primarily with the support of Saudi Arabia and Pakistan, and, to some extent, Turkey.

Whatever one's criticism of the Taliban, they had a clear philosophy and approach towards national consolidation and reforms. Their aim was to create a strong orthodox Afghan Islamic nation state. They believed, and wisely, that the stability of Afghanistan could be guaranteed only when Afghan politics is dominated by the Pushtoons, who constitute the majority of the population of Afghanistan. Neither the Taliban leadership nor the Taliban cadres had any interest in, or knowledge about, national consolidation and reconstruction in modern terms. They did not have any interest in evolving a composite national identity cutting across the ethnic and subordinate national identities of different sections of Afghan civil society.

While the Taliban brought some stability and law and order inside Afghanistan, there was no attempt at social reforms or developmental work to remedy the results of the destruction of the previous seventeen years. In fact, the Taliban were purposefully opposed to the creation of a modern civil society or nation state. They had no commitment to international norms of human rights. They were officially discriminatory against women. They were determined to establish an Islamic State on the basis of their warped antediluvian interpretation of Islam. The Taliban's ideology and intellectual orientation were in tune with violent and orthodox Islamic extremist movements in different parts of the world. In consequence, while consolidating themselves in power in Afghanistan, the Taliban also developed close contacts with extremist Islamic militant groups who were operating across the globe from Afghanistan in the West to the Philippines in the East. It is in this process that the Taliban government provided bases to Osama bin Laden and forged links with the Al Qaeda movement. Spreading the message of Islam through violent and aggressive means became a matter that received greater attention than dealing with the problems and processes of Afghanistan's national consolidation.

The Western democracies, particularly the USA, had no interest in the political destiny of the Afghanistan people during this period. Their only concern was that the Taliban, or whichever government was in Afghanistan, was not allowed to help in revival of Russian strategic influence in Afghanistan and the Gulf. A more important interest of the Western democracies was to have a friendly regime in Afghanistan that would be sufficiently stable to support US policies of outsourcing oil and hydrocarbon energy resources from Turkmenistan, Uzbekistan, and Kazakhstan.

The pipeline through which oil and natural gas could be supplied by American multinationals to the vast markets in South Asia had to come through Afghanistan. So the limited purpose and logic of the interests of the Western countries in Afghanistan was obvious. There were not even formal advocacies to the Taliban government to mend its ways and to allow the Afghan civil society to function normally. The US State Department and some US multinational corporations, which had initiated contacts with the Taliban government for this purpose between 1996–7, backed out because of the continuous civil war situation in Afghanistan and incremental worries about extremist Islam on the part of the USA.

Disappointed at the USA's withdrawing support, the Taliban proceeded to generate financial resources by entering into the world drug market. Afghanistan became the second largest producer of opium poppy crop after India. But unlike the controlled production in India, the Taliban government openly utilized the crop to generate cash flow through manufacture and trading of narcotics. This money was also made available to extremist Islamic militant groups operating from bases in Afghanistan and in other countries of West Asia. Irrationally fanatical Islamization, active involvement in terrorist movements, and conscious rejection of modern norms of building up of a civil society characterized the Taliban regime.

The terrorist attacks in New York and Washington on 11 September 2001 were the culmination of the Taliban's involvement in terrorist activities in Kenya, Uganda, and in the Muslim countries of Maghreb and West Asia. This is apart from logistical and training support for violent Muslim mercenaries who operate against India in Jammu and Kashmir. The political conundrum was that while during the late 1970s to 1996, external involvement in Afghanistan derailed national consolidation, from 1996 till October 2001, it is the engagement of Western democracies that isolated the Taliban regime, making it follow insular and antediluvian policies leaving all processes of national consolidation in disarray, neglect, and total confusion.

After October 2001

This brings us to the latest stage in Afghanistan developments. The international anti-terrorist military campaign led by the US has ousted the Taliban from power. There is intensely active external involvement in Afghanistan with three dimensions—(a) the continuing campaign against Al Qaeda and Taliban cadres, (b) providing internal security to the Afghan government and the Afghan State, and (c) stabilizing the new Afghanistan political dispensation and parallely providing across-the-board assistance for national reconstruction, economic development, and the creation of stable democratic institutions.

Another exercise in national consolidation commenced after the Bonn Conference on Afghanistan in October 2002. The *Loya Jirga* or the National Assembly session that concluded on 18 June 2002 made some very tenuous beginnings to move forward towards stabilizing Afghanistan.

The ground realities in Afghanistan remain volatile. Though the *Loya Jirga* took decisions about convening the Parliament, creating of a government, etc., factional contradictions remain rampant in Afghanistan. The Afghan Minister for Civil Aviation and Vice-President of the government were killed. Important political leaders like Rashid Dostum, Gulbuddin Hekmatyar, Barhanuddin Rabbani, remain disaffected. The rivalries and suspicions between Pushtoon and non-Pushtoon ethnic power structures remain a pernicious influence against political consolidation. The Afghan government's writ does not run beyond Kabul and its surroundings. The large amount of economic aid promised at the Tokyo Confernece cannot be effectively utilized in these circumstances, although some projects have been initiated. Tensions have emerged between the Afghan common citizens and the foreign forces operating under US and British command in the country. Programmes for training and creation of a new police and military force and administrative cadres are facing problems of ethnic tension and divided loyalties of the trainees belonging to different factions.

It is in this context that one assesses the impact of external forces on the nation-building processes in Afghanistan. The most important external entity involved in this process is the USA. Keeping in mind developments and ingredients of US policies so far, the presence of US and other allied foreign entities in Afghanistan could be analysed in terms of discernible objectives.

In terms of inter se priorities, the more immediate objective of the US presence is to mop up remnants of Taliban and Al Qaeda forces in Afghanistan and in north-western parts of Pakistan, to the extent possible. That this campaign still continues, is clarified by a Commanding General of the Central Command of the US, Lt. General Tommy Franks, in March 2003. The US bombing and ground action in eastern Afghanistan throughout the first half of March confirms this situation.

Another factor that compounds the negative situation is that large numbers of Taliban and Al Qaeda cadres who had escaped from the US-led military campaign, with their arms intact, have merged with the local population. Latest reports indicate that these cadres, some of whom are also based in north-western parts of Pakistan, have regrouped and have commenced guerrilla warfare to which the United States is reacting.

It is important to note that the major powers led by the United States envisage two distinctiv roles—one is an US-led coalition military force, which would be concentrating on the anti-terrorist war, and the second is a combined military force led by Britain consisting of troops from Western democracies who would function as a peacekeeping and internal security force for the stabilization of Afghanistan. It is logical, therefore, to conclude that the US-led anti-terrorist force would play a strategic role in Afghanistan while the other coalition force led by Britain would play the role of stabilizing the politics of the country, supporting the interim Afghan government till such time when it is no longer needed.

It is the broader objectives of the US military presence in different parts of Pakistan (Peshawar, Quetta, Pesni, Gwador, and Karachi), Uzbekistan, Azerbaijan, and the Gulf countries that merit a rational speculative prognosis to the extent possible.

US political and military leaders led by President Bush, as well as Prime Minister Tony Blair of the UK, have publicly stated that the war against terrorism would be a 'long struggle'. President Bush has been more specific, talking about the 'Axis of Eveil' mentioning North Korea, Iran, and Iraq, indicating that these countries could be the next target of US military operations. There are currently seven countries on the USA's list of terrorism sponsoring States: Cuba, Iran, Iraq, Libya, North Korea, Sudan, and Syria. Out of these, only Cuba and Libya lie outside the geographical limits of Central and West Asia. The augmented US military presence from Turkey in the north to the Philippines in South-East Asia, is clearly a physical manifestation of strategic and security understandings which the US has reached with various countries of this region to contain religious extremism and violence as well as to stabilize the region with a view to ensuring long-term energy and economic security for the international community, particularly, the security of Western democracies and their allies.

It must also be realized that three out of five central Asian countries are also members of the Partnership for Peace arrangements of NATO. The twin macro-level strategic objectives of the Amercian politico-strategic presence in the region (it is indicated that this would be a long-term presence) are, in a manner, an exercise to balance off or prevent any excessive domination or influence by China and Russia on the countries of the region. The second objective is to secure the energy resources of the Gulf and to have long-term access to the proven hydrocarbon and mineral resources of the central Asian countries. This is apart from the attraction of investment opportunities and the markets of Central Asia. Equally relevant is the US objective of stabilizing the nuclear weapons and missiles security environment in the region. The presence of US troops and creation of a pattern of political and security concentration, positions the US to effectively intervene in any nuclear confrontation between India and Pakistan. Such an exercise could contribute to gradual capping of *Sanitaire* nuclear weapons and missile capacities of these two countries and to persuade them to undertake effective arms control measures within the framework of the international Non-Proliferation Agenda determined by the five permanent members of the UN Security Council. The *Cordon Sanitaire,* or the structuring the politico-military stabilization of the security environment, being put in the place by the US would also be a more direct instrument in preventing the horizontal proliferation of weapons of mass destruction in countries stretching from North Korea to Iran. This assessment is not purely speculative. This message has been inherent in public pronouncements of President Bush, US Defence Secretary Donald Rumsfeld, and the testimonies given by the senior officials of the US government to various committees of the US Congress. More recent reports of the Congressional Research Service on Terrorism and Non-violence imply these underlying objectives of the US policies.

In the short term, the major powers of the region, Russia and China, seem to have reconciled themselves to these new equations being forged under the leadership of the United States. It is also obvious that these policy orientations will face resentment and dissent not only from these major powers, and to some extent from India, but also from important European powers like Germany and France.

Developments since 11 September 2001 are not limited to international consensus about fighting terrorism. They also signal critical changes in the strategic and security environment in the Asian region and in the new global order aimed at by the United States. The major task of Indian foreign and strategic policies now is to carefully assess the extent to which these new arrangements would benefit India or militate against India's substantive security interests and freedom of options. It is obvious that in the short and medium term, positive equation with the US is the practical option.

Many important and detailed aspects of the manner in which external entities would influence the dynamics of nation-building and the creation of democracy in Afghanistan have not been covered here. The most important point to remember, however, is that the fractious politics of Afghanistan cannot be overcome by imposed prescriptions, or political and organizational steps, emanating from foreign powers or external entities. It should also be remembered that beyond certain thresholds, and leaving aside Afghanistan's immediate neighbours, the other external entities would not be too interested or involved in the difficult task of Afghanistan's national consolidation. The responsibility for national consolidation rests primarily with the emerging Afghan leadership at present.

There is no doubt that overcoming their inner contradictions is going to be a daunting task, which will involve the setting aside of historical memories and burdens, and purposefully transcending current contradictions and narrower vested interests. The role of foreign powers, however, remains significant in one respect, i.e. they have an interests in a stable Afghanistan in the context of their immediate and long-term objectives. Karzai and other leaders of Afghanistan should take full advantage of this factor to further the processes of national consolidation by ensuring external support to policies of national reconstruction, which should be rational, practical, properly prioritized, and responsive to the aspirations and needs of the Afghan people as a whole.

The War in Afghanistan and US Policy Towards India and Pakistan

KANTI BAJPAI

In the days and weeks after 9/11, as the US prepared to go to war in Afghanistan to root out Al Qaeda, it was forced to think about how it would handle its relations with India and Pakistan. The war in Afghanistan could not bypass these two regional States. It would in any case have consequences for them. What kinds of considerations went into US thinking as it crafted its South Asia policy? And with what consequences? When a 'sheriff', however reluctant, comes riding into town to clean it up, there will be violence[1] despite the hope that peace and order will follow. In the same way, US's involvement in South Asia has not brought peace and order to this troubled region. Indeed, it has made violence more attractive for India, Pakistan, and various terrorist groups.

We are very close to the events of 11 September 2001 (9/11), and the motives, intentions, and policies of the US as well as India and Pakistan are not definitively known.[2] This essay is therefore largely a thought experiment. It is an attempt to imagine how the US and the South Asian dramatis personae 'must' have thought in response to various challenges and opportunities after the extraordinary events of 9/11. My reconstruction depends on a set of assumptions about the nature of US, Indian, and Pakistan thinking as well as bits and pieces of evidence gleaned from what has appeared in print plus interactions with diplomats in New Delhi. I make no stronger claim for it.

The first two sections of this paper deal with US views of India and Pakistan after 9/11. The next three sections relate to the consequences or effects of the US war in Afghanistan in terms of the challenges and opportunities identified by the Indian and Pakistani governments as well as various terrorist organizations operating in Kashmir.

Pakistan as a Liability and as an Asset

In the aftermath of the terrorist strikes in New York and Washington, the US government, broadly speaking, perceived General Musharraf's government in Pakistan as both a liability and an asset—a liability that could also be an asset.

From Washington's point of view, Pakistan represented a liability in three ways. First, Pakistan was implicated in, if it was not part of, the terror network of Al Qaeda and Taliban. To the extent that this was correct, it might continue to sustain the network covertly. Islamabad was involved with both groups in the sense that Pakistani authorities, civilian and military, at various times had knowledge of the terrorist nature of their activities. The Pakistani government, and agencies like the Inter Service Intelligence (ISI) of the Pakistan armed forces, had been involved in training and supplying the Taliban from its inception. There was little doubt therefore that the highest organs of government in Pakistan, and the ISI in particular, knew that the Taliban was hosting and collaborating with Al Qaeda. In the larger sense of the term, Pakistan had 'harboured' the two organizations.[3] The danger was that Pakistani agencies would continue to cooperate with Al Qaeda or Taliban elements. They might warn them of US plans; they might mislead the US about the whereabouts and capabilities of both groups, throwing the US off the trail; and they might continue to supply them with material.[4]

Second, as soon as the US determined that military action in Afghanistan was imperative, Pakistan appeared as a potential liability to the extent that it served as a safety valve for fleeing Al Qaeda and Taliban personnel.[5] Washington had no doubt that some of the terrorists would not stand and fight to the end. They would, instead, make their way out of Afghanistan, either to fight in nearby theatres—Indian Kashmir or even Xinjiang in China—or to regroup and continue their fight from other parts of the world, mostly from bases and safe places in Asia, Africa, and the Middle East. US fears were proven correct. Al Qaeda and Taliban personnel did indeed cross over into Pakistan—some to stay and operate from there, some to fan out to Kashmir, and some to fight in other areas. It has been suggested that the US was well aware of the fact that Pakistan had played an active role in arranging for the exit of Al Qaeda and Taliban elements and stood passively by as retreating terrorists and militants made their way into Pakistan.[6] Washington may have had to pay this price in order for the larger operation in Afghanistan to proceed. US decision makers may well have decided that, as long as the top leadership of Al Qaeda and Taliban was not knowingly allowed into Pakistan by General Musharraf's government, the larger US interest was served. The General might have to be given some 'wiggle room' in order for him to sign up for the US war on terrorism.

Third, Pakistan could become a liability if it collapsed politically. Popular opposition to the US presence and to Pakistan's role in the war on terrorism, a wave of violence unleashed by Islamic extremists in reaction to US actions, and dissent within the Pakistani army could lead to a political meltdown within Pakistan.[7] This would complicate US military operations, indeed it might be fatal to their success. Worse, there was the possibility that state failure might entail a loss of control over Pakistan's nuclear weapons. A political collapse of the Musharraf regime and the consequent fragmentation of political authority and power could have two consequences. One, a more right-wing government might come to power; two, a state of anarchy might be unleashed in Pakistan. Particularly in the second case, there was the danger that extremists, either within the military or amongst the Islamic right, would get hold of at least some nuclear weapons.[8] Should these weapons get into the hands of terrorists in Pakistan or elsewhere, the security threat to US troops, allies, and the continental United States homeland would be greatly magnified.

In the wake of 9/11, Pakistan was clearly not just a liability for the US. It was also a potential strategic asset. Here again, there were three kinds of calculations. First, Pakistani territory was vital in order to prosecute the war in Afghanistan. The US needed Pakistan for at least two reasons—overflights and bases. US warships stationed off the coast of Pakistan would have to be used as platforms from which to launch bombing runs and tactical support for ground operations. The shortest flight times were those over Pakistani territory. The US might launch air operations from air bases in the Gulf and Turkey, but these would be longer journeys. Theoretically, India was another possibility—within hours of the 9/11 strikes the Indian government had offered the Amercians any and all facilities.[9] However, as a non-Muslim country, one that was in the line of fire of Muslim extremists, India was something of a political liability. In any case, flying times from India would necessarily be longer. Then, too, while the US military had worked with Pakistani counterparts for years, they did not know Indian officers and Indian systems, and a crisis was not the best time to get acquainted. In sum, India was never a very serious option.

Pakistan was a potential asset for the US in a second, more perverse sense. Precisely because the Pakistani government had harboured the Taliban and must have knowledge of the Taliban's links to Al Qaeda and, by extension, of Osama bin Laden's organization, it was a crucial element in the war in Afghanistan. Pakistani intelligence, especially ISI, was indispensable. While it would have to be watched closely to ensure that it did not play a double game, it was the best source on the Taliban as also, in all probability Al Qaeda, a source that would have to be thoroughly mined.[10]

Third, Pakistan was a possible asset as a 'moderate' Islamic state in this crucial part of the world. Through much of the Cold War, Pakistan had been regarded as an asset in as much as it was a moderate Islamic country, one that was located at a vital geopolitical crossroads. Increasingly in the 1980s and 1990s, and then into the new century, Pakistan's credentials as a moderate state had degraded. President Zia-ul-Haq's Islamicization programme of the 1980s had been largely overlooked by Washington because Pakistan was a frontline state against Soviet-controlled Afghanistan and also because Islam was the rallying cry for the Mujahideen that were fighting the Soviets. In the 1990s, after the Soviet withdrawal from Afghanistan, Pakistan's Islamic turn was a growing embarrassment if it was not positively dangerous. By the end of the second Clinton presidency, Washington very much feared that Pakistan was on its way to becoming radical and ungovernable and that in combination this might lead it into extremism or collapse or both.[11] Pakistan, therefore, had to be re-engaged diplomatically, its military had to be brought out of its isolation, and its civic and educational institutions had to be strengthened against radical Islam. After 9/11, as the US prepared for war in Afghanistan and the larger war on terrorism that involved confronting radical Islam, Washington needed Muslim friends.[12] Turkey was one such friend. Indonesia might have been a friend as well, but it was too far from the main theatre of radicalism and was in any case deeply troubled internally. Malaysia under Mahathir was unpredictable, to say the least. The Central Asians lacked influence in the Islamic world. The Saudis were an asset, but after 9/11, the House of Saud was under a cloud in Washington—so many of the hijackers were Saudi or had Saudi connections, and Osama bin Laden and his family were Saudi. Egypt was an ally, but the Palestinian–Israeli troubles and Mubarak's own domestic fragility compromised Cairo's effectiveness. As the second largest Islamic country, one that had been a US partner for many years, Pakistan was crucial. It had to be reconstituted and reformed politically so as to strengthen the moderates. General Musharraf had signalled his desire to take Pakistan in just such a direction since taking power in October 1999.

After 9/11, US power and imagination had to be used to turn Pakistan away from radicalism and back towards a more respectable form of Islamic governance in order for it to function as a bulwark against extremism and terror.

Not surprisingly, in the wake of 9/11, US policy towards Pakistan had a dual character. On the one hand, the US made it absolutely clear to General Musharraf that he would have to be an integral part of the war against terrorism and that the US was prepared to take extreme measures in order to ensure Pakistan's cooperation: Washington may have gone so far as to threaten to destroy Pakistan's nuclear arsenal to get compliance.[13] Compliance meant that Pakistan had to ensure that it cut its links to the Taliban and Al Qaeda, to share information about those organizations, and to stop terrorists and extremists from Afghanistan crossing over into Pakistan. Islamabad also had to permit overflights and provide basing and other military facilities for US forces.[14] On the other hand, once Musharraf was coopeative, he would be rewarded politically and economically.[15] Military contacts with the Pakistani armed forces, which had declined palpably in the 1990s, would be renewed. There would be no more talk of the need to hold elections and hurry the transition to democracy. Pakistan's diplomatic near-isolation, evident after the Kargil War in particular, would be ended; indeed a very high level of diplomatic engagement would now be essential. Pakistan's complaints about India and its handling of Kashmir would get a better hearing, and India would be urged to begin a dialogue on the future of the state.[16] On the economic front, the US would get together with other rich countries to put together a foreign aid package of Overseas Development Assistance (ODA), loans, and debt rescheduling.[17]

India as an Asset and as a Liability

If Pakistan was a strategic liability that could also be turned into an asset, India was a strategic asset that could turn into a liability for the US. On the asset side of the ledger, first of all, India might, like Pakistan, be an intelligence source on Afghanistan and on terrorism in the region more generally. Within days of 9/11, India and the US began to share intelligence information on Afghanistan and terrorism. The two countries probably also shared information on Pakistan.[18] This was useful for the US, which could check on the veracity of information it was getting from Pakistan (and other countries) against Indian data.

Second, India's links with the Northern Alliance, which the US had cut adrift from, was an asset from the point of view of gaining a military foothold in Afghanistan. The Taliban were solidly entrenched in most of the country, particularly the south, which borders Pakistan. To launch US operations from the south would be difficult. To begin in the north, where the Alliance held on to a narrow strip of territory, was more feasible. India might have a diplomatic role in smoothening US contacts with the Alliance, contacts that had frayed considerably after the Soviet withdrawal from Afghanistan. In any case, Indian intelligence on the Alliance would be useful as Washington prepared to make contact.

Third, and perhaps most importantly, India was a possible alternative to Pakistan as a military launch pad if Islamabad was unable to deliver. As noted earlier, India was not ideal from a number of points of view. Militarily, operating from India would mean longer sorties for the aircraft. Given that India is not contiguous to Afghanistan, ground operaions from its territory were not feasible (even if India was ready to accept US ground troops). Politically, attacking Afghanistan from 'Hindu' India might complicate Washington's diplomacy with the Muslim world. Still, India had its attractions. One attraction was Indian naval facilities on the western seaboard as well as airfields in western and north-western India, which might come in handy depending on US needs. At the very least, Indian seaports and airports might be used for refuelling and maintenance purposes. Politically, India, as a victim of terrorism, was 'on the same side' as the US, and New Delhi therefore had a clear and parallel interest in seeing an end to the Taliban and Al Qaeda. Perhaps more than anything else, though, India was attractive politically in quite another sense. Flirting with India strategically was a potent reminder to General Musharraf and the Pakistani armed forces that the US could turn to Pakistan's enemy to fulfil its mission in the region, with the threat that the US and India would be partners for the longer term.[19]

While India was an asset, it was also potentially a liability for the US war in Afghanistan. In the first place, and perhaps most importantly, India might choose to take advantage of the US war in Afghanistan to attack—or threaten to attack—Pakistan over cross-border terrorism in Kashmir. Indian decision makers could well argue that if the US could justify an attack on Afghanistan after the 9/11 strikes, then New Delhi was justified in taking strong measures against Pakistan. Indian analysts almost immediately after 9/11 did indeed make exactly these kinds of arguments.[20] It did not take much imagination to see how a confrontation might develop. Suppose, after a terrorist outrage, India decided to resort to a hot pursuit or punitive attack against Pakistan. Pakistan might then retaliate. India might in turn raise the military stakes. An escalatory spiral might ratchet up into a nuclear standoff. A nuclear crisis would be impossible to ignore and would distract the US from its endeavours in Afghanistan. An Indian raid—for example, India airstrikes against Pakistani military sites and facilities—might hit US troops stationed in Pakistan. Pakistani troops guarding the border with Afghanistan might have to be shifted to the Indian border in these circumstances, leaving the northern border open to Taliban and Al Qaeda infiltration.[21]

India might also be a liability in its more general posture towards Pakistan. With the US presence in the region, India might choose to harden its diplomatic stance vis-à-vis Pakistan. The Agra Summit in July 2001 had led to considerable bad feeling in India, and there was not much interest in a dialogue with Pakistan. New Delhi might become even more obdurate as the US and Pakistan drew closer together in the wake of 9/11. It might even demand that the US adopt a very tough line against Pakistan given that Pakistan had helped the Taliban and had links to terrorism. US *demarches* to Pakistan in response to Indian demands for action would make General Musharraf's domestic political situation more tenuous. Indian diplomacy, which huffed and puffed too much about terrorism in Pakistan, might have the effect of undermining the position of the moderates and strengthening the hold of right-wing elements within Pakistan.

Finally, India might complicate US diplomacy in the Muslim world. In going to war against the Taliban and Al Qaeda, the US ran the risk of alienating the Muslim world as never before. Religious leaders and extremists in Muslim societies were likely to see US actions as a civilizational war. Islamic reaction throughout the world—including the US itself—was worrisome for Washington. It might well produce even more terrorists who at some future date would once again target the US homeland. In addition, the US's various Muslim allies might be endangered. Drawing too close to India ran the risk of confirming fears of civilizational conflict. The US, a Western Christian power, allied with Zionist Israel and Hindu India against the Muslim world, could become a powerful call to jihad in the Islamic countries. US power notwithstanding, Washington needed friends and stability in the Muslim world.[22] If India launched military strikes against Pakistan or called for sanctions against Islamabad for its support of cross-border terrorism, the US would find itself in a diplomatic quandary, not the least because a quasi-alliance with India against Muslim Pakistan might conjure up images of a civilizational ganging-up on Islam.

US policy towards India, like its policy towards Pakistan, was ambivalent and consisted of two elements. The first element was to initiate a process of limited strategic cooperation with the promise that bigger things were in motion. Thus, India and the US would share intelligence on terrorist-related matters. Washington would ask for Indian military facilities if and when necessary. Most importantly, though, the US would emphasize that its relations with India and Pakistan were not zero-sum, that good relations with one country did not mean bad relations with the other, and that in particular India–US relations went beyond South Asia.[23] India was an emerging power, and the US conceived India's role in a much larger strategic setting, especially in the rest of Asia, as the Bush administration had suggested prior to 9/11. The second element of US policy, though, was directed at ensuring that India did not strike out against Pakistan. Privately, US diplomats cautioned India against resorting to force with Pakistan in emulation of American actions in Afghanistan. India's concerns were understandable, but there was every possibility that the effect of the US war in Afghanistan would be to dry up the swamp of terrorism in Pakistan. India stood to benefit from US military action if only it was patient. In any case, there would be a second phase in the war on terrorism that would take care of India's concerns about cross-border incursions.[24] In addition, Washington urged New Delhi to reopen a dialogue with Pakistan, assuring India that the US would exert itself to curb Pakistani support for the terrorists in Kashmir.

Pakistan's New Strategic Situation

The US war on terrorism had several effects on Pakistan that in combination strengthened Pakistan strategically. First of all, US military operations in Afghanistan destroyed the Taliban and Al Qaeda that were increasingly becoming a liability for Pakistan. Pakistan's support of the Taliban was well known; whether or not, Islamabad had links to Al Qaeda was less well known. Nevertheless, the destruction of both organizations was beneficial for Pakistan. The Taliban was a drain on resources and a diplomatic embarrassment (Pakistan was one of the few countries in the world that had formally recognized it as the government of Afghanistan). Al Qaeda, with its links to the Taliban, was at the very least a growing political problem for Pakistan given the organization's increasingly public links to worldwide terrorism and its hostility to the US.[25]

Secondly, the US–Pakistan link in the wake of 9/11 dramatically changed Pakistan's diplomatic position. Prior to 9/11, Islamabad found itself in a state of some isolation. There were a number of factors responsible for this. For one thing, after the Cold War, Pakistan was no longer of such strategic importance, particularly to the US. The US had used Pakistan as a base against the Soviets in Afghanistan in the latter part of the Cold War. Pakistan was also important for the Gulf. It was touted as a moderate Islamic state, and cooperating with it and propping it up had ideological advantages as well, particularly in relation to radical Iran as also emerging extremist forces in Central Asia. As the 1990s unfolded, however, Pakistan's image underwent considerable change. With the withdrawal of the Soviet Union from Afghanistan, and indeed as Afghanistan ceased to matter strategically to the US after 1990, Pakistan was no longer a frontline State. After the Gulf War of 1991, naval facilities in Pakistan were of no great import: US air power had done most of the damage and did not require Pakistani facilities. The US, in any case, had alternative bases in Saudi Arabia, Kuwait, and other emirates. Lastly, it was increasingly difficult to claim that Pakistan was a moderate Islamic country. Islamic extremism was flourishing under the shadow of the Pakistani state. Pakistan's ability to serve as an ideological counterpoint to Iran and Central Asian extremists was limited. Indeed, Pakistan was more a threat than a solution in this regard. With 9/11, Pakistan's isolation in international society ended instantly.

The US war on terrorism benefited the Pakistani government in a third way—by strengthening the hands of General Musharraf and the military. Musharraf had come to power in October 1999 with the promise that he would hand back the reins of office to a civilian administration within a few months. In September 2001, he had been in power nearly two years. The international and domestic pressures on him to transfer power were growing. In all likelihood, these pressures would have intensified. The events of 11 September brought about a dramatic change. The US war on terrorism and Pakistan's vital role in it ensured that the international pressures on him evaporated. Washington needed an effective strongman in Pakistan, and Musharraf fit the bill.[26] Domestically, too the pressures suddenly declined. With both Benazir Bhutto and Nawaz Sharif in exile, there was no powerful figure to rally the opposition to Musharraf. Indeed, after 9/11, given the complexities and dangers in which Pakistan found itself, there was little prospect that anyone, even Benazir or Nawaz, would come forward to seriously challenge Musharraf.

The Rising Tempo of Terrorist Violence

While the US war on terrorism was successful in destroying the Taliban government and disrupting Al Qaeda in Afghanistan, it was not successful in dissuading terrorists from striking at India. Indeed, the US intervention in Afghanistan was accompanied by a series of terrorist attacks that were more provocative than before.

After 9/11, terrorist violence in India grew palpably more audacious. On 1 October 2001, terrorists attacked the Kashmir Assembly in Srinagar killing more than 30 people. Two months later, on 13 December, terrorists tried to storm the Indian Parliament. On 14 May 2002, terrorists attacked an army camp that housed women and children. Days later, they killed Abdul Ghani Lone, perhaps the most moderate leader in the separatist All Party Hurriyat Conference (APHC). In the months that followed, they attacked Hindu pilgrims on their way to the sacred Amarnath temple in Kashmir and the Akshardham temple in the religiously-charged state of Gujarat. The last major attack was on the Raghunath temple in the city of Jammu.

The new wave of terrorist attacks had the following characteristics—First, the terrorists targeted political institutions such as the Kashmir Assembly and Indian Parliament and high-level political leaders. Second, they increased the targeting of religious sites, particularly Hindu sites, as also members of the Hindu community. Third, they deliberately chose to attack the most vulnerable (women, children, pilgrims, and temple-goers). Fourth, they increasingly resorted to suicide attacks. In short, terrorism improvised and enlarged its field even as the world's only superpower was engaged in a war on terror a mere 500 km. away!

Why were the terrorists able to carry out these kinds of attacks, indeed why did they chose to expand their war? One, for all the promises of the Pakistani government, the terrorist groups continued to operate with impunity in Pakistan. Leaders and cadres of the Jaish-e-Mohammed and Lashkar-e-Toiba were arrested only to be released soon after.[27] Members of these groups were not disarmed. While the Pakistani government confiscated the money collection boxes that were displayed in shops and buildings and ordered the freezing of assets, the major organizations were not hurt financially.[28] A second factor in their continuing war was the cache of weapons and other materials that they had stashed away. A third factor was their calculation that Washington's primary focus was Afghanistan and not Pakistan or Kashmir. Fourth, the events of 9/11 inspired them to more ambitious and sacrificial attacks. Fifth, they seemed determined to provoke India into attacking Pakistan and thereby precipitating crisis and war. Terrorists gain by publicity, the ratcheting up of violence, and anger on the part of government authorities. The Indian military mobilization of January and then May 2002 played spectacularly into their hands: it publicized the Kashmiri cause as nothing had over the past thirteen years; it threatened to escalate the level of violence all the way up to the nuclear level; and it was accompanied by intemperate statements by Indian leaders and officials.[29] Sixth, the terrorists sought to embarrass General Musharraf who had promised to end terrorism from Pakistani soil. The destabilization of not just India but also of Pakistan was in the interest of some terrorists who saw in Pakistan's internal troubles an opportunity to snatch power from the military and political moderates.

India Responds with Coercive Diplomacy

The Indian response to Pakistan's new strategic situation as well as the rising tempo of terrorist violence was two-fold—to insist that the US war on terrorism should include Pakistan amongst its objects; and, most importantly, to threaten to retaliate militarily against Islamabad. US pressures on Pakistan to stop the flow of terrorists into Kashmir did not satisfy India or significantly reduce the incidence of terrorist violence. As a result, Indian policy became increasingly belligerent, culminating in the threat of war in the summer of 2002.

On 11 September just hours after the terrorists strikes in the US, India offered to help Washington in any way it could, including the use of Indian facilities. India's offer was based on sympathy for America's plight but also on a calculation that this would underline India's interests in a strategic relationship with the US. Only months earlier, New Delhi had been the first country to come out in support of missile defence, just days after President George Bush had announced his new strategic initiative. Indian support was conditioned on the need to build an unprecedented strategic relationship with the world's only superpower.

The US's response to India's offer of support after 9/11 was cautious.

Indeed, for the first few days after 9/11 there was virtual silence from Washington. As it became clear that Pakistan once again would be a frontline state, Indian suspicions grew. New Delhi understood the reasoning behind the US decision to enlist Pakistan in the war on terrorism, but it feared a regress into the kind of situation that had prevailed in South Asia after the Soviet invasion of Afghanistan—a de facto US–Pakistan alliance that would harm Indian interests. In the 1980s, the price of Pakistani cooperation had been the supply of US arms and a blind eye to Islamabad's nuclear programme. After 9/11, New Delhi wondered what price Pakistan would exact. The Indian government hoped that the US would demand that Pakistan dismantle the terror network within its borders and that it stop supporting terrorism in Kashmir. Surely the US could not be indifferent any longer to what was happening in the Valley. Yet in the days and weeks after 9/11, it seemed that Pakistan had clinched a deal once again in ways that would ignore, indeed compromise, Indian interests. In return for Pakistan's cooperation with the US, it appeared that Washington would make a distinction between 'global' and other forms of terrorism (e.g. local, regional terrorism), prioritize the former, and therefore ignore India's concerns about Kashmir as one of the focal points of terror.[30]

Second, New Delhi feared that the US had agreed to use its influence with India to argue for the unconditional resumption of dialogue between India and Pakistan whereas India insisted that Pakistan had to bring cross-border terrorism under control before talks could be resumed.

New Delhi continued vigorously to argue against both notions. Indian officials and leaders argued that terrorism was the same everywhere and that a truly effective war on terrorism could not afford to make distinctions between global and other forms of terrorism. US interlocutors agreed in principle but insisted that in any campaign there had to be priorities. If the global menace of terrorism, currently located in Afghanistan, were destroyed, everyone would benefit, including India. Indeed, India would do very well since the fight in Kashmir was connected to Afghanistan—terrorists in Afghanistan were fighting in Kashmir and were training and inspiring Kashmiri terrorists. India also disagreed with the US notion that New Delhi and Islamabad should immediately return to a dialogue. Indian diplomats argued that Pakistan had to rein in the terrorists before this was possible. US diplomats suggested that Musharraf would be in a better position to do so if a dialogue resumed. Washington assured India that it would do everything it could do to dismantle the terror network in Pakistan. The Bush Administration reasoned though that General Musharraf was vulnerable to terrorists and extremists within Pakistan and to Pakistani public opinion, and he could therefore not be pushed too hard.

New Delhi remained unconvinced by these arguments. The Bush administration therefore shifted focus. It suggested that India–US relations could not be confined to South Asian issues and the war on terrorism and that the two countries should turn their attention to other matters as well, particularly in Asia, a code word in the India–US lexicon for rising Chinese power. The Bush administration had, from its entry into office, accorded India greater importance as a player in Asia and global security, and it was able to build on this promise in the difficult days after 9/11 as the India–US relationship grew increasingly troubled.[31] A number of high-level bilateral visits took place to give expression to the strategic shift that the US had touted since January 2001, and US officials publicly began to talk about the building of a long-term strategic relationship with India that would be 'non-hyphenated' (that is, not held prisoner to US–Pakistan relations) and would include much deeper military ties.

In the midst of these arguments and counter-arguments between India and the US, terrorists attacked the Indian Parliament on 13 December. Outraged by the boldness of the attack, the Indian government's actions became more not less aggressive. Within days of the attack, India took a number of steps in relation to Pakistan, which it held responsible for the attack. New Delhi recalled its High Commissioner in Islamabad, thus withdrawing Ambassadorial-level diplomatic representation in Pakistan. It ended all road, rail, and air traffic to Pakistan. It also threatened to revoke MFN status for Pakistani goods and to abrogate the Indus Water Treaty (which divided the waters of the Indus river system between the two countries and which had been signed with World Bank and US assistance in 1960). Most importantly, New Delhi ordered a general mobilization of its military forces for war. Indian ground, air, and sea forces were moved into forward battle positions and placed on the highest level of alert. Indian leaders demanded that Pakistan hand over twenty terrorists that it named, that it end infiltration across the Line of Control in Jammu and Kashmir and stop all terrorist strikes, that it dismantle the terrorist infrastructure within its borders, and that it seize the assets of terrorist organizations. In the event that Pakistan did not do so, India reserved the right to go to war.

Along with these bilateral steps, India launched an international campaign against Pakistan. The US was the focus of this campaign. New Delhi argued that the attack on Parliament was too outrageous to shrug off and that Pakistan was at least indirectly involved. Just as the US and Israel, in the wake of 9/11, had chosen to go on the offensive against those who sponsored or harboured terrorism, so too India had the right to take the fight to Pakistan. Even as the US counselled restraint, arguing in effect precisely what New Delhi feared, namely, that the global war on terrorism would be disrupted by India's more localized fight and that the latter therefore should be subordinated to the exigencies of the former, India demanded that the international community take action against Pakistan. Western pressures led to President Musharraf's 12 January 2002 address to his nation in which he pledged to stop terrorism from Pakistani soil. India's reaction to the speech was guarded: it sensed that the General's carefully-worded reference to Pakistani soil could exempt terrorist activity from the Pakistani side of Kashmir, which Islamabad could claim legally speaking is not a part of Pakistan.

In May 2002, as India and Pakistan traded charges on whether or not cross-border terrorism had been reduced or not in the wake of the 12 January speech, terrorists struck at the Indian army camp of Kaluchak killing the wives and children of personnel stationed there. Days later, the moderate Kashmiri separatist leader, Abdul Ghani Lone, who had signalled an interest in contesting the Kashmir elections to be held in October 2002, was assassinated. Indian leaders promised war, and the armed forces once again were placed on high alert. Pakistan warned India that any attack on it would be repulsed with any and all weapons at Islamabad's disposal.[32] The Indian Prime Minister in a public speech stated that Indians should be prepared for a 'decisive conflict' with Pakistan.[33] Indian analysts argued that Pakistani-backed terrorists had gone too far and that military strikes were the only way of punishing Pakistan and thus ending terrorism. Islamabad must know that it could not continue to hide behind nuclear weapons and that India was capable of punitive military action.

Two propositions were at the heart of the argument that India could use force under the shadow of nuclear weapons. First, India had 'escalation dominance' in relation to Pakistan. It could up the ante at every level of violence, including the nuclear. Pakistan, recognizing India's superiority, would not be able to use nuclear weapons against an Indian military attack, for fear of pushing India up the escalation ladder with the promise that any Pakistani counter would be met by further escalation. Hardline strategists argued that, if it came to nuclear war, India would be 'grievously' injured but Pakistan would cease to exist and that Islamabad would therefore have to fight India on terms set by India.[34] Secondly, the presence of US forces in Afghanistan and Pakistan ensured that Islamabad woud not use nuclear weapons. Washington would simply not tolerate Islamabad's threat or use of nuclear weapons in these circumstances.[35] If Pakistan was prevented from using its nuclear weapons, India could exploit the situation and launch punitive military strikes against its troublesome neighbour. Terrorist camps and infrastructure as also Pakistani military facilities were legitimate targets. In sum, India could do what it had promised to do after the Kargil War in 1999, namely, resort to 'limited war under nuclear conditions'.[36]

The international community led by the US, alarmed by the prospect of nuclear war in South Asia, became intensely involved diplomatically. Washington urged restraint on both sides while trying to persuade Islamabad to take steps to curb terrorism from Pakistan. General Musharraf promised once again to stop cross-border terrorism. In early July, the US and several other Western powers issued a travel advisory warning their citizens not to travel to India. Whether or not it was meant as a rebuke to India, it had the effect of shocking the Indian public and leadership.

The crisis now gradually wound down, although Indian and Pakistani forces remained eyeball to eyeball and terrorist attacks in India continued. A suicide squad attacked a Hindu temple at Akshardham in Gujarat. While this was a grave provocation in a state that had only just recovered from the worst communal rioting in India since Partition, the Indian government soft-pedalled Pakistan's involvement. Soon afterwards, in October 2002, elections were held in Kashmir. Election-related violence killed over 800 people, but the polls were generally regarded as the freest and fairest in Kashmiri history. The ruling National Conference that had held power since Kashmir's accession to India lost the elections; the separatist organization, the All Party Hurriyat Conference, did not participate in the elections and rejected the outcome as irrelevant; on the whole, though, Kashmiri opinion was not as negative. Just days after the results were announced, India stated that it would recall its forces from the international border. In early November 2002, terrorists struck once again in a major suicide attack, in Jammu, at the Raghunath temple. India accused Pakistan of being behind the attack but did not stop the process of military withdrawals.

While the international community continued to urge India to resume negotiations with Pakistan, New Delhi flatly rejected the idea until Pakistan stopped terrorism. Indian leaders indicated that they were still prepared to use force if terrorism did not ease. The Western powers argued that there had been a perceptible decline in terrorism, though Pakistan could do more to reduce violence. India appeared unsure of its stand on the incidence of terrorism. The Indian National Security Adviser, Brajesh Mishra, indicated that there was no change in the rate of terrorist infiltration.[37] The Indian Army Chief, on the other hand, claimed that there was a 50 per cent decline in infiltration compared to the previous year.[38]

By the end of 2002, relations between India and the Western powers, especially the US, were increasingly chippy. There was growing unhappiness in New Delhi over Western 'double standards' on terrorism and a tendency to make excuses for General Musharraf.[39] At the heart of the disagreement was the question of General Musharraf's political vulnerability. India argued that Musharraf had exaggerated the pressures on his regime in order to gain leverage with the Western powers who feared that if he was ousted, either political chaos or a more extremist regime would succeed him. The Western powers argued, by contrast, that while Musharraf may indeed have exaggerated his vulnerability, the threats to his regime were real, and political chaos or a right-wing takeover was a distinct possibility. As a result of these growing differences, a number of diplomatic spats occurred between India and the US in particular. For instance, the Indian Prime Minister was moved to say publicly that all countries, including Iraq, had the right to determine how to look after their security and that India would only support military action against Iraq if this was authorized by the UN.[40] The US, perhaps in retaliation, asked India to slow down its involvement in Afghanistan's reconstruction and to stop enlarging its diplomatic presence in that country in deference to Pakistani sensitivities.[41]

Conclusion

The US war on terrorism has had its successes, primarily the destruction of the Taliban and the disruption of Al Qaeda in Afghanistan. On the other hand, the region is not more peaceful. In particular, India–Pakistan relations have never been worse. Nor has terrorism been visibly reduced; indeed, right under the eyes of the greatest power on earth, terrorist groups have become more audacious than ever before. Put differently, the US has not been able to manage regional affairs terribly well. Managing South Asia was never going to be an easy task, and the US was well aware of the dangers and difficulties, but once it had made up its mind to go into Afghanistan there was little choice but to get more deeply involved in the domestic and international politics of the region. The future remains murky. The US will be in Afghanistan for the foreseeable future. It seems clear that Washington will continue to view Pakistan as a liability that could become an asset and India as an asset that could become a liability. India and Pakistan will continue to use the US for their own purposes if they can. The terrorists will continue to look for opportunities to hit India. A terrorist outrage could well lead to an Indian attack on Pakistan, Pakistani retaliation, and the threat of a nuclear confrontation. This is a constant, nagging fear for Washington. US policy makers want Pakistan to end its support to terrorism; and they would like India to begin a serious dialogue with Pakistan on the future of Kashmir. As things stand, Islamabad has not been able to—or has chosen not to—end its support to the terrorists; and New Delhi has refused to talk to Pakistan until it stops terrorism. The US seems to have run out of ideas and may well have decided that as long as both countries, in their different ways, cooperate with the US in *its* war on terrorism and avoid going to war with each other, there is little else that can be done—Washington needs Pakistan too much to discipline General Musharraf beyond a point—and it cannot be too harsh on India, which has been the victim of terrorism for over a decade and which has its own place in US grand strategy. As President Bush geared up for war against Iraq, the India–Pakistan problem receded in US thinking. Washington must be hoping that another crisis will not occur in South Asia, but the mood amongst US decision makers seems to be to deal with that eventuality if and when it occurs rather than formulate a comprehensive plan for peace and stability.

NOTES

1. I have drawn on the imagery of the Wild West from Richard Haas, *The Reluctant Sheriff*, New York: Council on Foreign Relations, 1997.
2. Bob Woodward, *Bush at War*, New York: Simon and Schuster, 2002, is an informed account of the first one hundred days of the Bush administration's handling of the war on terrorism. I use it rather extensively in this essay to give credence to some of my conclusions about US policy,

particularly towards Pakistan. Interestingly, the book hardly mentions India in US calculations. This suggests that India was not much of a factor as the US made up its mind on its course of action in the wake of 9/11.

3. Woodward, *Bush at War*, pp. 30–1 on how the Bush administration came to use the word 'harbour' in respect of those states that gave shelter to and otherwise helped or tolerated terrorist groups.
4. On US distrust of Pakistan intelligence, and in particular its ISI, see Woodward, *Bush at War*, pp. 162, 168, 214.
5. Ibid., p. 77.
6. Referring in particular to the Kunduz incident. See 'Northern Alliance Takes Kunduz', *BBC News*, 26 November 2001, http//news.bbc.co.uk/1/hii/world/south_asia/1674765.stm.
7. Woodward, *Bush at War*, p. 82.
8. Ibid.
9. Various Indian journalists and foreign diplomats in Delhi have confirmed the 'carte blanche' Indian offer of help to the US immediately after 9/11. See Chidananda Rajghatta, 'US Drive Will Cover J&K, India Assured', *Times of India*, 27 September 2001. Rajghatta notes that visiting National Security Adviser, Brajesh Mishra, reiterated India's unconditional offer of assistance including logistical support (e.g. overflight and refuelling facilities).
10. Woodward, *Bush at War*, pp. 32, 123.
11. See Jessica Stern, 'Pakistan's Jihad Culture', *Foreign Affairs*, vol. 79, no. 6, November/December 2000, pp. 115–26.
12. Woodward, *Bush at War* notes that US strategists were of the view that the war on terrorism should not be portrayed as a war against Islam or Afghans but rather against the Taliban and Al Qaeda (p. 115). When Pakistan's Foreign Ministry stated that it was satisfied with US evidence linking Al Qaeda to the events of 9/11, US officials were relieved. According to Woodward, 'The clear endorsement of the American case by a Muslim state was a boon' (p. 196).
13. There is no hard evidence of such a threat. The idea gained currency with General Musharraf's public statement that he had joined the US war on terrorism in order to protect Pakistan's 'strategic assets', a phrase that was interpreted to mean nuclear assets. In his first meeting with General Musharraf after 9/11, President Bush denied that the US had contingency plans to team up with Israel to take control of Pakistan's nuclear weapons. On this last point, see Woodward, *Bush at War*, p. 303.
14. Woodward, *Bush at War*, pp. 58–9 lists seven demands in all—stopping Al Qaeda operatives from coming into Pakistan, intercepting arms through Pakistan, and ending logistical support for bin Laden; blanket overflight and landing rights; access to Pakistani naval and air bases and border areas; 'immediate' intelligence and immigration information;

condemnation of the September 11 attacks and controlling domestic support for terrorism against the US, 'its allies or friends'; cutting off fuel shipments into Afghanistan and stopping Pakistanis from helping the Taliban; and ending recognition of the Taliban and assisting in its and bin Laden's destruction if it became clear that they had been involved in 9/11.

15. Woodward, *Bush at War*, pp. 82, 98, 114–15.
16. In the wake of 9/11, Secretary of State, Colin Powell, publicly reminded India of the need for dialogue on his various trips to the subcontinent. This angered India. New Delhi's view is that the State Department generally is more sympathetic to Pakistan than is warranted. South Block has noted that the US Department of Defence has usually been more 'pro India'. Powell's statements bear out the view, in India's estimation, that the US did a deal with Pakistan in the wake of 9/11. It is true of course that the US has always urged India to start a dialogue on Kashmir. However, after Bush's coming to power, India had expected the US to play this theme in a minor key.
17. Woodward, *Bush at War*, pp. 82, 98, 114–15.
18. Within hours of the attacks on the US, Indian intelligence warned US counterparts that there might be another attack on the White House in an effort to kill President George W. Bush. The US took the threat very seriously on the argument that India had good sources in Pakistan. See Woodward, *Bush at War*, pp. 55–6.
19. Shireen Mazari, 'Regional Security Issues and Concerns: A View From Pakistan,' in *South Asia and the War on Terrorism: Analysing the Implications of 11 September*, ed. Dipankar Banerjee and Gert W. Kueck, New Delhi: India Research Press, 2003, pp. 82–3.
20. G. Parthasarathy, 'US Action: A Lesson for India', *Hindustan Times*, 30 September 2001. Parthasarathy served in Pakistan as High Commissioner.
21. After the 13 December 2001 attack on the Indian Parliament, India mobilized its troops, threatening to take military action against Pakistan. Islamabad responded by moving its troops forward and redeploying units from the Afghan front. See Edward Cody and Kamran Khan, 'Pakistan Troop Shift Vexes US', *International Herald Tribune*, 2 January 2002.
22. This may well have been one of the reasons for Washington's slow response to the Indian offer of 'full support' to the US immediately after 9/11. The slowness of the response and the US's attempt to make amends when Vajpayee went to the US is noted in Satu P. Limaye, 'United States Security Policy Towards the Subcontinent After 9/11', in *South Asia and the War on Terrorism*, ed. Banerjee and Kueck, pp. 215–16.
23. Robert D. Blackwill, 'The United States, India, and Asian Security', 5th

Asian Security Conference, organized by the Institute for Defence Studies and Analyses (IDSA), New Delhi, 27 January 2003 downloaded from http://usembassy.state.gov/posts/in1/wwwh0127amb.html; Limaye, 'United States Security Policy Towards the Subcontinent After 9/11', in *South Asia and the War on Terrorism*, ed. Banerjee and Kueck, pp. 211–21.

24. Chidanand Rajghatta, 'US Drive Will Cover J&K, India Assured', *Times of India*, 27 September 2001.
25. Pervaiz Iqbal Cheema, 'Post-11 September Developments: A Pakistani Perspective', in *South Asian and the War on Terrorism*, ed. Banerjee and Kueck, pp. 43–5.
26. Woodward, *Bush at War*, p. 289.
27. B. Muralidhar Reddy, 'Masood Azhar Released', *The Hindu*, 15 December 2002.
28. Munir Ahmad, 'US, Pakistan Reach Accord on Operation Plan', *Times of India*, 27 September 2001; 'Sept 11: The Economic Fallout', *Tribune*, 12 September 2002.
29. For instance, the Indian Prime Minister told Indian troops in Kupwara to prepare for a 'decisive battle'. See Pramit Pal Chaudhary, 'India's Million-Man Gamble', *Hindustan Times*, 26 May 2002.
30. Varun Sahni, 'Fractured, Frightened and Frustrated: South Asia After 11 September, in *South Asia and the War on Terrorism*, ed. Banerjee and Kueck, pp. 99–100, footnote 6.
31. Blackwill, 'The United States, India and Asian Security', op. cit.
32. 'Musharraf Says Pakistan Was Ready to Use Nuclear Weapons', *CBC Corporate Radio-Canada*, http://www.cbc.ca/stories/2002/12/30/india_pakistan021230.
33. Pramit Pal Chaudhary, 'India's Million-Man Gamble', *Hindustan Times*, 26 May 2002.
34. Bharat Karnad of the Centre for Policy Research, New Delhi, has made this point most articulately. However, there are others who would agree. Defence Minister George Fernandes makes the point that it would be foolish for Pakistan to use nuclear weapons against India because while India would be hurt, Pakistan would be completely destroyed. Responding to President Musharraf's remarks that India would face 'non-conventional' war if it attacked Pakistan, the Defence Minister stated: 'The Pakistani leadership should not get into the idea of committing suicide because we [i.e. India] can take a bomb or two more.' See 'India Warning Over Nuclear War', *BBC News*, 7 January 2003, news.bbc.co.uk/1/hi/world/south_asia/2636157.htm.
35. Sahni, 'Fractured, Frightened and Frustrated', op. cit., pp. 95–6 goes so far as to speculate that Pakistan may have lost (some) operational control over its nuclear weapons after 9/11. However, he also makes the point

that with the US troop presence in Pakistan, India also has to be more restrained militarily.

36. The phrase was made famous by the Indian Army Chief, General V.P. Malik, after the Kargil conflict.
37. Shridhar Krishnaswami, 'US Could Not Make Pak. Give Up Terrorism: Brajesh,' *The Hindu*, 12 December 2002, http://www.thehindu.com/2002/12/12/stories/2002121204830l.htm.
38. 'Groping in the Dark', *Frontline*, 7–20 December 2002, http://www.frontlineonnet.com/f/1925/stories/20021220007412300.htm.
39. 'West Needs to Get Tougher With Pakistan: Sinha', *Times of India*, 25 November 2002.
40. As late as February 2003, India maintained that there should be a peaceful resolution of the issue with Iraq even if the UN authorized the use of force. See 'India for Peaceful Resolution to Iraq Crisis', *The Hindu*, 4 February 2003.
41. In early December 2002, the Indian press reported that the US had sent a *demarche* to India asking it to reduce its involvement in Afghanistan in deference to Pakistani sensitivities. India acted frostily to the US action. Washington stated that it had not sent a *demarche* to India. During his visit to Washington in December 2002, Brajesh Mishra downplayed the incident. See Shridhar Krishnaswami, op. cit.

American Wars on its Flanks: Iranian Perceptions and Policies

GULSHAN DIETL

As the American battle drums are beating on Iran's western flank all over again, it is necessary to look back at the two earlier wars that the Americans waged on its borders in the past decade: the war against Iraq in 1991 and the war in Afghanistan a decade later. The exercise would provide comparative perspectives, may yield parallels, and could lead to signposts for the future.

The Gulf War: A Retrospection

The Iranian foreign policy in the Gulf marked a drastic change with the inception of the Islamic Republic in 1979. The relations between the Arab rulers on the western shore of the Gulf and the Shah on the eastern shore were never entirely devoid of rivalry and suspicion. However, maintaining the status quo was the common broad aim within which the rivalries were contained. With the Shah's departure from the scene, the situation changed completely. Preservation of the status quo was thrown overboard as the revolutionary concept of the struggle of the *mustazafeen* (the exploited) against the *mustaqbareen* (the exploiters) was articulated and actively promoted. A decade later, the revolution had stabilized, the Iran–Iraq war had ended, and Khomeini had died. Each of these developments left an imprint on the Iranian foreign policy. Iran's response to the Gulf War evolved in this context.

The Iraqi occupation of Kuwait sent shivers down the spines of the Iranians, and the subsequent US determination to punish Saddam Hussein thrilled their hearts. These circumstances helped Iran break out of the old foreign policy straitjacket of exporting the revolution. Its stand on the issue stemmed from its smugness at having proved correct in its assessment of Saddam Hussein. 'We told you so' was the consistent Iranian refrain every time an accusation was levelled against him. He had finally proved that Iran had fought its own war against him on moral grounds for a just cause. He himself confirmed this when he agreed to return the Iranian territory and Iranian Prisoners of War (PoWs) and retreat to the Thalweg demarcation of the river Shatt al-Arab between the two.

The evolving Iranian policy on the issue marked a radical departure from its earlier Islamic revolutionary ideology on many points. In sharp contrast with its consistent position of keeping the Gulf out of bounds for foreign military presence, President Ali Akbar Hashemi Rafsanjani came close to accepting it as a necessary evil in the circumstances. 'We have no objection to them obstructing aggression; anybody may help in any way. However, it would have been better if the regional countries had done so', he said at a Friday sermon as the multinational forces started landing in the area.[1] An equally radical departure from the earlier Iranian position of one indivisible Islamic umma and the artificiality of nation states was its concern over even a slight change in the political map of the region. In an interview with the French daily *Le Monde*, Rafsanjani opposed any territorial compromise. 'If Kuwait were to go ahead and cede Bubian to Saddam all the same, we would act within our means to stop it', he warned.[2] Iran's earlier defiance of the United Nations and its questioning of its very legitimacy gave way to its acceptance and enforcement of all UN resolutions on the crisis. Its UN envoy, Kamal Kharrazi, went out of his way to underscore Iran's compliance with the UN resolutions. 'No Iraqi oil was exported through Iran and the Iranian authorities had arrested 430 persons on the charge of attempted smuggling of food to Iraq', he declared.[3]

Iran and Iraq

On 14 August 1990, a little more than a week after he invaded Kuwait, Saddam Hussein wrote a letter to Rafsanjani in which he appeared to meet all of Iran's conditions for a peace treaty formally ending the Iran–Iraq war. He said that he would begin an unconditional withdrawal of Iraqi troops from Iran's territory within three days, start exchanging the PoWs at the same time, and negotiate their boundary in the Shatt al-Arab river on the basis of the Algiers Accord of 1975.[4]

The offer was clearly related to the invasion of Kuwait. He wished to secure his eastern flank, to ensure that Iran did not join in any military offensive against Iraq, and to free his troops for redeployment on the Kuwait–Saudi border.[5] He conceded as much in his letter to Rafsanjani. He was making his offer, he said, 'so as not to keep any of Iraq's potentials disrupted outside the field of the great battle, and to mobilize these potentials in the direction of the objectives on whose correctness honest Muslims and Arabs are unanimous'. In the weeks that followed, Iraq made swift progress in withdrawing troops and releasing Iranian captives.

The pace slackened soon thereafter. Iran showed no inclination to stand up for Iraq. An unconditional Iraqi withdrawal from Kuwait was the consistent Iranian demand throughout the entire crisis. As the war began in mid-January 1991 with an Allied air bombardment of Iraq, Saddam made one last attempt to involve Iran on its side of the conflict—he sent some 165 warplanes to Iran in the hope that they would join the war from Iranian territory at a later date and drag Iran into the fray in the process. Iran did not let that happen. In fact it confiscated the planes 'as part payment' of the war reparations it had demanded from Iraq![6]

As things stand today, there are far too many outstanding contentious issues between the two countries that preclude any possibility of an early rapprochement. Technically they are still in a state of war with each other. The territorial dispute and the issue of the Thalweg demarcation are not yet resolved. Iranian PoWs are still in Iraq and the Iraqi PoWs in Iran. The Iranians refused to return the Iraqi warplanes, and as we have already noted, confiscated them in part payment of the war reparations allegedly due from Iraq. The issue of reparations itself is rife with complications. Lastly, Iraq has granted asylum to Iranian dissidents, the Mujahideen-e Khalq; Iran on its part has granted asylum to Iraqi dissidents, the SAIRI.

Iran and the GCC

As Saddam sought to woo the Iranians by his peace offer, the Gulf Cooperation Council (GCC) rushed in to outbid him. The Kuwaiti Foreign Minister, Sheikh Sabah, visited Tehran on 22 August 1990 and met his counterpart, Ali Akbar Velayeti, with a message for Rafsanjani. He expressed his regrets for the 'past mistakes' of Kuwaiti support to Iraq during the Iran–Iraq war, which the Iranians accepted.[7] In the following month, there was a constant one-way traffic of visiting high-level GCC dignitaries to Tehran. The culmination came on 29 September 1990, when the Foreign Ministers of the GCC countriesmet Velayeti in the Iranian office at UN Headquarters in New York. On 19 November 1990, Fawzi al-Jasii presented his credentials in Tehran as the new Kuwaiti Ambassador.

Beginning 12 December 1990, Iran launched a big air, sea, and military exercise involving nine thousand troops, fifty warships, several helicopters, and hundreds of speedboats in the Gulf and the Gulf of Oman. Codenamed *Piroozi*, it lasted ten days. Velayeti then set off on his tour of the GCC capitals. Firepower and diplomacy were both geared to secure a role for Iran in the security arrangement in the Gulf. His visit took place on the eve of the next GCC Summit and he used his visit to stress the need to convene a 7-member GCC session. He wanted such sessions to be held regularly.[8]

The GCC Summit met at Doha, Qatar, from 22 to 25 December 1990. In an unusual move, the Iranian Ambassador to Qatar, Nasrollah Mirzaiee Nasir, was invited to attend one of its sessions. The Summit communique contained a special section on 'Relations with Iran' in which the GCC welcomed the Iranian desire to improve its relations with all GCC countires and stressed its own desire to establish relations with Iran on the basis of 'good neighbourliness, non-interference in domestic affairs and respect for sovereignty, independence, and peaceful coexistence deriving from the bonds of religion and heritage that link the countries of the region'. Further, it underlined the importance of serious and realistic action to settle all outstanding differences between Iran and the GCC.[9]

The Doha Summit marked the high point of Iran's reconciliation with the GCC. The differences inherent in the world view of Iran and the GCC countries and their mutual suspicions of the roles they aspired to play in the regional power game were irreconcilable. In any case, Iran simply stayed out of the war. It kept up its search for a rapprochement with individual GCC states in the aftermath of the war.

The post-War Gulf in American Perspective

With the disintegration of the Soviet Union, the doctrine of containment became passé. The Clinton administration sought to formulate a strategic doctrine that would be particularly relevant to the post-Cold War world. Anthony Lake, Assistant to the President for National Security Affairs, who consciously stepped into the oversized shoes of George F. Kennan, envisaged an enlargement of the family of nations 'committed to the pursuit of democratic institutions, the expansion of free markets, the peaceful settlement of conflicts and the promotion of collective security.'[10] While containment was aimed at exclusion, enlargement was aimed at inclusion.

Lake warned against recalcitrant and outlaw states that not only chose to remain outside the family, but also assault its basic values. Not only did these states lack the resources of a Superpower that would enable them to seriously threaten the democratic order being created around them, but their behaviour too was often aggressive and defiant. The ties between them were growing as they sought to thwart or quarantine themselves from a global trend to which they seemed incapable of adapting. Lake chose to call them the backlash states. According to him, they consisted of Cuba, Libya, North Korea, Iran, and Iraq.[11]

How did that globe-encompassing doctrine translate in the regional context? Its assessment of the previous US administration in that regard was harsh. President George Bush 'had a preference for the status quo, and its actions fell short of its ambitious objectives. It sought more to stabilize the old order than to remake the Middle East in its own preferred image', it concluded.[12]

Martin Indyk, the then Executive Director of the Washington Institute for Near East Policy, did substantial prescriptive writings on the Clinton administration's policy in the region. According to him, there is a choice: 'We can preserve our strategic interests by attempting to quarantine the region, or we can undertake a more arduous effort to begin the transformation of the Middle East from a balance of power system to one based more on notions of collective security.'[13]

The latter approach generated an ambitious agenda, i.e. the removal of Saddam Hussein from power, the control of weapons of mass destruction in the region, support for greater political participation in the Arab states, and the encouragement of the Arab regimes to deal with the basic needs of their constituents. 'If the United States chose not to take that road, and the balance of power in the Middle East again disrupted, it would be remembered that there was a time when the United States was in a position to restructure the regional order, but chose not to do so', he said.

Narrowing the focus further to the Gulf region, he warned, 'While keeping Iraq weak, the US will also have to be watchful of Iran.'[14] Just as the Reagan and Bush administrations allowed their antagonism towards Iran to blind them to the rising danger of a powerful Iraq, so too was it important to avoid allowing an obsession with Saddam Hussein to blind American policy makers to the dangers of the balance in the Gulf tipping in favour of a revisionist Iran, he argued.

Indyk was appointed Special Assistant to the President for Near East and South Asian Affairs in the National Security Council shortly thereafter. It was in that official capacity that he went back to the Washington Institute for Near East Policy to deliver a speech on 18 May 1993 in which he propounded the doctrine of dual containment vis-à-vis Iran and Iraq.[15]

Anthony Lake brought forth five specific charges against Iran while calling it a backlash state: (a) Iran is actively engaged in clandestine efforts to acquire nuclear and other unconventional weapons and long-range missile delivery systems; (b) It is the foremost sponsor of terrorism and assassination worldwide; (c) It is violently and vitriolically opposed to the Arab–Israeli peace process; (d) It seeks to subvert friendly governments across the Middle East and in parts of Africa; and (e) It is attempting to acquire offensive conventional capabilities to threaten its neighbours. Its record as regards its treatment of its own citizens, especially women and minorities, is deeply disturbing.[16]

The War in Afghanistan

Iran and Afghanistan are neighbours along a long land border. They share a common history going all the way back to antiquity. Religion, language, and ethnicity are additional common factors binding the two countries. In the aftermath of the American war in Afghanistan, there has been a complete transformation in the Afghan political system and a dramatic realignment of forces in the region. Iran has been deeply impacted by these developments. They have spelt economic opportunities, political openings, strategic uncertainties, and most significantly, geopolitical and energy-related challenges.

Iran and Afghanistan: An Overview

Iran's relations with Afghanistan have been influenced more by external factors than bilateral issues.[17] In ancient times, great empires straddled the two countries. In the eighteenth and nineteenth centuries, Iran was struggling to deal with the expanding Russian and Ottoman empires while Afghanistan was engaged in the Indian subcontinent. Soon, the two were drawn into the 'Great Game' between Russia and Britain. The term refers to the struggle for supremacy in Central Asia between London and Moscow in the nineteenth century. The vast chessboard on which it took place stretched from the Caucasus in the west along great deserts and mountain ranges to Tibet in the east. It involved espionage and adventure in equal measure. The end result of the game was a historic compromise between the British and the Russian empires under which the Russians were given a free hand in Central Asia and India remained a jewel in the British crown.

In 1921, two years after Afghanistan gained independence from Britain, it signed a treaty of neutrality and friendship with the Qajar rulers in Iran. In 1927, a treaty of friendship and security was signed—this time with Reza Shah Pahlavi. Ten years later, the two signed the Saadabad treaty of non-aggression and cooperation. The Cold War period set them on divergent courses—Iran joining the US-led security structures in the region and Afghanistan opting for non-alignment. The military coup in Afghanistan that overthrew King Zahir in 1973 aroused security concerns in Iran—because a fellow king was overthrown and because the new ruler Sardar Daud Khan went on to improve relations with the Soviet Union.

By the end of the 1970s, the situation in Iran as well as in Afghanistan underwent a dramatic transformation. Iran was vociferous in condemning the Soviet invasion of Afghanistan and the Soviet-backed regime in Kabul. Its support of the opposition Mujahideen forces, however, suffered from two debilitating weaknesses—its own war with Iraq and its confrontation with the United States.[18] Within these limitations, it supported the anti-Soviet struggle, created and sustained its own Mujahideen factions, and hosted two to three million Afghan refugees. Iran commanded respect and influence in Afghanistan after the Soviets left.

With the establishment of the Taliban regime in Kabul, its sphere of influence shrank to the northern areas of the country held by the former Mujahideen, who united under a tenuous 'Northern Alliance'. Iran perceived the Taliban to be a creation of Pakistan and Saudi Arabia with US support. It was convinced that the Taliban was put together not just to contain the Iranian role in Afghan affairs, but more specifically, to use it as a south-bound route of the Central Asian oil and gas—a route that would be projected and promoted in lieu of the Iranian route.[19]

Iran's paranoia went even further. The Taliban was perceived to be a 'trap' set up by the US, Saudi Arabia, and Pakistan to drag Iran into a war with Afghanistan. A conspiracy theory sought to explain that since the Gulf War of 1991, US was trying to lure Iran into some war or the other that would serve as an opportunity to destroy its renovated military machine and further exhaust its economy—with the overall objective of restoring Iran to its former status as a piece on the US strategic chessboard. And since the US would prefer to distance the war as far as possible from the Gulf region—to avoid repercussions that might prove hard to control later—a war between Iran and Afghanistan would be ideal.[20]

Iran shares a 900 km border on the east with Afghanistan. The relations between the two reached the nadir in late 1998, when ten Iranian diplomats and a journalist in Mazar-i-Sharif went missing, and were presumed to be killed. Iran amassed 70,000 Revolutionary Guards and conducted the largest ever ground and air exercise on its Afghan border. As the relations continued to deteriorate, Iran deployed a 42,000-strong Baseej force and armed 1,100 villages along the border to fight against drug and ransom offences.

Iran has been hosting several leaders of the Afghan opposition including the Northern Alliance President, Barhanuddin Rabbani, and the Prime Minister, Gulbuddin Hekmatyar. Simutaneously, it has been playing an active role in all the multilateral efforts to resolve the Afghan problem. Most importantly, the UN-sponsored 6 + 2 group (Iran, Pakistan, Tajikistan, Turkmenistan, Uzbekistan, China + USA and Russia).

There are more than two million Afghan refugees in the country even today. Their presence has led to general resentment and occasional demonstrations. As they are increasingly blamed for drug addiction[21] and unemployment, the government has been seeking to repatriate them. A law passed in May 2001 imposes fines on Iranian employers hiring Afghans. According to the Director-General of the Foreign Nationals and Expatriate Affairs Department at the Interior Ministry, Iran spends US $4.5 million annually on them.[22] In August 2001, a year-long immigrant census was held during which 2.6 million Afghans registered themselves. As the census process came to an end on 27 August 2002, Iran decided to arrest and deport the unregistered Afghans and deny admission to their children in schools. The government contended that at least 2,50,000 Afghans have not registered in the census.[23]

Geopolitics

Civil wars and social fragmentation in failed states have invariably led to the rise of warlords who benefit from a prolonged strife. Whether it is Congo, Sierra Leone, Somalia or Liberia, it is the same story of poppy cultivation, drug traffic, gun running, protection money, and control of scarce resources in the context of acute shortages. In such a situation, the warlords acquire an abiding interest in perpetuating insecurity.[24] The Afghan situation is no different; only a lot more complicated. The Afghan population is an ethnic mosaic: the Pashtuns constitute 38 per cent of the population, the Tajiks 25, Hazaras 19 and the Uzbeks 5. The ethnic diversity of the country elevates the status of a local warlord to that of a community leader.

Ismail Khan, the Governor of Herat province, is the most powerful warlord in Afghanistan today. Situated in the north-west of the country, Herat is close to the Iranian border. Iran is one of the few countries, according to field researchers, that is making good on its financial commitment of US $560 million made at the Donors' Conference that met in Tokyo in January 2003.[25] Much of that monetary assistance is spent in Herat. There is a low-key competition between the Iranian and the US diplomats in Herat, both visible and active in the reconstruction work. The Iranian Pasdaran (The Iranian Revolutionary Guard Corps) provide a stark contrast and seek to offer a countervailing force to the US Special Forces. Iran is busy building a road connecting Herat to the Iranian city of Mashhad. Samina Ahmed, an Afghanistan watcher for the International Crisis Group, a research and advocacy organization, calls it a new Great Game. 'It is a political game, but it is being played in an economic sphere.'[26]

Every single day, between 100 and 400 trucks pass to and from Iran. The goods range from food to airconditioned cars from Dubai. They reach local markets within the country and in Pakistan. According to one estimate, as many as 500 cars from Dubai reach Pakistan via Herat every day. The transit has contributed toward making Herat one of the richest regions and a major port of entry. Presiding over this thriving trade route is Ismail Khan. Justly proud of post-war reconstruction going on in his region, he says, 'Before it was a jihad of blood. Today, it is a jihad of sweat.'[27] He is reported to be earning as much as US $60 million to US $80 million annually from the customs duty he collects from the trade. His refusal to hand over the tax revenue or even a part thereof has been a constant source of helplessness to the national government in Kabul.

Resurgence of warlordism is fuelled by international factors. The US policy of committing minimum US troops has resulted in reliance on local warlords to provide security and help with the ground operations. In the aftermath of Operation Enduring Freedom, the US Central Intelligence Agency (CIA) established a 150-strong Special Activities Division (SAD) consisting largely of the veterans from the

1980s anti-Soviet campaign in Afghanistan working in civilian clothes. While the US government is committed to organizing and training an army for the country, the SAD continues to pay the local warlords and use the local troops—particularly in the south and the east of the country—to locate the Al Qaeda. Ismail Khan continues to remind the world that only 5 per cent of the Al Qaeda are captured to date. They still pose a threat, and need to be confronted, according to him. His ability to keep the rival Americans and Iranians at bay and defy Kabul at the same time cannot be totally attributed to his financial independence, not even to his well-equipped and well-paid 30,000-strong army—stronger than Kabul's ragtag troops of a similar number. There are larger issues and external actors involved in the game.

In early July, there were fierce clashes between the forces of Ismail Khan and those of Farah province's Pashtoon commander, Amanullah Khan. The fighting centred on Shindand, an area where the Tajik dominated north-west and Pashtoon dominated south-east converge. It was an inevitable conflict. First, it was a war between the two warlords at the most basic level. Second, it was a national showdown between the two major ethnic components of the population: Tajik and Pashtoon. Third, it was widely believed to be a proxy war between Iran and Pakistan. Lastly, it had beyond-the-region implications as well—Shindand is at the centre of the proposed natural gas pipeline and the oil consortiums would find it difficult to obtain finances in circumstances of strife and uncertainty.

The Pipeline Politics

The pipeline politics continues to remain an intractable problem. The three possible routes are via Turkey to the Mediterranean,[28] via Georgia and Russia to the Black Sea and via Iran to the Gulf. The US has consistently championed the route through Turkey even though it is the least feasible of the options. And it has equally consistently blocked any move towards the route via Iran, even though it is the shortest and cheapest of the options. The oil companies have sought a compromise by advocating the Georgia–Russia–Black Sea route—without winning the argument so far. The Caspian Pipeline Consortium is, none the less, finalizing plans for a private 1.34 million barrels a day (mbd) pipeline from the Tengiz field in Kazakhstan to the Russian port of Novorossisk, utilizing an existing Russian line from Tengiz to Grozny.

There already is a pipeline from Baku to Novorossisk through Chechnya, which could be updated.

In 1995, the Centgas consortium initiated by the US oil company, Unocal—in collaboration with Saudi Arabia's Delta Oil, Argentina's Bridas, Turkmenistan's Turkmenrosgaz, Russia's Gazprom and others—proposed and aggressively pursued a fourth route. It envisaged a double pipeline. An oil pipeline could transport some 50 million tonnes of oil per year from the Turkmen oilfield of Chardzou to a terminal located on Pakistan's Indian Ocean coast. From there the oil could be exported to the rest of the world including India. A gas pipeline could transport some 20 billion cubic metres annually from the Daulatabad gasfield in south-east Turkmenistan to Multan in Pakistan through Herat and Kandahar in Afghanistan.[29] The optimism of Turkmenistan and the oil companies was rooted in their cynical realization that the Afghan warlords needed the funds generated by the pipeline for the purchase of armaments.[30] After lengthy negotiations, in January 1998, the Taliban formally agreed to the pipeline project and pledged to provide full security for it.

The project would have required US $2.5 billion external financing. The international lending agencies determined that the situation in Afghanistan precluded lending until such time as a stable regime had been established, the Unocal admitted.[31] Insecurity could range from the kidnapping of the expatriate staff, to financial blackmailing, to blowing up pipelines.[32]

Such a project would deprive Iran of transit fees, of the South Asian markets for its own oil and gas, and most importantly, of a potential political and trade influence in South Asia. All its attempts to forge new links with Asia in order to break out of the US containment policy would come to zilch. The economic strangulation, if anything, would get worse.[33]

The plan was suddenly abandoned by the Unocal in 1998, when the bombing of two US embassies in Africa was linked to Osama bin Laden in Afghanistan. The next year, the then US President, Bill Clinton, banned US investments in Taliban-controlled areas in Afghanistan. None of these calamities was to dampen the Turkmen President Saparmurad Niyazov's hopes to build the pipeline. In May 1999, Turkmen and Taliban officials sought to revive the project amid Niyazov's continued efforts to mediate between the warring Afghan factions. 'If they have gone, others will come in. We are already being approached and talks are going on. Several companies want to come in place of Unocal', said the Turkmen Oil Minister, Arazov Redjebai.[34] The trans-Afghan pipeline project was also discussed at the May 2000 meeting between Niyazov and the Pakistani ruler, General Pervez Musharraf.[35]

Just a couple of days after the terrorist attacks on the US on 11 September 2001, Unocal reiterated its complete dissociation from the project: 'We withdrew from that project in 1998, and do not have—nor plan to have—any projects in that country. We do not support the Taliban in any way.'[36]

The war in Afghanistan revived the Iranian suspicions regarding the pipeline. It feared a long-term US hegemony in Afghanistan and a fierce competition for Central Asian energy resources among American multinational companies. In view of the US determination to block the route through Iran, the Afghanistan–Pakistan corridor could emerge as the only alternative to unleash Central Asian energy potential. Kamal Kharrazi, the Iranian Foreign Minister, expressed his anxiety as also a hope that the territorial realities and security of the competing countries would finally determine the race in favour of Iran.

The Central Asian states have been receptive to the Afghan route in varying degrees. Niyazov has urged the UN to consider supporting the Afghan pipeline project as a way of bringing stability to the country. The Kazakh President Noorsultan Nazarbaev, has also shown interest in exploring the Afghan option to export his country's energy resources. His preference remains the route over Iran, none the less. In a joint press conference with the visiting US Secretary of State, Colin Powell, he stated that the investors consider the route to the Persian Gulf the most beneficial. 'The American companies think this', he added for extra emphasis.[37]

The Iranians closely monitored the war in Afghanistan as it progressed. Within hours of the fall of Kabul, the Interior Minister, Abdolvahed Mousavi-Lari left on an unexpected visit to Pakistan. Two weeks later, Kamal Kharrazi visited Pakistan. The result was the formation of two committees: one, to coordinate aid for reconstruction of Afghanistan; and the other to look into the Iranian gas pipeline. The Oil Minister, Bijan Zangeneh, stated that Iran was reviewing the feasibility studies on the undersea gas pipeline to India.

In addition to politics, the issue of the pipeline seems to have also become a point of prestige for the advocates of different routes. In view of the fact that the oil market has remained unpredictable, there probably is no need for a grand pipeline project. It also still remains unclear whether there will be large enough flows of oil from the region to the potential markets. Economic rationale should suggest short haul solutions to the countries concerned. In a few instances, that has already been the reality on the gound.

Post-War Iran in American Perspective

President Bush defined the future contours of US-Iran relations in his State of the Union address of 29 January 2002 in which he delivered the now famous phrase—the 'Axis of Evil'. Iran, Iraq, and North Korea constituted that axis. 'By seeking weapons of mass destruction, these regimes pose a grave and growing danger. They could provide these arms to terrorists, giving them the means to match their hatred. They could attack our allies or attempt to blackmail the US', he declared.[38] On Iran specifically, he also added the charge that 'an unelected few repress the Iranian people's hope for freedom'. The two countries were back on square one after this.

When the European Union foreign ministers reached an agreement in June to open talks with Iran on a trade and cooperation pact that would also include a political annexe, the US reacted by obliquely threatening to invoke the ILSA. When the Sheer Energy Company of Canada agreed to an US $ 80 million development project with the National Iranian Oil Company, the US reaction was the same. In July, however, the US sent a plane carrying US $3,00,000 worth of aid to Tehran to help with the earthquake relief.

Since then, the highest echelons of the US administration have been speaking up within the officially laid down context—Iran is accumulating weapons of mass destruction, is sponsoring terrorism, is hindering Israel–Palestine normalization, is creating problems in Lebanon through its support of Hizbollah, and most importantly, is smothering the democratic urge of its people. The Afghanistan-specific charges have been that Iran hosts the Al Qaeda and Taliban and helps them escape through its territory to other countries; that it provides weapons to Afghan warlords and urges them not to cooperate with the Afghan authority. The US Department of State has listed Iran as the most active state sponsor of terrorism in its annual report of 2002.

In June 2002, Bush unveiled a long-awaited peace plan for the Israel–Palestine problem. While the plan itself was almost non-existent, the speech referred to Iran in a harsher than hitherto tone. 'Every nation committed to peace must block the shipment of Iranian supplies to these groups', he said referring to Hamas and the Islamic jihad. 'Power is concentrated in the hands of an unaccountable few', he stated. The speech ended with an ominous warning. Quoting from the Bible, he said, 'I have set before you life and death; therefore choose life'. On 11 July 2002, the White House issued a statement to coincide with the third anniversary of the students' demonstration in Iran. Reformers and pro-democracy students have 'no better friend than the US' in their efforts to bring about change. 'The unelected people who really rule Iran have silenced or ignored the overwhelming call for reform evident in recent presidential, parliamentary and local elections. People of Iran want the same freedoms, human rights and opportunities as people around the world', it stated.[39]

That set the stage for the conservatives in Iran to assert their independence, cast aspersions of the reformers' integrity and mobilize the masses for a massive show of strength. President Khatami infused a sense of unity in the project by saying that there was no dispute over confronting insults and foreign interference. On 19 July 2002, tens of thousands of Iranians demonstrated in Tehran against the United States. The net result of the entire episode has been that the conservatives are better entrenched and the reformers find themselves on the defensive.

War on the Western Front, Again?

While the Iranian conservatives were busy turning their criticism by the Americans into a domestic bonanza, the *Tehran Times* reported that Washington had sent a confidential message to Tehran to ascertain Iran's stand on the US plan to attack Iraq. The letter was being discussed by the high-ranking Iranian officials, it said.[40] Whether the letter was genuine at all or whether it was a concoction to fuel the rage that was building up in the wake of the protest marches is not relevant. What has become relevant is a gradual evolution of the domestic debate on the impending US war against Iraq.

That Saddam is not a friend has never been in doubt. Saddam, however, is weak, embattled, and isolated. His replacement will necessarily be an Iraqi Hamid Karzai, completely beholden to the Americans. Certainly not a comforting thought for the Iranians, be they conservatives or reformists. In addition, once Saddam is out of the way, the next target might well be Iran. As things stand, there are frequent voices in the American media keeping the agenda alive: 'Talk of Iraq, but think of Iran.' On the other hand, Iran does perceive a minor gain from an operation against Iraq. Since the US has already branded the Iraq-based Iranian Mujahideen dissidents a terrorist outfit, Iran would be rid of it without any effort on its part.

Once the action starts, Saddam would be compelled to reach out to Iran all over again. If his behaviour on the eve of the Gulf War is a guide, then securing his eastern front with Iran would again be an important strategic goal for him this time as well.

If the war does take place, however, it is not likely to be another ultimate perfect war that Gulf War was. There are far too many unseen and unexpected variables this time that could swing the outcome along a very broad spectrum.

CONCLUSIONS

In the past decade, the Americans have fought two wars on Iran's borders with Iran's enemies. In a way, they fought the Iranian wars, or at least, the wars that Iran would have liked to fight itself and the wars that Iran reaped benefits from.

American support to Iraq during the Iran–Iraq war was all too evident. Its cautious opening towards the Taliban has been well recorded by now. Iran could justly claim to be right, whereas the US has had to radically revise its policies in both instances.

Iran chose to watch the Gulf War from the sidelines as two of its enemies fought it out. A decade later, it went a step further. Without getting actively involved in the action, it lent support to the US-led war. The Amercian soldiers entering Iranian territory in hot pursuit of the Al Qaeda and Taliban or the American crew of the downed aircraft were promised assistance. Iran played a positive role at the Bonn Conference that put together the Afghan Interim Authority. It pledged and contributed generously to the reconstruction efforts in Afghanistan.

An assessment of the Iranian prospects in Afghanistan can only be made with reference to the US policies. While the defeat of the Taliban is a major gain for the Iranian foreign policy, there are serious challenges ahead. Iranian influence in Herat may yet depend on the power struggle between Hamid Karzai and Ismail Khan as also on competitive favours granted to the latter by the US and Iran. A tenuous toehold in Herat may exact high costs on several fronts from Iran. The re-emergence of the Afghan option as a South-bound pipeline could finally seal the fate of the Iran option; worse still, the US oil lobby may ease its pressure on the US Congress and the Government to lift sanctions against Iran. And finally, it could mean an extension of the US reach in the region and literally all around Iran.

The Americans singled out Iran and Iraq as the targets of their dual containment policy at the end of the Gulf War. After the war in Afghanistan, Korea was added to the list in Bush's formulation of the Axis of Evil. Iran's neutrality in the first instance and its active assistance in the second did not matter. The next time around, things are not likely to be any different.

NOTES

1. *Survey of World Broadcasts—Middle East*, London, 22 August 1990, cited hereinafter as *SWB—ME*.
2. *Le Monde*, Paris, 9 October. Quoted in *Middle East Economic Digest*, London, 19 October 1990, p. 26.
3. *SWB—ME*, 21 December 1990.
4. Quoted in Shaul Bakhash, 'Iran: War Ended, Hostility Continued', in *Iraq's Road to War*, ed. Amatzia Baram and Barry Rubin, Hampshire: Macmillan, 1994, p. 219.
5. Ibid., 220.
6. *Iran Focus*, vol. 10, no. 9, October 1997, p. 12; and vol. 11, no. 8, September 1998, p. 14. The number of planes has varied according to differing estimates. Iran maintains that there are only 22 aircraft on its soil.
7. *SWB—ME*, 24 August 1990.
8. Islamic Republic of Iran Radio. Quoted in *SWB—ME*, 19 December 1990.
9. For the text of the communique, see *SWB—ME*, 29 December 1990.
10. Anthony Lake, 'Confronting Backlash States,' *Foreign Affairs*, New York, vol. 73, no. 2, 1994, p. 45.
11. Ibid.
12. Martin Indyk, 'Watershed in the Middle East', ibid., vol. 71, no. 1, 1992, pp. 70–1.
13. Martin Indyk, 'Beyond the Balance of Power: America's Choice in the Middle East', *The National Interest*, Washington, DC, Winter 1991–2, p. 42.
14. Ibid., p. 41.
15. 'Special Report: Clinton Administration Policy toward the Middle East', *Policy Watch*, Washington Institute for Near East Policy, 21 May 1993.

Quoted in F. Gregory Gause III, 'The Illogic of Dual Containment', *Foreign Affairs*, vol. 73, no. 2, 1994, pp. 57–8.

16. Lake, op.cit., no. 28, pp. 52–3.
17. Ali A. Jalali, 'A Historical Perspective on Iran–Afghan Relations', in Ali Mohammadi and Anoushiravan Ehteshami, *Iran and Eurasia*, Reading: Garnet Publishing Limited, 2000, p. 139.
18. At that time, the Soviets had expressed willingness to offer strategic military armaments to Iran and halt the sale of long-range missiles and jet fighters to Iraq, provided the Iranians turned a blind eye to the developments in Afghanistan. Ali Khorram, 'Afghanistan and the National Security of the Islamic Republic of Iran', *Amu Darya*, vol. 1, no. 2, Tehran, Summer and Fall 1996, p. 226.
19. 'By marginalizing Iran in Afghanistan and by bypassing Iran as a route for an oil and gas pipeline, US strategists assume they stand a better chance to contain Iran', according to Kamal Kharrazi, the then Iranian Ambassador to the UN and the present Iranian Foreign Minister, *Washington Post*, 4 November 1996.
20. Adam Tarock, 'The Politics of the Pipeline: The Iran and Afghanistan Conflict', *Third World Quarterly*, vol. 20, no. 4, London, September–December 1999, p. 813.
21. Two to three million Iranians are estimated to be drug–addicts, which works out to 5 per cent of the population. Sixty per cent of the prison inmates are on drug-related charges.
22. *IRNA*, Tehran, 7 August 2002.
23. *New York Times*, 15 August 2002.
24. Mohammed Ayoob, 'South-West Asia after the Taliban', *Survival*, London, vol. 44, no. 10, Spring 2002, p. 53.
25. The international community promised to give US $4.5 billion towards reconstruction in Afghanistan.
26. Bay Fang, 'The US and Iran Jockey for Influence in Western Iran', *US News and World Report*, Washington, DC, 12 August 2002.
27. Ibid.
28. The Turkish option envisions gathering the oil exports at Baku in Azerbaijan, thereafter crossing either Georgia, Armenia, or Iran to terminate at Ceyhan in Turkey's Gulf of Iskenderan on the Mediterranean. The British Petroleum-led Azerbaijan International Operating Company has refused to build the 2,000 km. Baku–Ceyhan pipeline. The Azeris are searching for options, including forming their own company to do it. www. turkestan-n@vm.ege.edu.tr, vol. 98, pp. 207–21, December 1998.
29. Frederic Grare, 'Meeting India's Energy Needs: What Role for Central Asia?', in *India's Energy: Essays on Sustainable Development*, Pierre Audinent, P.R. Shukla and Frederic Grare, eds., Delhi: Manohar, 2000, pp. 247–8.

30. R. Hrair Dekmejian and Hovann H. Simonian, *Troubled Waters: The Geopolitics of the Caspian Region*, London: I.B. Tauris, 2001, p. 100.
31. Unocal Bharat Limited, *Energy Solutions for India*, New Delhi, March 1998, p. 3.
32. Tarock, n. 4, p. 817.
33. Ibid., p. 816.
34. Sreedhar and Mahendra Ved, *Afghan Buzkashi: Power Games and Gamesmen*, Delhi: Wordsmiths, 2000, pp. 254–5.
35. R. Hrair Dekmejin and Hovann H. Simonian, *Troubled Waters: The Geopolitics of the Caspian Region*, London: I.B. Tauris, 2001, p. 101.
36. www.unocal.com, 24 December 2001.
37. *New York Times*, 10 December 2001.
38. www.whitehouse.gov/news/releases/2002/01/20020129/html.
39. *Los Angeles Times*, 13 July 2002.
40. *Tehran Times*, 16 July 2002.

The Geopolitical and Socio-Economic Implications of USA's Involvement in Afghanistan

JAGAT S. MEHTA

The crisis in Afghanistan not only illustrates the abiding lessons distilled from history but also shows how, with change in politics and technology, the bequeathed hypnosis from the past can lead to fateful errors in contemporary judgement. Located on the crossroads of Asia and the route to the invasions of the subcontinent, Afghanistan has had great strategic importance through millennia. It is thus surprising that while most countries of Asia succumbed to European imperialism, Afghanistan managed to preserve its independence. With exceptional courage and cunning, it defeated the covetous ambitions of both Czarist expansionism from the north and British Indian forward policy from the south. The conservative Afghan tribes had a reputation of interminable bloody feuds with each other but also of unity whenever threatened by foreign intrusions. There is enormous ethnic plurality in the country, with the Pushtoons being the most dominant, and it is Islam which provided the bedrock of Afghan unity. Some sects, especially the Hazara Shias in the west and the Tajiks and Uzbeks in the north, had assertive identities but, in general, Afghans were comparatively moderate in their religious practices. It was the combination of all these factors that helped Afghanistan remain detached in both World Wars even in the face of pressures and inducements. By 1919, the international community had come to recognize and respect the Afghan desire for an independent foreign policy. After the Romanov dynasty was wiped out in the October revolution, as early as 1925 Amanullah was the first monarch to visit Moscow; indeed he negotiated an arms supply agreement with the USSR. Long before non-aligned principles and the fraternity was established as a movement, Afghanistan practiced neutrality and detachment between the great powers. It was, therefore, a tragedy, and an avoidable one, that a country with such a uniquely proud history should have suffered destruction, and that too in the

1970s when the non-aligned approach was on the way to be universalized. This needless tragedy can be traced to the mindset conditioned by the fallacies of the Cold War, compounded by the accidents of chronology and the failure of diplomatic judgements.[1]

Afghanistan's international problems had got greatly accentuated after the partition of India in 1947. Afghan Pathans had never got reconciled to the Durand Line imposed by the British in 1892 but Pakistan refused to reopen the inherited delineation. Afghanistan found itself even more sharply at cross-purposes with Pakistan when the latter joined the anti-communist alliances, which even led to the temporary stoppage of its sea-borne trade. Even so, in the 1970s, the situation in the country evoked no serious anxiety for its neighbours or for the great powers. Indeed, over the years, a pattern of cooperative coexistence on aid and development had evolved, with the USSR aiding projects north of the Hindu Kush and the United States assisting in education and economic progress in the south and the east of the country.

While the Afghan will to political independence had remained strong, the socio-economic progress towards modernization was sluggish, with only occasional half-hearted attempts at democratization, which were insufficient to defuse the growing disaffection in the body politic of Afghanistan. Considering its location on the Cold War frontier, different intelligence organizations had always remained active and in contact with amenable domestic factions who looked to extra-constitutional political opportunities. It was the combination of these factors that led Mohammed Daud to oust his own brother-in-law King Zahir Shah and proclaim the country a Republic in 1973. There was, however, no apprehension of another radical change in the country when, in April 1978, the Saur Revolution erupted and brutally assassinated President Daud and his cabinet. The People's Democratic Party of Afghanistan (PDPA) headed by Noor Mohammed Tarakki, which initially had the support of both the leftist Khalq and Parcham political factions, was proclaimed the ruling group. By prophylactic diplomacy on behalf of India, the ascendancy of the pro-Soviet regime in Kabul did not provoke an American alarm nor did it lead to sharp deterioration in the India–Pakistan relation, which had improved significantly after the 1976 normalization during Mrs Gandhi's Prime Ministership. However, at the end of 1979 (when Charan Singh headed an interim government), there was a fateful triple coincidence.

In November 1979, the American embassy in Teheran was stormed and the diplomats were taken hostage by Ayatollah Khomeini's supporters; on Christmas Day, the Soviet Union massively intervened in Afghanistan; and on 3 January 1980, Mrs Gandhi was re-elected Prime Minister of India. Evidence was available to all concerned governments even then that these developments had independent and unrelated dynamics but in Cold War tailored-reactions, objectivity and sagacity were nervously surrendered. The developments in Iran were, in fact, part of the US–Iranian politics following the overthrow of the Shah; the Soviet invasion of Afghanistan flowed from the ideological militancy and dictatorial propensity of Hafizullah Amin, which created the ironical situation that the ascendancy of Socialism ignited anti-Soviet insurgency amongst the conservative Afghan tribes.

The electioneering pledges of Mrs Gandhi got her committed to improving relations with the Soviet Union but she and her advisers had never anticipated that as soon as she came back to power, she would be facing international horror against Soviet Union and that she would have to give directions for the debate in the General Assembly at the first violation of the Great Power demarcations agreed at Yalta in 1945. The US proved to be wholly mistaken in seeing the Soviet action as a strategic threat with the intention of holding a tourniquet on the oil artery flowing through the Gulf: it was not difficult for professionals to see that it was for internal political damage control and not, as argued, to pre-empt a CIA conspiracy that the Soviet Union undertook this ill-conceived intervention. India too was mistaken in believing that this might lead to a clash of superpowers around South Asia and thus in turn, feeling it would be prudent to side with the Soviet Union, a long trusted friend. As it happened, in the process India departed from its Cherished non-aligned principle of non-aggression. In these ill-considered reactions, Indians like the Soviets, overlooked the lessons of history, and alienated the Pathans with whom there were old affinities. In the beginning, Pakistan genuinely feared a direct threat from the USSR but when it became clear that such a danger was non-existent, it decided to seize it as an opportunity to rebuild the frayed relations with the United States administration.

I had ceased to be Foreign Secretary in November 1979 but before that I had seen some thoughtful reports from our embassy that the developments in Kabul warranted no international or strategic alarm. Anyway it came as no surprise that the Soviet operations were restricted to the Afghan borders. When the Reagan administration came to power in 1981, embedded with old rigid Cold War attitudes, Pakistan was seen as a front line state against the 'Evil Empire' and the Congress was persuaded to vote in two instalments a total of nearly US $7 billion of military aid to Pakistan. In addition, during the next few years, separate allocations totalling US $600 million were made to the Mujahideen fighting the Soviet forces. The militarization of Pakistan, in turn, correspondingly increased the defence budget of India, except that India's burden fell on its own hard-earned foreign exchange earnings. Incidentally India lost the most propitious opportunity ever—even better than at Simla in 1972—to consolidate India–Pakistan relations, including rationalizing to confirm the Line of Control, which *de facto* was being fully respected as it was an internationally recognized frontier. The intelligence organizations, true to their habit of being wedded to the worst-case scenarios, aggravated the disastrous consequences. The CIA handpicked thousands of Islamic militants from all over the Arab world, brought them to Pakistan where, after training, they were inducted into Afghanistan to fight with the Mujahideens. (These were to be the nucleus of the terrorists who eventually would attack American installations in 1998 and plan 9/11 in 2001.) Vast numbers of Korans were printed and smuggled into Central Asia to inflame the Muslims in the Central Asian Soviet Republics. Even after it was clear that there was no strategic threat to the oil artery, there was still a malevolent satisfaction to see the Soviet Union being bogged down in its own 'Vietnam'. Pakistan got burdened with millions of Afghan refugees and found its administration and political economy under strain from narco-terrorism and the Kalashnikov culture but it still rejoiced at the flow of dollars and arms as worth the price to be paid for its bolstered security capability vis-à-vis India. Unfortunately contacts with the mainstream Afghans were marginalized as the country got identified with the 'communist infidels'. Pakistan fully exploited India's non-critical attitude at Soviet intervention globally.

For the first time, India found itself out of step with all its neighbours and most of its friends. Its approach was projected as an example of sharing with the Soviet Union the belief in the *droit de limitrophe*—that a big country could exercise the right of intervention if it felt its own security was under threat. This distortion, compounded by other reasons, specially after Sheikh Abdullah, the then Chief Minister of Jammu & Kashmir passed away in 1982, began the process of undermining the political stability in the Valley. A recent independent study[2] by a Swedish scholar Sten Widmalm, argues that just when, after the fair and free elections of 1977 and 1983, political stability was taking root, there was 'decline of democracy' between 1983–9. The National Conference was splintered; the elections in 1987 were heavily rigged and all this precipitated the outbreak of insurgency in 1989. The insurgency was started by disaffected Kashmiri youth but then the ISI seized the opportunity and ever since has fuelled it from across the Line of Control. The alienation of Afghan Mujahideen from India and the corruption of democracy in Kashmir were no doubt separate phenomena but they got enmeshed and crystallized into anti-Indian sentiments in the minds of Islamic jihadis. One could plausibly speculate that, though surreptitious infiltration was consistent with Pakistan's old ambitions in Kashmir, there might not have been non-Pakistani volunteers across the line of control in Kargil in 1999 if India had not stood aloof from the international consensus against the Soviet invasion in 1980. Islamic countries were not always enthusiastic supporters of India on Kashmir but in recognition of the country's leadership on decolonization, it had come to command widespread respect of many countries; however, after its abstention on the vote of Afghanistan (which was repeated year after year till 1989), India laid itself open to criticism in the Third World and lost ground on international support on Kashmir.

Gorbachev after coming to power in 1985 was quick to recognize that, notwithstanding a loss of pride in the Kremlin at the failure of the coup planned in Moscow in September 1979 and the goals of political damage control, Brezhnev was guilty of serious impetuosity in authorizing the Soviet invasion in December 1979. A great deal of detail is now publicly available from KGB records. In 1986, Gorbachev confidentially requested India to help in taking a hand in restoring stability to Afghanistan but India did not respond positively. It was apparently hoping the Soviet supported government in Kabul would prevail. India even invited President Najibullah on an official visit to Delhi in 1988 in the hope that secularism and non-militant Islam would triumph even after the Soviet forces withdrew. Najibullah was unpopular with the Mujahideen and was obliged to take refuge in the UN compound in 1992. He was looked upon as a renegade, and was pulled out and brutally killed by the Taliban in 1996. By an agreement brokered by the UN in 1988, the Soviet Union and the USA had decided on a symmetrical termination of involvement in Afghanistan by 1989. After withdrawal, both the superpowers immediately switched their attention to their own agenda of detente, showing disregard at leaving Afghanistan in chaos and civil strife. The competition to command the sinews of power between different ethnic factions in Kabul continued. Initially through a *shura*, Pakistan did make efforts to bring together the seven eastern factions but manoeuvred to have Gulbuddin Hekmatyar, favoured by the Inter Services Intelligence (ISI) of Pakistan, to lead the coalition. It was in fact Rabbani of the Tajik minority who succeeded in establishing himself in Kabul with Ahmed Shah Massoud as the most effective military commander.

It was at this stage that, as a corrective to the ugly rivalries and lawlessness of the Mujahideen factions, the idea of recruiting Taliban youth from the mosques and madrasas was conceived. These youth were more religiously motivated and disciplined. Recognizing their enthusiasm, arms, training, and officer leadership was provided to them by the ISI. The Taliban were able to establish themselves in Kandahar in 1994 and displace Rabbani in Kabul by 1996, and except for a small area in the north, virtually the whole country came under their administrative control. Wherever they prevailed, they enforced what they considered to be the Sharia pattern of law and governance. They closed all girls' schools, banished women from work places, and frowned on most kinds of entertainment and avenues of relaxation. They showed their fidelity to militant Islam, which was very different from the traditional practice in Afghanistan. In 1991 the US had launched the Gulf War against Iraq and, in pursuit of these military operations, an agreement had been reached with Saudi Arabia to use the holy land of Arabia in attacking Iraq. The old jihadis who had been assembled from the Muslim world to fight the 'infidels' in Afghanistan now switched their hate from the Soviets to the Americans.

This is a story of compounded misjudgements. It is hard to think of bigger political U-turns than what has characterized US and Pakistan policy towards Afghanistan within no more than 10–12 years. If political and professional attitudes of outside nations had not been propelled by outdated fears, Afghanistan might not have suffered so fatally. The United States instead of simply walking out should have remained committed to restore stability and economic viability of the kind now being marshalled. Pakistan if only by distilling lessons from history should have desisted from the temptation of looking upon Afghanistan as a pliable surrogate that could give it strategic depth vis-à-vis India. If India had persisted with patient diplomacy, India–Pakistan relations might not have degenerated and Islamic radicalism would not have destabilized South Asia. All this is not so far-fetched as it seems; nor is it only hindsight wisdom. Following the comprehensive normalization in 1976 under Mrs Gandhi's governmental authorization, several bilateral problems, grid-locked for eight years, were sorted out through constructive successful negotiations. The improvement also gathered bipartisan legitimacy under the Janata government. Pakistan still looks upon the visit of A.B. Vajpayee as Foreign Minister to Islamabad in 1978 as the high point of good relations with India—an old Jansanghi burdened with a 20-year anti-Pakistan record, after a 3-day visit was able to sublimate the hostility into trust and friendliness. History obviously cannot be unwritten but if we want to give better shape to the future, one must not blink over crass blunders of the past. Indeed one cannot help regretting that there is a convenient amnesia and arbitarily selective chronology, which overlooks positive successes of the past and the adverse consequences of fateful mistakes. Even while conceding the imperatives of public relations to feed the domestic constituency, there is room and need for confidential confession to facilitate catharsis and to help correct the course in order to safeguard national interests.

It was not just the USA but there was a broad band of culpability for the destruction of Afghanistan. One cannot, for example, overlook that the leadership of the Khalq and Parcham, specifically Hafizullah Amin, Rabbani, Hekmatyar, Babrak Karmal, Najibullah, etc., were not free of guilt in failing to understand the hold of Islam in their own country's national personality. The Saur Revolution was precipitated by a handful of Leftists, not at the Kremlin's prompting. It was a folly to try to graft a 'foreign' ideology in a conservative tribal milieu. In the 1970s, Afghanistan had secondary importance for US as well as the USSR. There was of course intelligence vigil but no great anxiety for either superpower. However, in the 1980s Afghanistan became a battleground for confrontation in one of the last encounters of the Cold War and misjudgements put into train the subsequent disaster.

The strategic importance of Afghanistan got dramatically enlarged following the disintegration of the Soviet Union in the early 1990s, especially as it came along with the confirmation of substantial reserves of oil and gas in the landlocked Central Asian region. The US was quick to establish diplomatic relations and sought to explore the economic potential in all the ex-Soviet republics. Initially the reports suggested that these energy reserves could equal that of the Middle East. Although these estimates were found to be exaggerated but still the estimates were substantial enough to invite a rush of multinational corporations with plans of transporting it to the big markets of Japan and the West. Even if there were no political crisis in Afghanistan, the Central Asian region would not now be left alone because of its new-found economic importance. Afghanistan thus finds itself between two globally important energy sources—the Gulf and Central Asia. While the crisis in Afghanistan in 1979–80 started with the false alarm of USSR threatening the Gulf artery, now for its own viability Afghanistan may have a vested interest in the world demand for oil and gas and to become the favoured conduit for the flow to the international markets. The possibility of this happening, however, hinges on the political stability of Central Asia as well as Afghanistan.

In the decade after liberation/independence, none of these countries—Uzbekistan, Kazakhstan, Tajikistan, Kyrgistan and Turkmenistan—has so far shown promise of requisite internal dynamism. There is only limited development of the infrastructure necessary for being on the international investment radar screen. (Turkmenistan and Uzbekistan may be marginal exceptions.) In most countries, dictatorships continue, often harking back to the Communist Party's exclusive control, and Uzbekistan is giving signs of wanting to become a regional hegemon. What is common to the entire region is that Islam is on the ascendant, with varying degrees of contaminated militancy. Al Qaeda and suspected Taliban recruits are alleged to be part of the insurgent challenge to Soviet power in Chechnya. Islam is also of nervous concern to China because of the linkages with Sinkiang and therefore it hosts the Shanghai group that tries to coordinate efforts to meet the (Islamic) terrorist threat. What is relevant in our context is that some of the Central Asian republics have traditional connections with minority diaspora resident within the established boundaries of Afghanistan. The United States has now reached agreements with some countries to establish a military presence to facilitate operations against Al Qaeda inside Afghanistan. The problem may be that the politics and operations of anti-terror and the economics of energy exploitation may be at cross purposes—hunting the terrorists may be a short-term priority but it could undermine the long-term goals of energy export and stability and reconstruction of Afghanistan.

Ahmed Rashid in his well-researched study on the Taliban[4] details how after the USSR splintered, some MNCs, specifically the Unocal of the United States and Bridas of Argentina, tried to reach exploratory agreements for routing the energy exports. Apart from Turkmenistan, Kazakhstan and Russia, China, Iran as also the United States are in the twenty-first century variant of the Great Game. Turkey has been interested in providing terminal points in the Mediterranean at the port of Ceyhan. Officials of the Clinton administration even canvassed support for the MNCs in Pakistan and India, which suggests that the US, at one time at least, had accepted that the Taliban regime was providing the requisite measure of long-term stability to permit pipeline installations running through Afghanistan. All this, however, changed after the attack on the American embassies in Africa in 1998 which was traced to have originated in the mastermind and financial resources of Osama bin Laden sitting in some hideout in Afghanistan. The US finally came to face with the dilemma that the economic benefits from the Central Asia may face Islamic militants. The negotiations for oil and gas pipelines across Afghanistan seem to have taken a back seat in the post 9/11 situation.

This warrants a digression on the nature and reach of terror in the twenty-first century. The attack on the World Trade Centre and the Pentagon planned in the Tora Bora caves showed that Islamic militants were led by people from educated middle class families who had sophisticated comprehension of the technological potential of modern communications. At one stroke they buried the illusion of geographical invulnerability and the comfort of purely military superiority of America. Religious fanaticism is not the only tinder to terrorism—strength also comes from desperation of poverty and other grievances against the West. The United States is now perceived as the new Imperialist arrogantly exploiting the world in the confidence of being the victorious sole superpower. The future of Afghanistan is perceived only as a means to the end of the forces hostile to United States. Fighting terror effectively presents not only operational but also political problems. In this priority, the Bush administration has to rely heavily on General Musharraf. One cannot help wondering if the US understands the dangerous dilemma being posed for the General at being perceived as no more than an American satrap. Even after the Bonn Conference and the *Loya Jirga* in Kabul, the legitimacy of the interim government of Hamid Karzai, although multi-ethnic, is dominated by the Northern Alliance. It is hugely dependent on non-national protection by an international contingent and the reach of this force is restricted to Kabul only. Karzai seems a brave, patriotic leader but his cabinet consists of not-so-wholesome representatives. Economic support for Karzai is crucial but the promised aid is not being delivered in the measure committed by the international community. Of the US $4.5 billion pledged in Tokyo, US $1.8 billion was to be disbursed in the current year but barely 30 per cent of that figure has so far reached Kabul. It is more than likely that if political stability and reconstructed economic infrastructure are not effectively and expeditiously created and justly distributed, Afghanistan may not only remain a long-term basketcase but militant terror would fuel dissatisfaction and stalk the country itself, aside from conspiring in dark corners of the world.

The economy of Afghanistan was never strong. The 18 million Afghans were dependent on a subsistence agricultural, pastoral economy, and narcotic smuggling. Exports from Afghanistan before 1979 were chiefly carpets and dried fruits. These would take some time to pick up but even then they will be meagre in relation to the country's needs. Aside from aid, and that was at low level, there was practically no foreign direct investment. The one great hope for the eventual and self-supporting viability and the rebuilding of Afghanistan is that the country could provide the shortest possible route for export of the oil and gas from Central Asia. This could be a bonanza of new earnings, possibly worth several hundred million dollars a year. However, with the current instability in much of the country, a pipeline traversing the country may well look like a poor investment to the MNCs. Even though it may be a longer route, the alignment ending in Turkey may be preferred because of more stable conditions. It is plain that smothering of terror in Afghanistan itself will be helped politically by collateral social and economic progress, and therefore should weigh positively with the international community, but until stability returns, the MNCs may feel safer in choosing the east–west alignment. In sum, there might be an incipient conflict of interests between help to the interim government in Afghanistan and the interest of US MNCs, where profit may be the overriding consideration.

This brings us to the major collateral problem of Afghanistan—the question that arises from India–Pakistan relations and the dilemmas and prospects that the hostility may pose to the viability of Afghanistan. As hinted, partition of the subcontinent exacerbated the problem of landlocked Afghanistan. Crudely summarized, in India, Afghanistan was perceived, in Chanakya's terms, potentially the enemy's enemy. Afghanistan did not subscribe to nationhood based on religion and also subscribed to non-alignment. Moreover, India instinctively supported the claim to Pakhthunistan and may even have tried to discreetly fuel it. Pakistan has the ultimate advantage of contiguity (as India has with landlocked Nepal). In Pakistan—as it came out in the last two decades—notwithstanding centrifugal dissatisfaction in Baluchistan, Sindh, as well as the Frontier Province, there was reliance on ethnic and religious kinship with Afghanistan compensating for its own fundamental strategic vulnerability with all national economic lifelines, notably the communication grid, the Indus river, for a thousand odd miles running parallel to the frontier with India. As stated earlier, India blundered in 1980 when it sacrificed its political affinities with Afghan nationalism and it has yet to live down the political fallout. Pakistan on the other hand, by showing genuine sympathy initially, scored over India by giving shelter and sympathy to millions of refugees who fled east. However, this great advantage got dissipated by the reversal when Pakistan first bolstered the Taliban and then, in 2001, at the behest of the US, branded them as terrorists. At least in private Pakistan must have invited the accusation of treacherous betrayal of the fraternal and friendly Pathans. For a long time to come, Pakistan will have to walk a tightrope of fighting Al Qaeda and disowning the remnants of the Taliban to earn dollar indulgence on the one hand and not wanting to be seen as a renegade to Islam on the other.

Pakistan and India became the real victims of the needless crisis. India–Pakistan relations deteriorated grievously around Afghanistan. Just when they held promise of firm improvement, both sacrificed the imperative of permanent good relations with the people of Afghanistan, not for objective but ulterior reasons. The deterioration was initially not because of Kashmir or any bilateral problems but the mindset of beggaring each other. India and Pakistan are now at the nadir of their relations, at least since 1971. Following 9/11, the US has tried hard through pressure and powerful inducements to promote a dialogue between these hostile neighbours, now armed with nuclear weapons.

Is it not the time for detached reflection within the two countries on their respective national interests when the hopes, fears and fallacies of the Cold War stand exposed? Afghanistan always belonged to South Asia and its continued instability will affect the stability of Pakistan and indirectly also of India. No other country, except perhaps Iran, has as great a permanent interest in the resurrection and rebuilding of Afghanistan as Pakistan and India. It is far greater than that of the United States, Russia or even the Arab world. Diplomatic and economic competition between India and Pakistan has delayed and in the future will only further delay the restoration of Afghanistan to stability. In 1997 itself, even while the Taliban controlled much of the country, as a humanitarian initiative, India and Pakistan should have jointly offered to deploy teams of sappers to sweep the 10 million odd landmines randomly strewn in the fields and pathways of Afghanistan, which may well make Afghanistan the biggest accidental killing field of the world. Symbolically this would have been indicative that both countries have separate and common interest in helping Afghanistan.

Pakistan alone provides the most convenient access for Afghanistan to the blue waters and is therefore irreplaceably more important. However, even at the best of times, even if its economy gets into better shape, Pakistan cannot carry the burden of rehabilitating Afghanistan alone. Afghanistan too has already shown that, along with UN and international assistance, it wants economic support from India. India can provide material and human resources at lesser cost than any other of Afghanistan's neighbours. India has also taken initiatives to give earnest proof of its capability and goodwill. India is, however, being debarred from land transit for regular trade and the alternative routes for aid support and trade are needlessly more expensive. It is fortunate that India is not involved in any anti-terror operations in or on the borders of Afghanistan. Sooner or later, for Pakistan too, anti-terrorism must be put second to the economic reconstruction of Afghanistan and the promotion of peoples' friendliness for their kinsmen, and this may require visibly distancing itself from the priorities and politics of USA. American and international support for Afghanistan itself could get diluted and deflected if a terrorist outrage takes place somewhere else in the world or operations are launched against Saddam Hussein's Iraq. Only if India and Pakistan recognize their common interest and jointly approach Afghanistan can Afghanistan argue with the US on the obvious economic rationale for oil and gas pipelines from Central Asia using the southern route for export to the thirsty markets within South Asia and across the oceans. The US should also understand that its own fight against Al Qaeda and defusing rampant anti-Americanism in Afghanistan will have greater credibility if it is seen to be promoting Afghanistan's economic viability. Donor aid by itself will never be enough—it will be highly problematic in the long run to keep up with the enormous needs. There is a congruence of interests of Afghanistan, Pakistan, and India but it squarely requires overcoming seated prejudice and suspicions.

The logic of the foregoing paragraph, at this moment, is probably like a pie in the sky. To think of India–Pakistan launching a joint initiative towards regional cooperation to help Afghanistan or to canvass a profitable outlet for Central Asia is absurdly idealistic when SAARC (and SAPTA) have made poor progress. But if any lessons can be learnt from the past fifty-five years, in the final analysis—this is a deliberate oversimplification—geography of contiguity has proved more telling than history and the logic of globalized economics has prevailed over borrowed ideology and distant politics. Just as Pakistan can only develop nuisance value through its connections with Bangladesh and Nepal, India has not, and will not in the future, be able to politically or economically hurdle jump to Afghanistan (or Central Asia) without the beneficial and willing cooperation of Pakistan. Even US would agree that Pakistan's viability depends on a stable South Asia more than on US dollars. Pakistan must or should avoid standing in the way of the new Afghan government. Progress of course hinges on the Indo–Pakistan conflict resolution coupled with the ascendancy of moderate Islam in Pakistan itself. It also implies that Pakistan should not continue to risk straining India's secularism in Kashmir or outrage democracy in India. Statesmanship has to raise aloft the long-term vision of a cooperative policy for the region as a whole. In the new world, the hypnosis from the past has to be 'plucked from the brain like a rooted sorrow'.

It follows that it is in India's long-term interest that Pakistan should be reassured that India has no designs to unscramble the existing divisions of the subcontinent. India must demonstrate to a hostile people—as happened between Germany and France, USA and Russia (after the Cold War) and other international reconciliations—the finality of 1947 and 1971 divisions. The long-term answer now is not confederation but beneficial functional cooperation between India and Pakistan that could develop into regionalism. Pakistan has to finally come to terms with the fundamental dilemma of its own identity; nationalism in the country has to go beyond negative 'anti-Indianism' and the ambition to directly or indirectly wrench Kashmir. In the recent book on 'Pakistan: Nationalism without a Nation?' edited by Christophe Jaffrelot, a French scholar[5] (only one out of many scholar contributors) Pierre Lafrance sees the possibility of Pakistan escaping the trap of 'anti-Indianness' and finding a positive identity as a nation. He argues that Pakistan should see itself as the heir to the Gandharva civilization around the Indus Valley. Indian diplomacy must see more honestly its own self-interest in assuaging Pakistan's anxiety but Pakistan must not persist with the counsel of desperation, which could cause it even more decades of frustration. The subcontinent has really no constructive alternative but to end the long process of compartmentalized and competitive manoeuvring. India–Pakistan relations were mangled in 1979 by the coincidence of developments in Afghanistan—it would surprise the world if there was recognition that the advent of terror is seen as a threat to entire institutionalized civil society including independent governments in both India and Pakistan. The spirit of 1976 should be recaptured and the shift away from Jinnah's vision articulated on the 14 August 1947 and Pandit Nehru's promise of the tryst with destiny must be finally reversed.

The whole world has suffered from having taken too seriously the hyperbole and fears of the Cold War. Afghanistan has been the grossest mistake in international politics of the post-War years and alas an wholly avoidable one. It showed that the Information Revolution has sharpened peoples' political awareness and nationalism can be scotched but not smothered by superior force. Even in the face of increased sophistication of weapons and condign capabilities of the state, interventions have invariably proved counter-productive—be they in Vietnam (1965–73), Czechoslovakia (1968), IPKF in Sri Lanka (1987–9) or in Afghanistan (1979–89). The fig leaf of intervention by invitation has always eventually got exposed. The crisis in Afghanistan started a two-decade-long sorry trail but the story has not ended with the military response to the attack on the World Trade Centre and the Pentagon. The operations against Al Qaeda have stretched longer than was promised and terror may continue through the century. The cancer of terror may again require surgery; it demands prophylactic diplomacy and extended therapy of enlightened internationalism. Apart from religious fanaticism, desperation is born of anger of deprivation. Imported ideologies grafted in foreign mud do not bear root. It is also the legacy of the Cold War to blame domestic failures on foreign manipulations. The Afghan people defiantly kept their independence for two centuries; they must now unitedly refashion their own socio-economic future. They will have to rediscover the balance between nationalism and tribal warlordism. The international community must not tire of building a world climate sympathetic to constructive national aspirations but, regardless of failure at Kyoto and Johannesburg international conferences for economic equity, we have to persist against odds bequeathed by history and exert maximum efforts to show that we are the masters of our own national fates. Terror, desperation, and the diplomacy of complaint and accusations provide no answers.

NOTES

1. *The March of Folly in Afghanistan: 1978–2001*, Delhi: Manohar, 2002.
2. Sten Widmalm, *Kashmir in Comparative Perspective*, New York: Routledge Curzon, 2002.
3. Vasily Mitrokhin, 'The KGB in Afghanistan', in Cold War International History Project, ed. Christian F. Osterman and Odd Anne Westad, W. Wilson Centre for Scholars, Feb. 2002, in MS.
4. Ahmed Rashid, *Taliban: Islam, Oil and the New Great Game in Central Asia*, London: I.B. Tauris, 2002.
5. Christophe Jafferlot, ed., *Pakistan: Nationalism Without a Nation?*, Delhi: Manohar, 2000.

India and US Involvement in Afghanistan

V.P. DUTT

The terrorist attack against the United States was a horrendous event. It was almost incredible that the greatest power of earth, perhaps since the beginning of history, was made to look so vulnerable. The attack was as daring as it was dastardly. Thousands of innocent people, many from other countries, lost their lives. It was the latest display of evil power by the terrorist organizations that were burgeoning all over the world. The world was shocked, and so was India. The repeated filming of the incredible event over the television sets brought home the enormity of the event.

The United States had now come face to face with the menace of terrorism of which India had ample experience in the last three decades. India had been a victim of terrorism nurtured, fed, and equipped from across the border. Terrorists coming into India through the Kashmir border came from Pakistan but most were being trained in Afghanistan. It was, therefore, natural that India should feel a kinship with the victim of terrorism, anywhere in the world. It was also clear to India that the United States would be taking all possible steps, including an attack on Taliban-ruled Afghanistan.

The Indian government conveyed to the United States the deep sense of shock and sympathy that was generally felt all over the country.[1] India, however, did not wait to see how the US would subsequently react, what retaliatory action it planned, and what role it could play in it. Within two days, the government had offered all logistic help to Washington. The Foreign Minister disclosed that India had established contacts at all political, executive, and operational levels and that India had expressed its readiness not just to give logistic help but also provide the staging ground for the US military operations.[2]

The Prime Minister also addressed the nation and declared India's intention to be with the global coalition against terrorism. He pointed out that India's neighbourhood was a hub of terrorism and that India would give unstinted support to the global war against terrorism.[3]

India's reaction must also be seen in the background of what the Taliban and the Al Qaeda leadership was proclaiming. Osama bin Laden named India along with USA, Russia, and Israel as responsible for world terrorism and, ipso facto, legitimate targets for terrorist attacks.[4]

It is necessary here to analyse the various factors that prompted the government to adopt such an open-ended approach, even when the US had not yet fully indicated its future course of action and had not even indicated what support it expected from India.

One factor, of course, was the prolonged war, at the India–Pakistan border, and the suffering it entailed. Sometimes this struggle was a rather lonely one, with the big powers generally offering lip-sympathy but taking little concrete action. It almost appeared that the terrorism that was striking India was not a matter of great concern to the superpowers. Now, the situation seemed to have undergone an overnight transformation. The foremost power of the world was a victim too and this seemed to provide a great opportunity to wage a common war against terrorism. The US itself began talking of a prolonged struggle to eradicate terrorism all over the world, which appeared to include terrorism in India too. The government believed that through this open-ended approach a new alignment had been created with the United States in combating terrorism.

The Pakistan factor in New Delhi's reckoning could also not be ignored. Since most terrorist groups were raised, trained, and financed by Pakistan, there was a general perception, both within the government and outside, that through this 101 per cent support to the US, terrorism from Pakistan could finally be scotched. The entire geopolitical situation in the region was believed to have undergone a sea change.

The same logic appeared to hold vis-à-vis the Taliban-controlled Afghanistan. The Taliban was not only an extremist, obscurantist, and fanatical regime that had prompted a sense of revulsion in much of the world but was also a source of spreading jihadi culture. A number of militants fighting in Kashmir had come from and had been trained in Afghanistan. It was in India's interest that such a fanatical government should not be allowed to spread mayhem in other countries.

All these considerations provided the rationale for the almost one-sided support that India had offered to Washington. The issue was not that of denouncing terrorist attacks against the US or even that of joining a worldwide coalition against it—There was no question that India, which had experienced prolonged terrorism, would be siding with those who were now leading this struggle and would be a part of the international front against terrorism and its sources. The issue was whether it was in India's interests to have given the impression that it was offering itself almost as a battlefield to the US without waiting for the unfolding of further developments in the region. Was it necessary to appear so obsequious? Would it not have been better if India had pondered over more deeply about the geopolitical realities and the limitations on any ground role for it?

Nevertheless, Prime Minister Vajpayee told an all-party meeting on 27 September 2001 that India had not given any assurance 'either directly or indirectly on the use of its air bases'.[5] A month later, the Defence Minister, George Fernandes, on a visit to that country revealed that the United States wanted Indian air and naval facilities for military operations in the region.[6] Many of these statements were in fact confusing rather than clarifyng the grounds of interaction between India and US. It was also be noted that India had to keep it clear that this was a war against the Taliban and the Al Qaeda terrorists and not a war against Islam. India had to make clear that terrorists had no religion and that religion was used only as a facade for gaining power. Vajpayee himself told the all-party meeting that 'we must tell the people that Islam has nothing to do with terrorism'. This was particularly important not only in the light of certain paranoiac developments in the United States soon after the 11 September attacks but also because many sections of society in India, and some other countries, were trying to divert the struggle against terrorism into a general condemnation of one religion. It should, however, be noted that, as a noted US commentator subsequently pointed out, not a single Indian Muslim went to Afghanistan to join the Taliban or the Al Qaeda war.[7]

While rushing to offer its services to the United States, India forgot the geopolitical realities. It was Pakistan that had physical proximity to Afghanistan. The US needed Pakistan more than India for its operations in Afghanistan. As Jim Hoagland of the *Washington Post* put it, 'Wars run on expediency and not on logic', no matter whether it was a Faustian bargain.[8] A point-blank US notice to General Pervez Musharraf (are you with us or not?) resulted in a 180° turn in Pakistan's policy and Musharraf declared himself to be a partner in the international coalition agaisnt terrorism.

Before we consider some ramifications of US involvement in Afghanistan from the Indo–Pakistan angle, we may note that there certainly was an independent dimension to India's relations with Afghanistan. India had had considerable interaction with the leaders of the Northern Alliance much before the collapse of the Taliban. India had provided notable assistance in keeping the Alliance afloat during times of adversity. India had put in considerable effort in sustaining Ahmad Shah Massoud and his forces. India was reported to have spent 'tens of crores of rupees' per year to purchase arms and other equipments for the Northern Alliance.[9] The families of many leaders of the Northern Alliance were given protection by India and had been living unobtrusively in the country. Even Hamid Karzai had studied unobtrusively in Himachal University.

India did play some role in the war strategy against the Taliban. Initially the US tried to carry on its war without too much interaction with the Northern Alliance but soon discovered that it was getting nowhere, and it then, perhaps as India had advised, utilized the Northern Alliance to break the hold of the Taliban and its ally Al Qaeda. Also, India, through its special emissary for Afghanistan Satindra Lambah, contributed not insignificantly to the formation of a new government in Kabul as well as in strengthening ties between the new Afghan authorities and India. Many of the new Afghan leaders, like the defence, foreign, and interior ministers paid their first visit abroad to India.

Coming back to the US strategy, it was clear that, in addition to use of its aircraft carriers, the war could be pursued most effectively only through the use of Pakistan's territory and airspace. In fact, within days of the attack on the WTC, USA began intensive talks with Islamabad demanding Pakistan's agreement for American ground troops and special forces units to operate from there. The Pakistan regime was told that they must allow the use of Pakistan's airspace and military airfields, as well as its military intelligence apparatus, for targeting Taliban and Al Qaeda bases the Afghanistan. Pakistan was also asked to deny use of Pakistan's airspace to the Taliban and to halt all other forms of support.[10]

Americans had no doubt that without Pakistan the Taliban could never have swept across Afghanistan and imposed their regressive rule. President Pervez Musharraf and a group of his fellow generals met on 14 September 2001 in what was described as 'a tense 7-hour conference at army headquarters' and realized that they had only got one option before them, and that was to accede to the US demands. The Americans wanted access to everything that Pakistan's shadowy military intelligence agency, the Inter Services Intelligence (ISI), knew about the bin Laden network.[11]

The American government might have underplayed the shakiness of the General's regime at that particular point of time, but they needed to bolster it for conducting the war in Afghanistan. As a well-known foreign journalist put it, 'for years, Pakistan has seemed a place about to blow. Bankruptcy is at the door; angry mullahs are at the gate. The corruption of the powerful is epic, the poverty of the masses crushing. The army has taken charge, again putting democracy on the shelf. More people own guns than refrigerators.' Yet it was conceded, Pakistan was 'a rediscovered crony from America's cold war days, forced back into the friendship at gunpoint to fight terrorism'. As Musharraf explained in his 19 September speech to the nation, he was facing an American ultimatum—'join us or fight us'—and that he felt that 'the country's very survival was at risk'.[12] It was further conceded that 'one of this region's many open secrets is that the Pakistani government itself has armed Islamic militants, sending them off to fight the Indian authorities in Kashmir. But whatever the government's past relationship, the US, in its new determination to combat terrorism, has sided with the military government that has not been averse to backing insurgency in Kashmir.'[13]

Necessarily, the US had to put together an aid package for Pakistan that would keep it afloat and that was likely to add up to several billion dollars and included sweeping debt rescheduling, grants spreading over many years, and trade benefits as a reward for its support against terrorism. The US administration's package came up as the 'largest mobilization of low-interest loans and debt relief' since the aid extended to Egypt during the Persian Gulf War.[14]

It would be naive to believe that this 'alliance' would be short-term, temporary and evanescent. As Jim Hoagland of the *Washington Post,* quoting Napoleon, put it, 'nothing lasts as long as the temporary'. This perceptive comment came notwithstanding his own view that the United States had assembled in all necessary haste coalition regimes 'that practise or tolerate terrorism as a matter of policy. The inclusion of such States at the centre of the coalition undermines the sweeping war aims enunciated by Bush, who has promised not to divide terrorists into bad and good camps.' He described the US hesitations about the Pakistan-based militants that had wrecked the State Assembly in Srinagar as 'diplomacy without vision'.[15]

In a similar vein, after the attack on the Indian Parliament, Selig Harrison had implored the Bush administration to proceed with caution and not advance military assistance to Pakistan without first ensuring its abandonment of the terrorists' route.[16]

Similar other voices could be heard in the United States from outside the government. Ted Galen Carpenter, Vice-President for Defence and Foreign Policy Studies at the Cato Institute, Washington, described as 'doubtful' the willingness of some members of the coalition to actually combat terrorism, mentioning Saudi Arabia, Pakistan, and China in this connection, and holding that they were part of the problem and not part of the solution.

In Ted Carpenter's view, the Saudi government had been 'the principal financial backer of Afghanistan's odious Taliban movement since at least 1996' and that 'Pakistan's guilt is nearly as great as Saudi Arabias. Without the support of the government in Islamabad, it is doubtful whether the Taliban could ever have come to power in Afghanistan'. He also said Afghanistan was not the only place where Pakistani leaders had 'flirted with terrorist toys, for they had assisted rebel forces in Kashmir even though these groups had committed terrorist acts against civilians'.[17]

In the short-run, in any case, the US had 'other priorities' and Indo–US military (or even political) cooperation could not go too far.[18] USA was at this stage largely interested in using this opportunity to enhance its influence over India and in fact become the final arbiter, and so far as cooperation with India in the wake of the Afghan operations was concerned, US desired intelligence sharing[19] more than anything else and in having the friendliest possible government in India that did not impact its new relationship with Pakistan.

Privately, the United States was giving assurances to India, particularly through its Ambassador in New Delhi, that the priority of the moment was the operation in Afghanistan and the need to eliminate Al Qaeda, but that there would be a phase-II, in which India's concerns on terrorism would be dealt with. As evidence of it, the pressure being applied by the United States on General Musharraf to declare himself unequivocally against Jihad was being cited.[20]

How this phase-II would eventually unfold was left for the future, but the present reality was that US needed Pakistan as much as Pakistan needed US. US was no doubt concerned about the terrorism in Kashmir but could not forego its relationship with Pakistan. As Richard Haas, Director of US Foreign Planning and Coordinator for Afghanistan, told his Indian interlocutors in Delhi, Kashmir was not an issue for which Americans were going to jeopardize their 'good relations' with Pakistan at this stage. Similarly, the US National Security Adviser, Condeleeza Rice told the BBC that 'Pakistan is not just a credible ally, but an ally who is proving itself everyday in its support for the coalition;

President Musharraf has been forthcoming'. She however added that this was not a one-note war and that US had told the Indian government that it intended to fight terrorism 'wherever we see it', which included India.[21] More significantly, Condeleeza Rice told the Pakistan Television that the United States' new interaction with Pakistan was not going to be a temporary affair and that the US would have long-term ties with Pakistan. Washington would not turn away once the present crisis was over, she asserted.[22]

We can note here the initial disconnect between US military advance in Afghanistan and its diplomatic hopes. Diplomatically, the United States was not too eager to fight its war in tandem with the Northern Alliance, which was not only dominated by non-Pushtoon elements but was also clearly anti-Pakistan in its approach. The US wished to accommodate Pakistani apprehensions and sensitivity, but the military requirement determined otherwise.

The US had to overcome its inhibitions in the context of Pakistan's sensitivities and to start providing assistance to the Northern Alliance as well as using its foot soldiers to advance into Kabul and break the hold of the Kabul and Kandahar-based Taliban and their Al Qaeda supporters. Pakistan's effort was to sneak in some Taliban representation, keep to the minimum the Northern Alliance representation, and to keep India out of the process of consultations in the formation of a new government in Afghanistan. The US made a vain effort to accommodate Pakistani sensitivity in the matter and to search for possible elements from the Taliban for inclusion in an interim government. The pervasiveness of the US influence would be seen from the Prime Minister Vajpayee's assent that reform-minded elements from the Taliban could be included in the interim government.[23] Eventually, however, it was obvious that just like terrorists, the Taliban could not be divided among 'good' and 'bad' elements. As Colin Powell himself acknowledged, Pakistan's viewpoint should be taken into account, but it could not dictate what the new government of Afghanistan should be.[24] The Northern Alliance secured key portfolios, including defence, interior, and foreign affairs—an arrangement that continued with slight changes even after the *Loya Jirga* set up a new government in June, 2002.

As events unfolded, victory in Afghanistan remained partial and somewhat murky. Mullah Omar and Osama bin Laden remained elusive and the military campaign continued, though desultorily. The US need for Pakistan's cooperation did not diminish as many Al Qaeda elements fled into Pakistan's tribal areas and subsequently fanned into the cities of Pakistan (as well as into areas in Kashmir occupied by Pakistan—PoK). There was no way the US could go after them without Pakistan's cooperation. General Tommy Franks, the Chief Military Commander for the war in Afghanistan, told the Associated Press that Pakistan had agreed to allow US troops in Afghanistan to cross the border in pursuit of the fugitive Al Qaeda and Taliban leaders. In some cases the Pakistani military could pursue such targets, and in some other cases, US troops could do that, General Franks said. An undisclosed number of US Special Forces soldiers were in Pakistan to coordinate with the Pakistani army there. He credited Pakistan with having gone to extraordinary lengths in support of the US campaign to hunt down and capture or kill Osama bin Laden and his top lieutenants.[25]

Although Pakistan was unhappy over the US statements and denied US participation in these operations, there was strong evidence from the US press about these developments. A Western report, for instance, said that American advisers had been granted permission to accompany Pakistani troops into tribal areas of Pakistan on raids of suspected Taliban and Al Qaeda hideouts, according to senior Pakistani officials.[26] Another report, revealed through an internet traffic detected by the US, indicated that many Al Qaeda followers and elements of the terror network were trying to re-group in remote sanctuaries in Pakistan near the Afghan border.[27] These reports led to some kind of a joint operation against the Taliban and the Al Qaeda elements in the tribal areas of Pakistan.

Another report mentioned that, protected by 'sympathetic clerics', up to 1,000 Taliban and Al Qaeda leaders were hiding in Pakistan and planning for a comeback. A certain Mullah Towha, former chief of security for the Taliban Governor of Afghanistan's Nangharahar province, told a Western correspondent that he was waiting for the day when America and Britain would leave and 'then we will have a jihad against those Afghans who fought with them against other Muslims'. The Mullah was living in Pakistani tribal areas.[28]

Similarly there were confirmed reports about infiltration of the Al Qaeda into the cities of Pakistan. Dexter Filkins reported to the *New York Times* from Islamabad that American law enforcement agencies had been working in tandem with the American military in Pakistan in 'an unusual and sustained effort to hunt down fighters of Al Qaeda who fled their sanctuaries in Afghanistan and are struggling to revive their group'. In Pakistani cities, agents of the Federal Bureau of Investigation helped the local police and provided information—in rare instances even personnel—to break up what senior American intelligence and law enforcement officials regarded as a 'depleted but still dangerous network'. The report claimed that 'Pakistan has become a laboratory for how American power could be used to combat terror'. A Pakistani journalist in Wana in the heart of Pakistan's tribal areas told Dexter Filkins that 'most of the Al Qaeda did not stay here. They kept going into the cities'. Senior Pakistani officials also told the correspondent that FBI agents were taking part in raids with the local authorities. 'They help us break down doors. They go with Pakistani law enforcement authorities when a raid is necessary, and they carry guns.'[29]

The arguments advanced by many analysts in India and abroad that, as a consequence of 9/11 and the war in Afghanistan, the US approach had changed so radically that India and US were now virtually allies in the new struggle and that it was US and Indian interests that had now converged and not US and Pakistani interests, was only half correct. The US could no longer afford to turn a blind eye to terrorism in Kashmir and Pakistan's role in it but nor could it ignore Pakistan's needs and interests. This explains the dual-track policy adopted by it towards this subcontinent in the wake of its involvement in Afghanistan.

The new strategy was perhaps most aptly summed up by David Sanger of the *New York Times*. In the weeks following the deadly attack on the Indian Parliament, President Bush and his foreign policy team have scrambled to avoid war in South Asia with a simple formula: 'daily phone calls to both sides'. Sanger might have added fortnightly visits by high dignitaries, such as Secretary of State, Secretary of Defence, Deputy Secretary of State and many other lesser functionaries. 'They have tried to reframe the conflict as a battle over terrorism, not territory', Sanger wrote. 'Instead, they have acted as if the Islamic extremists' groups accused of carrying out the assault were stateless terrorists similar to Al Qaeda and perhaps linked to it—and that they threatened the stability of Pakistan, where they are based, as surely as they threatened India.' Sanger himself acknowledged that it was partly 'a convenient fiction'. President Bush made no public mention of the fact that 'the terrorists' groups he wants to be crushed had often acted as a surrogate for Pakistan's intelligence service'.[30]

The dual-track policy was further reflected in the dual pressure, exercised by the United States, on the one hand on Pakistan and on the other on India. It is another matter that this policy also revealed contradiction and distortions in the US policy, what noted analyst Nicholas Kristoff described as 'our friends, the terrorists'. In any case, the American administration and President Bush himself leaned on

General Musharraf to discourage and cease the export of terrorism from Pakistan, but equally leaned on India to resist from taking any aggressive action in response to Pakistan-based terrorist activities in India and to open a dialogue with Islamabad on Kashmir and other issues. The US could no longer afford to accept, even tacitly, the view that one terrorism was terrorism while another terrorism was a struggle for freedom. The terrorist attack on the Indian Parliament—the heart of Indian democracy—became a defining moment and required US intercession with Islamabad lest things should get out of hand.

President Bush told General Musharraf that he must prove that he was fighting terrorism, even while the State Department heaped praise on the General for his cooperation in the fight against terrorism.[31] The US presence and pressure placed some limits on the activities of the militants and the ISI. This was, from the Indian point of view, a positive consequence of the American involvement in Afghanistan. General Musharraf's speech of 12 January 2002 came as a result of this American pressure. The General cleverly focused his speech on domestic terrorism, but he had to make public disavowal of assistance to terrorism abroad (i.e. in India, including Kashmir). The ball game in Kashmir, therefore, changed in some fundamental respects. Militancy in Kashmir could hardly be sustained by the Pakistani government at the same level.

Another spin-off of US involvement in Afghanistan was the tremendous improvement in Indo–US relations. Apart from closing the chapter of US sanctions following India's nuclear tests, the two also initiated a military relationship.

Yet, unfortunately, US involvement in the Afghanistan war also made India's foreign policy as well as making its US policy Pakistan-specific. Like USA, India too suffered from its own contradictions and distortions. India's dilemma resided between the desire for involving US intercession for pressurizing Pakistan in regard to cross-border terrorism and the fear of inviting US mediation in the Kashmir dispute. On the one hand, India was cautioning that its patience was running out and was virtually pleading with Washington to prevail upon Pakistan to desist from stoking the forces of cross-border terrorism. Yet, on the other hand, India studiously denied any mediatory role for America in the resolution of the Kashmir dispute. Although New Delhi perceived a difference between the two propositions, the line separating the two was getting thinner and thinner.

In any case, India was not impressed to the same extent by Musharraf's

12 January speech as the US administration was. Necessarily India wanted to first watch for a genuine change in the ground realities in Kashmir. But Washington now leaned on the Vajpayee government, and as US Secretary of State, Colin Powell, put it, the onus was on India to de-escalate the tensions.[32] The alternate, and sometimes simultaneous, pressure on India and Pakistan vastly enhanced the US leverage in the subcontinent.

Then came the vicious killing of families of army personnel in Kashmir resulting in a flashpoint in the deterioration of relations between India and Pakistan.

Elites in many countries of the world panicked over the prospects of a nuclear Armageddon between India and Pakistan. Yet there could not have been a more phoney war scare in modern history than the Indo–Pakistan standoff. Has one ever heard of a country threatening war, massing troops on the border, and then waiting for weeks and months to allow the other side to mobilize a similar force and be equally ready for war? Even that might have been considered feasible in the pre-Second World War situation but not in the post-11 September world. The government had hardly any intention of actually starting a war. The entire strategy was to deeply involve if not frighten the Americans into action, so that Washington's pressure would dissuade President Musharraf from sending any more militants into India, including Kashmir. The high-voltage rhetoric (in which both the Prime Minister and the Defence Minister have specialized—'the troops must be ready for a decisive and triumphant final battle'!) and the media hype could suitably impress people about India's determination to teach Pakistan a lesson.

The strategy worked up to a point. After the taming (and destruction) of Afghanistan, the Americans had eased up on General Musharraf and on the continuing cross-border terrorism. But the Indian reaction to a series of heinous terrorist acts in Kashmir and the mobilization that took place in its wake galvanized Washington (as India had hoped it would), partially because of apprehension that in such situations even 'a single spark can set the prairie on fire' and partially because of the opportunity it offered.

President Bush reportedly warned General Musharraf that cross-border terrorism must end before a meaningful dialogue could take place between India and Pakistan.[33] This was accompanied not only by the pressure on India to refrain from escalating the tensions but also by a continuation of the shuttle diplomacy bringing high-level dignitaries to India and Pakistan. President Bush repeated the warning to the Pakistani President in early June on the eve of a visit to the two countries by Deputy Secretary of State, Richard L Armitage, in a more vigorous attempt to ease the tensions. Armitage was reported to have engaged with the Pakistani authorities in blunt talk and detailed demands. He elaborated on the private message delivered by telephone earlier by President Bush and handed over a dossier containing the details of the border areas where, in the US view, Pakistan was continuing to assist Kashmir militants.[34] He made public a pledge supposedly given by President Musharraf that there would be a 'permanent' cession of assistance to cross-border terrorism.

So Musharraf and the ISI were obliged to promise to lay off—for a while in any case—and India could claim that its strategy had worked. Pakistan too used the opportunity to strive for same gains for itself from the rather messy situation that it had perforce landed itself in since the campaign against Osama bin Laden and the Taliban. All the dark hints that were dropped, and sometimes crude statements that came from Pakistan about its willigness to resort to its nuclear armoury 'under certain extreme circumstances' were meant not so much to deter India (the Pakistani generals were as aware of the phoney war scare as the Indian government leaders) as to impress the Americans that the 'grave' situation called for their immediate intervention. The 'extreme conditions' referred to the threat to Pakistan's existence as a State, that is, in the event of India's attempt to conquer Pakistan. The generals in Islamabad knew very well that even the most rabid politicians in India were not so insane as to make any such attempt—and that too while the American military was posted within Pakistan and many of its air fields were under its control. Nor were the Pakistani military leaders so insane as to begin a suicidal nuclear holocaust in a limited war with India.

General Musharraf was realizing that in the new world situation in the wake of the Afghanistan war, terrorism, no matter under what garb, would not be defended, much less condoned, and therefore in return for some concessions that he would have to make, he must secure a heavier US involvement in the Kashmir issue. So, Pakistan too has some gains to show. It had to give more trustworthy assurances to the US to prevent infiltration of militants into India from the Pakistani side (at least temporarily), but it may have ensured long-term US involvement in the region, which gives Washington the kind of leverage that it never had so far. What this means for Pakistan's own sovereignty is quite another matter.

Prime Minister Vajpayee indicated this much when he bemoaned that India should have taken action after the terrorists attack on Parliament on 13 December. He was expressing both his helplessness and his desperation. Middle-class India just had no understanding of what a modern war means. Many of them think that hey can go to war and watch it on television. Even the 1965 and the 1971 wars, although they inflicted very considerable damage on the Indian economy, could not have brought home the destructiveness of modern warfare. Wars can take place in the contemporary conditions only if either warring country has preponderant power or if it can use the opportunity of unpreparedness of the other side through recourse to the ancient strategy of secrecy and deception.

Middle-class India also drew entirely fallacious conclusions from the American war in Afghanistan and the Israeli knockout of Palestine. 'If America can do it, if Israel was allowed, why not India?'—was the constant refrain of middle-class India, including the media. This showed scant comprehension of the revolution in military affairs. USA had overwhelming power, Afghanistan was hapless, despite the viciousness of the Taliban. Israel had a great many instruments of modern warfare, Palestine had none. Pakistan and India just do not fall in the same category.

However, both India and Pakistan achieved one result—they became totally dependent on the US to pull their chestnuts out of the fire. In any case, India made its relations hostage to the US role in Kashmir. A defiance could cost heavily externally and a compliance could cost heavily internally. This is for the first time since independence that India's decision-making autonomy in foreign policy, including policy towards neighbours, has been eroded so substantially. The issue is not that USA has any hostile intentions (I believe it does not have) but that it is the first time that India has lost so much leverage in foreign policy. General Musharraf is desperately trying to turn to his advantage the role that the USA has assigned him by resorting to blatant unconstitutional means to stamp out opposition to him. How Pakistan is to recover its sovereignty is for the people of Pakistan to decide. But it is in India's fundamental interests to strive for the complete and genuine restoration of democracy in Pakistan. Only after such restoration can India innovatively search for a détente with the people of Pakistan.

NOTES

1. *Hindustan Times*, 12 September 2001.
2. Jaswant Singh, in interview with *Times of India*, 14 September 2001.
3. *Hindustan Times*, 15 September 2001.
4. *The Sunday Times*, 28 October.
5. *The Hindu*, 28 September 2001.
6. *Asian Age*, 11 November 2001.
7. Thomas Friedman in *New York Times*, 14 August 2002.
8. *Washington Post*, 8 November 2001.
9. Manoj Joshi, in *Times of India*, 16 October 2001.
10. *Washington Post*, 14 September 2001.
11. *New York Times*, 15 September 2001.
12. Barry Bearak in *New York Times*, 2 October 2001.
13. Ibid.
14. *New York Times*, 27 October 2001.
15. Jim Hoagland, re-produced in *Times of India*, 4 October 2001.
16. *International Herald Tribune*, 20 December 2001.
17. Cato Institute, electronically, 21 November 2001.
18. Ted Carpenter, quoted in *Asian Age*, 21 November 2001.
19. John Pike, quoted in *Asian Age*, November 2001.
20. Raja Mohan in *The Hindu*, 2 February 2002.
21. *Asian Age*, 9 November 2001.
22. *The Hindu*, 3 December 2001.
23. *Hindustan Times*, 3 November 2001.
24. *Time of India*, 24 October 2001.
25. Associated Press interview, quoted in *Asian Age*, 9 January 2002.
26. *New York Times*, 24 April 2002.
27. *The Times of India*, 7 March 2002.
28. Kathy Gannon of the Associated Press, quoted in *Asian Age*, 21 March 2002.
29. Dexter Filkins, *New York Times*, 14 July 2002.
30. David E. Sanger, *New York Times*, 7 January 2002.
31. *Hindustan Times*, 9 January 2002.
32. *Times of India*, 16 January 2002.
33. *Times of India*, 9 March 2002.
34. *New York Times*, 7 June 2002.

US Perspectives in a Global and South Asian Context: Before and After 11 September

ACHIN VANAIK

The methodological approach for the task at hand is rather simple. The political culture of foreign offices, including that of the US, is straightforwardly realist. It is the way foreign-policy shapers, makers, and implementers think. That the world order or global context is shaped rather differently cannot seriously be taken into account when such is the dominant paradigm of thought. Whatever the short-term hopes, expectations, and results of specific foreign policy ambitions and practices of even the most powerful states, in the medium and longer term, what emerges from the always complex intersection and interaction of a very wide array of forces and actors (not just states) between, across, and within states, are mostly *unanticipated outcomes and unintended consequences*. The rise of Islamic terrorist groups once aided by the US, now out to target it, is but another example of this 'law' of international relations.

To properly trace US global perspectives after the end of the Cold War, and the changes or adjustments to that post-Cold War strategy after September 11, we need only to think like realists. But not just like the common or garden variety of realists that proliferate everywhere. We have to think like the most ruthless and hardheaded American does. To understand the true purposes and ambitions of this US foreign policy behaviour, we must never make the mistake of taking American liberals (and their liberalism) seriously. Unlike their role in domestic affairs where no balanced assessment can ever preclude their importance, in the external behaviour of the US State, they invariably lose out barring occasional and brief periods of influence. Their principal function is to establish the outer limits of acceptable dissent and its related terms of discourse for declaratory and media purposes. For the last half-a-century (if not for far longer), and certainly since the end of the Cold War, it is the hard right that has determined the strategic goals of US foreign policy and the most important tactics to be adopted in their pursuit. What then was the new post-Cold War strategy and perspective to be?

END OF THE COLD WAR: FROM SOVIET BREAK UP TO 11 SEPTEMBER 2001

John L. Gaddis, the noted US diplomatic historian, once talked of the dog-car syndrome. The dog chases the car but never really thinks about what it will do if it ever catches up with the car. This was an apt characterization of the US between 1945 and 1991 when it was chasing victory in the Cold War but never really expected victory, nor thought of what it would do if it won. Post 1991 it had to start thinking. After only a brief interlude where some uncertainty prevailed and more magnanimous visions of collective security through cooperation with other states (including former rivals) were entertained, the US established its basic strategic goal—world dominance through determined unilateralism. It correctly recognized the unique situation existing.

In the system of nation states, nothing like this had ever existed before, certainly not over the last 150 years of modern history. Between 1870, at the height of British imperial power, and the First World War, there was the rising challenge of Germany and the US to worry about. Between the First and Second World Wars, a declining Britain and France were faced with a rising US, Germany, Japan, and USSR. After World War II, the US was confronted militarily–strategically–politically by the USSR, and economically by Germany and Japan, both of which made substantial relative gains vis-à-vis the US. After 1991, and for the foreseeable future, the US simply has no political–strategic–military rival. Its annual military budget of over US $380 billion dollars cannot be matched by the next fifteen countries put together (Russia's annual budget is around US $7 billion and India's today at around $14 billion). Yet, at around 5 per cent, this is by no means an excessive percentage of its total GDP. Such a situation of overwhelming military power over all actual or potential rivals has never before existed.

This unique situation of exceptional dominance must be sustained as far as possible against both allies and rivals. Of that the strong conservative right has no doubts. Witness what two hard-nosed commentators Robert Kagan and William Kristol (*National Interest*, Spring 2000) have to say: 'Today's international system is built not around a balance of power but around American hegemony. The international financial institutions were fashioned by American interests and serve American interests. The international security structures are chiefly a collection of American-led alliances. . . . Since today's relatively benevolent circumstances are the product of our hegemonic influence, any loosening of that influence will allow others to play a larger part in shaping the world to suit their needs. . . . American hegemony, then, must be actively maintained, just as it was actively obtained.'

And this is what the post-Cold War period has been all about. Here domination of the world economy and geostrategic domination of the Eurasian landmass have been the key goals to be pursued, with the add-on provided by the search for nuclear, and general military, pre-eminence in space to be achieved through its long-term programme of 'full-spectrum dominance'.[1] Again, the American hard right makes no bones about it. Sub-Saharan Africa is, strategically speaking, irrelevant, which is why the massacres in Rwanda did not call for urgent military intervention (unlike the Balkans) by the West, or more specifically the US, in the name of protecting humanitarian principles. South and Central America, as also Australasia, are similarly of no real strategic importance and are dominated by the US anyway save the odd irritant in Cuba and one or two other minor countries in the Southern hemisphere. It is Eurasia that is crucial. Here, through NATO, the western flank is secured by the US. On Eurasia's eastern flank there are the US-dominated security pacts with Japan, South Korea, and Taiwan. And in the heart of this Eurasian landmass, in the all-important oil-rich Middle East, US dominance is secured through its tripod of client regimes—Israel, Egypt, Saudi Arabia. The first is the most militarily powerful regional satrap. The second is the one Arab state with the population and potential technological, scientific, and military resources to provide the nucleus of a real and collective Arab resistance to Israel and the US. The third controls 50-60 per cent of the world's known oil reserves (its wealth is also responsible for maintaining various Gulf sheikdoms, themselves generously endowed with oil) and whose internal corruption and conservatism is matched only by their general subservience to US dictates and inclinations.

To quote Brzezinski: 'Its [US's] military legions are firmly perched on the western and eastern extremities of Eurasia, and they also control the Persian Gulf. American vassals and tributaries, some yearning to be embraced by even more formal ties to Washington, dot the entire Eurasian continent.'[2] The bluntness of the language used is not accidental. For Brzezinski divides the system of nation states into four types—the vassals (Western Europe, Australia, Japan, Canada), the tributaries (much of the rest of the world), left-out aspirants seeking tributary and vassal status (India would easily find a place here), and potentially serious though not yet actual rivals (Russia, China, and Iran).[3] The job is 'to prevent collusion and maintain security dependence among the vassals, to keep tributaries pliant and protected, and to keep the barbarians from coming together'.[4] Since 1991, US foreign policy behaviour on various fronts has conformed to this overarching US perspective.

The World Economy: Neo-liberal Economic Globalization

Those who have a vested interest in supporting the particular (neo-liberal) form of economic globalization that has taken place since the beginning of the 1980s would like nothing better than to portray this process as inevitable and therefore unavoidable, thereby weakening efforts at resistance to it. For the truth is that even within the framework of capitalist globalization processes there are other directions that could be taken, alternative combinations of 'market forces' and 'state powers'. Indeed, to the key questions that might be posed of this globalization—How big? How wide? How new?—the general answers contradict much of the received wisdom. In terms of the goods and services produced or traded outside one's country as a proportion of world output and trade, it is neither remarkable nor novel as compared to earlier periods such as the pre-World War I world economy. If there is a growing integration of many national economies, there is also growing marginalization and exclusion of others, and certainly not the simplistic model of straightforward and growing convergence and inclusion of peoples and economies. External investment of a genuinely productive kind is not, in relative terms, more marked or distinctive in this era as compared to previous ones.[5]

Yet there are certain undeniably novel aspects of this period of neo-liberal economic globalization that must be grasped, as also the connection between this 'global trend' and the very 'specific' interests of the US State and Capital. We can register four distinctive aspects of qualitative importance in today's form of economic globalization. (a) There is much greater concentration of capital expressed in the absolute and relative growth in importance and power of transnational corporations (TNCs) as compared to other economic actors. (b) There is not just the growing transnationalization of production relations, something that characterizes previous eras as well, but the considerable transnationalization of the production *process* itself. (c) There is both growing integration and inclusiveness of certain economies and societies accompanied by growing exclusiveness and marginalization of others. That is to say, the historic pattern of uneven and unequal capitalist development is now rendered qualitatively greater. (d) Finally, there is the most important development of all, the one without real historical precedent. This is the truly dramatic burgeoning and loosening of financial capital/financial markets from the real economy/markets/ flows of production and productive investment as well as the incredible involution of activity within the former.

This last named development is what we must try and understand if we are to have any kind of a handle on what US efforts to dominate the world economy are all about. It really started in 1971 and the abandonment of the Gold Standard for the international monetary regime. The shift then to a pure Dollar Standard (with peripheral roles for the German Mark and the Japanese Yen once the effort at establishing IMF controlled Special Drawing Rights or SDRs as a new form of international currency fell into oblivion) marked the point when a new kind of US dominance of the world financial and economic system became a possibility. It still remained to thoroughly dismantle the Bretton Woods system of fixed exchange rates and its maintenance of powerful constraints on the international movement of private capital for speculative purposes. It was in the 1980s that this neo-liberal form of financial globalization became a reality. The overall result was the establishment of what aptly has been called the Dollar Wall Street Regime (DWSR).[6]

With the dollar central to the international monetary system, more and more people turn to Wall Street (and to what is, in effect, its offshore junior partner, London) to hold their reserves. Many commodities are also priced in dollars so much of trade finance too will take place there. The bigger and stronger the financial market (and Wall Street is far and away the biggest), the easier and safer it is for investors to buy and sell all kinds of securities, and the more likely that rates will be competitive for borrowing. Throughout the 1980s and 1990s, the world's 'capital markets' became an arena where the channelling of funds/ savings and credit creation for productive purposes became increasingly dwarfed by financial activity of an essentially speculative nature with no positive functional connection with the real economy. The priority was no longer *capital formation* but money movements and transfers of capital ownership. This is a world where over 90 per cent of financial activity has to do (a) with trading in the secondary securities markets (a great variety of financial 'instruments', e.g. derivatives, junk bonds, etc., were created in the last two decades) whose main purpose is not to help in the creation of new value but to participate in the buying and selling of *claims on future value* yet to be produced; (b) foreign exchange and currency speculation; (c) hot money flows. And all of this in search of short-term rentier and arbitrage profits, namely buying cheap, selling dear. This is about money to be made out of money itself, from its velocity of circulation, from even the smallest variations geographically in its pricing, i.e. interest rates, from speculative pressures on exchange rates themselves promoting speculatively cashed-in profits.

Since the dollar is the key currency in which most such activity takes place, the US enjoys the unique advantage of seignorage—it does not face the balance of payments constraints of other countries.[7] It can spend far more abroad than it earns, e.g. for financing military bases, for helping its TNCs buy up other companies, or for engaging in foreign direct investment, whether of the portfolio type or for the much rarer 'greenfield' investments. The US financial system becomes the world's main source of credit. The DWSR becomes the battering ram to open up other countries/region's financial systems and subject them to the procedures and aims of the DWSR. The US financial system, which is shaped by the relationship between the government (the Federal Reserve) and the DWSR determines credit nationally, and in doing so, determines, to a great extent, credit availability and terms internationally. When US government bonds become the most prized financial asset internationally, then a low-saving US economy is guaranteed the necessary external investment to keep going.

This is a world economy where the greatest 'virtue' to be secured above all else, is that capital can be at its most mobile and therefore allows for the quickest and maximal money profits *unconnected* to the inescapably far slower rhythms of actual production of publicly consumable goods and services. Why do other elites and capitals of other countries go along with this neo-liberal project whose benefits are most strongly biased towards US capital and US-based TNCs?[8] Partly because they can also benefit from such an unconstrained financial set-up. There is no simple separation between productive and unproductive units of capital. TNCs and companies responsible for productive activity garner much of their profits from unproductive ones as well. The same applies to banks and mutual funds. In what used to be called second or third world countries, domestic capitals and capitalists, even as they sell out rather than compete with more powerful foreign companies, benefit from the existence of the DWSR by simply and substantially transforming themselves into the newer kind of international rentier capitalists benefiting from this neo-liberal financial order.

Even so, European capital enjoyed partial protection from this growing US dominance because of the EU. But the most important challenge to American economic pre-eminence was coming in the 1980 and 1990s from East Asia (including China and Japan). At the beginning of the 1980s, East Asia (minus Japan, Australia, New Zealand) accounted for one-sixth of world output. By the mid-1990s, this region (in purchasing power parity terms) was accounting for one-fourth of world output. By 2005, on then existing trends it would have accounted for one-third of global output. If Japan's output was added to this, then clearly there was a real likelihood that for the first time in 500 years, the centre of the entire world economy would have shifted away from the Atlantic and from the bloc of countries of what came to be called after 1945, the Atlantic Alliance. Between 1990–7, East Asia accounted for two-thirds of new global investment and around half of total growth of world GDP!

The Clinton administration was fully aware of the East Asian economic challenge and consciously pursued what it called 'geo-economics'—a systematic drive to open up the world economy to US goods, services, and capital. Japan could not yet be frontally challenged since its key source of dynamism lay within its own borders. At any rate, since the beginning of the 1990s, Japan has entered an exceptionally long cycle of stagnation to the relative advantage of the US. It was its eminence in East Asia (outside China), namely its role as a productive–investment motor for the whole of the region, that had to be challenged and this required not a head-on confrontation with Japan but the undermining of the key country of South Korea.

In the 1980s under Reagan, the US discovered that Structural Adjustment Programmes (SAPs) of the IMF/WB could be the lever to prise open third world economies to American benefit, hence the value of US dominance of these two institutions.[9] To take on East Asia the US had to do more. Washington successfully changed the purposes of the IMF/World Bank. In 1997, the IMF Articles of Agreement were changed to press for dismantling of capital controls in all member countries. In the same year, the World Trade Organization (WTO) in its terms of operation, legitimized and pressed for global liberalization of financial services. Yet the US will not accept WTO rulings if these are deemed 'unfair' to the US by the government.

Under Clinton, the US waged a trade war on South Korea in the name of 'anti-dumping' and 'voluntary export restraints' on steel, textiles, and clothing. It also used its Super-301 clause against 'unfair' practices by Koreans. Thus a Korean trade surplus of US $9.6 billion in 1987 became a US $4 billion trade deficit with the US by 1996. After 1995, the US pushed the dollar exchange rate higher relative to the yen undermining East Asia's (outside Japan) exports denominated in dollars. Private inflows of dollars into East Asian economies raised exchange rates and domestic inflation. The financial squeeze resulting from lower exports, higher domestic prices pushed East Asians to borrow more from the US, Europe, and Japan. All this created a dangerous situation in the currency markets. Massive speculation against East Asian currencies (Baht, Rupiah, and the Won) precipitated the collapse of currencies and the financial system in the region. So currency rates swung wildly around a declining overall trend, and hot money/short-term loans were pulled out. The US, in particular, used the 1997 East Asian crisis to finish off the challenge of the Korean Chaebols and to buy into Korean assets on a very significant scale. Meanwhile, a major reworking of East Asia's financial systems took place to make it like the US/UK systems with much freer entry and exit for external capitals.

The overall US strategy with regard to what it considers the 'big emerging markets'—Indonesia, Malaysia, Thailand, South Korea, China, India, Brazil, Poland, Mexico, and Argentina—is clear. With the EU basically allying itself with American capital in its zeal for predatory behaviour, these emerging markets are targeted for attempted 'takeover' through association and collaboration with local rentiers or those willing to become internationally mobile rentier capitalists. Since many of the governments and state apparatuses in these countries are manned at the top by those who, for one reason or the other, are quite willing to accept the neo-liberal economic agenda, the prospects for substantial success in pursuit of this strategy are certainly bright.

In short, economic neo-liberalism has behind it the conscious aim and power of the American state to promote its globalization. It is the way the US has been able since the end of the Cold War to partially retrieve ground lost earlier to its principal economic challengers, Germany and Japan; and to pave the way for its enhanced and continued economic dominance globally. Please note, however, that prosperity for corporate America does not mean prosperity for geographic America.

Geostrategic Perspectives

EUROPE

One of the first questions that emerged after the end of the Cold War was what should the new security architecture of Europe be, and on what should it be based? There were three possible answers—a greatly enhanced role for the Organization for Security and Cooperation in Europe (OSCE); or for the Western European Union (WEU); or continued reliance on an American dominated and led NATO. The clear logic of the first two approaches would have been to give a much more enhanced role and importance to Germany and Russia, and a concomitantly more reduced role for the US in Europe. The fundamental subtext of the Balkans eruption (the break up of Yugoslavia) was, in fact, the issue of whether the post-Cold War period would now see the emergence of a new dynamic characterized by enhanced Russian and German power in Europe with possibilities of even an eventual condominium between the two, or whether NATO would reassert itself as the principal framework of strategic–military–political control in Europe. The failure of the European powers to manage the Balkan crises on their own, and the continued internal suspicions within the EU about German aggrandizement in the future, effectively paved the way for NATO, and therefore the US, to reassert its primacy in the Balkans. Europe was still not able or willing to do without the US. The NATO project in Europe remained intact—to keep the US in, the Germans down, and the Russians out. But there was also more.

It was not enough just to maintain NATO. It had to be expanded eastwards if the opportunity provided by the collapse of the Soviet Union was to be taken proper advantage of. The point was not insurance against a possible Russian threat in the future but the folly otherwise of not trying to cash in on this remarkable period of great Russian weakness! Of course, this meant betrayal of earlier promises, but so what? At the time of unification of Germany, Russia had been assured informally that NATO would not expand eastwards. Later, Gorbachev was to publicly regret his failure to insist upon and obtain this reassurance in formalized treaty terms. It was, he was to declare, one of his great mistakes. By the mid-1990s, a near-consensus in the US 'foreign policy establishment' had decided that NATO must expand eastwards. The Russians would be fobbed off with the sop of 'consultative status' with NATO. Russian expressions of willingness to even join NATO were politely rebuffed. In the latest phase, a NATO–Russia Council has been set up giving the Russians a say and decision making powers in matters of 'common' concern, e.g. terrorism, etc. But the Russians are firmly excluded from any involvement in the internal functioning and decision-making of NATO itself. This Council arrangement is but another sop to sweeten the otherwise bitter pill that Russia must swallow. NATO will now expand even closer to Russia in the future, incorporating even the Baltic Republics eventually.

So weakened is Russia that it doesn't even possess the courage to protest seriously against what it knows full well is a long-term strategy directed against it. Under the Putin regime, it deems it preferable to settle for what it can get by way of capitulation disguised as a new and welcome era of 'mutual cooperation'. During the Cold War it was inaccurately held that the Warsaw Pact had a conventional military preponderance over NATO, which NATO's trip-wire of possible first use of nuclear weapons had to balance out. In reality, given the qualitative superiority of NATO's weaponry, there was a rough balance, even a slight advantage perhaps to NATO on the conventional military plane. But since 1989, there has been a dramatic change, no doubt the major reason why Russia has abandoned its former commitment to 'No First Use' of nuclear weapons against a nuclearly armed adversary. On the conventional military plane, NATO is today *three times* stronger than Russia and the Confederation of Independent States (CIS) put together! With the absorption of Poland and other Central and Eastern European States into NATO, it will become four times stronger.

And this extended absorption is very much on the cards. In fact, the long-term perspective of the US is to prevent any possibility of a future condominium between a developing Germany and a revived Russia. This means the US must politically–strategically occupy the space between the two, namely seek control over Poland and the Ukraine, the two most important and powerful States between them. The two most powerful countries to emerge from the wreckage of the Soviet Union were Russia and the Ukraine. One of the rare failures of the US in the post-Cold War period was its inability to wean Ukraine away from Russia. However, this failure remains a partial one. Ukraine has dropped its opposition to the expansion of NATO and even hinted that it might not be averse in the future to being part of it. But the incorporation of Poland into NATO and its expansion eastwards is bad enough for Russia. It means there is a mighty military (and nuclear-armed) entity on its very borders whose constituents and leadership have eyes on the energy-rich resources in its 'underbelly region' and will seek to extend their influence over Ukraine.

Poland, of course, has always been viewed by the US as a specially prized asset. It is not an accident that no other Central or Eastern European country after 1989 was awarded the same terms of massive debt write-offs and debt rescheduling that was given to Poland by the international financial institutions. As for Germany, its short-term desire for an extended buffer between it and Russia meant it would accept the incorporation of Poland into NATO. Moreover, since the US does not and cannot control the EU, which is also to be expanded through eventual inclusion of the Central and Eastern European countries, NATO incorporation of the latter gives it a leverage over the EU it would otherwise not have.

Disagreements between the US and its European allies, most often with France, should not be allowed to disguise the reality of Europe's subordination, geopolitically, to US perspectives. The differences express not a dispute about, or challenge to, the fact of such subordination, but express concerns about the terms on which such subordination is to be organized with the Europeans wanting multilateralist consultation and some limited influence on US decision making rather than having to simply line up behind US unilateralism. It remains to be seen whether these current differences will develop further to the point where there is a more serious and basic discord reflecting European willingness to challenge that subordination itself.

ASIA: FROM WEST TO EAST

Saddam Hussein had reasons to be shocked by the Gulf War of 1991. Here he was the favoured ally of the US against Khomeini's Iran in the 1980–8 war, or what was the second longest war of the twentieth century (Only the Sino–Japanese war of 1937–45 lasted a few months more). He had expected the US, if not to back him in his takeover of Kuwait, at least to turn a blind eye. What he failed to realize is that the US was bound to oppose him for the very same reason it had backed him against the Shia revolution of Iran under Khomeini. The strategic aims of the US in the Gulf have been threefold. First, to control not just the key sources of oil production but the direction and form of disposition of those vast rentier 'lakes' constituted by oil revenues. Second, to keep its most serious rival, the USSR/Russia, out of the region. A negotiated withdrawal of Iraqi forces from Kuwait and a re-establishment of the previous status quo had clearly become possible in the weeks preceding the initiation of the war. But the US wanted the war and acted to prevent any chance of a negotiated withdrawal.[10]

Third, to prevent any single power in the region from becoming too strong or otherwise threatening the 'moderate' (which means sufficiently servile to the US and not necessarily anti-Islamic fundamentalist) Arab regimes of the Gulf and the Middle East. This was the threat posed by post-Shah 'revolutionary' Iran, requiring US backing of Hussein's Iraq. It was, again, these very strategic guidelines that now required the brutal taming of Iraq. The seeming paradox of the US seeking the ouster of Saddam Hussein, yet allowing him to remain in power within his country for more than a decade after the Gulf War, is not difficult to explain. The problem is the strength internally of the Baathist regime in Iraq. What the US needs, but has not yet found, is an indigenous leadership, which can be an alternative to Hussein, that can at one and the same time provide a coherent Iraqi regime (its break up would unleash Kurdish and Shia forces that would exacerbate American difficulties in controlling the region) yet one that is also adequately subservient to the US.

The 1993 Oslo Peace Accords must be seen in the context of the post-Gulf War realignment of forces globally and regionally, one that greatly favoured Israel and the US. Fearful of his own and the PLO's growing irrelevance in the new situation, Arafat traded in his most important political--diplomatic asset—recognition of Israel—not for Israeli recognition of a fully sovereign and independent Palestinian state to emerge in the future, but (a) merely for recognition of the PLO as the authentic representative voice of the Palestinians; (b) the initiation of a process of negotiations leaving unspecified and vague what ultimate goal it would lead to—there was no promise then or now that full and proper sovereignty would ever be given or that there would ever be complete restoration of all territory illegally occupied by Israel after the 1967 war; and (c) acceptance of a gendarme and local administrative role by a newly founded Palestinian National Authority (PNA) over certain parts of the occupied West Bank and Gaza Strip.

The intent of the Oslo Accords, certainly on the part of Israel and the US, was that in accordance with the existing relationship of forces on the ground, some kind of 'final settlement' involving the effective Bantustanization of the West Bank and Gaza, but with superficial nationalist trappings (a flag, declaration of statehood, UN membership, etc.) could be secured through the Arafat leadership. In short, there would be the permanent subordination of the new 'state', economically and security-wise, to the power of Israel.

What has prevented this from taking place and indeed caused the complete collapse of the Oslo process has most certainly not been the principled resistance of the Arafat leadership but the remarkable refusal of the Palestinian people, despite the enormous odds against it and despite its international isolation, to accept this political trajectory of Bantustanization. Arafat is not in control of the Palestinian resistance, which in retaliation to the brutal and terrorist military assaults of the occupying forces of Israel has responded with a terrorism of its own—suicide bombings.[11] Today, a bitter and vicious Israeli leadership backed by an even more arrogant American leadership is further redefining the future prospects of Palestinians—if not an acceptance of Bantustanization, then their conceivable expulsion outside the West Bank to Jordan and elsewhere leaving behind only a small minority much more easily absorbable by the new Israel. This would be the fulfilment of the dream of at least some sections of Israeli Zionists—the establishment of an *Eretz* or Greater Israel over all of historic Palestine, and the elimination of the Palestinian problem through the elimination of the category of a territorial Palestine.

How do South and Central Asia fit into the wider picture of post-Cold War perspectives of the US? Immediately after the end of the Cold War, despite India's status as one of the 'big emerging markets' economically, in geo-strategic terms South Asia was actually somewhat downgraded. Throughout the Cold War period it was East Asia and the Middle East (West Asia) that were seen as the key areas of geopolitical concern. South Asia's importance was essentially derivative, coming from the fact that it was the site of Cold War rivalry involving the US, the USSR, and China. These rivalries were partly mediated through the India–Pakistan face-off. The end of the Cold War fundamentally eroded Sino–Russian rivalry in South Asia and elsewhere, as indeed US–Russian rivalry in South Asia.

The collapse of bloc rivalry, which had given an obvious relevance to India's foreign policy of non-alignment, meant that there would now be a search for a new and improved relationship between India and the

US, especially after the inauguration of the neo-liberal economic turn by India in 1991. Quite unsurprisingly, both countries now began talking of forging a new 'strategic friendship' with some voices even daring to talk of a new 'strategic partnership'. The problem, however, was always the terms on which such a friendship or partnership were to be forged. New Delhi wanted Washington to forego the charms of Islamabad for what it believed were its own more alluring charms. India as the pre-eminent power in the region, and now looking to establish a long-term relationship of friendship and cooperation with the West, especially the US, should be correspondingly favoured over the US–Pakistan link. Moreover, wasn't there much to be said about the usefulness of India as an Asian counterweight to China, now and in the future?

However, the fundamental asymmetry in power guaranteed that there was no reason why Washington should view the region, the Asian continent or the world, through the prism of New Delhi. The US as a world power had, and continues to have, many more options than an India, which is at best a potential major power, a potential that it may not even realize. Furthermore, for all its regional eminence, India was not a regional *hēgēmon*. There was the reality of a Pakistan that continued to challenge its authority. And if the 1987 Indo–Sri Lanka Accord marked the meridian of India's search for regional dominance, its subsequent collapse in a little over a year marked the failure of India to fulfil those ambitions.[12] In any case, the collapse of the Soviet Union had already indicated the fragility even of 'superpowerdom'. In short, the US need not take seriously Indian conditions for improving bilateral relations but could press its own terms of accommodation. If India was pleased that the US came down diplomatically on its side during the Kargil War of 1999, forcing Pakistan to withdraw and thus suffer a political-diplomatic defeat, though not a serious military one, this most certainly did not mean that the US was abandoning Pakistan for India.

Pakistan through the 1990s continued to serve US interests both with respect to the Middle East, where its historic connection with Saudi Arabia has always been useful to the US, and by its connections with Afghanistan, and through it to areas beyond. Even after the accession of the Taliban to power in Afghanistan in 1996, the US was by no means averse to improving relations with a Taliban-controlled Afghanistan, including giving formal diplomatic recognition. It came close to doing so on a number of occasions between 1996 and the 1998 bombings of the US embassies in East Africa. The bombings marked the point at which the US shifted its attitude towards the Taliban regime, now on its black book because of its informal support to Osama bin Laden. Prior to this, the Taliban regime was seen as a counterweight to Iranian influence in Afghanistan and hostile to the Russians, neither of which was seen as particularly negative attributes for a Washington keen to penetrate the Central Asian region with its oil–gas reserves and to establish pipelines that, by going through Afghanistan and Pakistan to the Indian Ocean, could bypass both Iran and Russia.

As for the China factor, the bird-in-the-hand reality of a complex and very important US–China relationship meant it was not something that would be jeopardized or sacrificed now for the bird-in-the-bush possibility that India (should it fulfil its potential for becoming a major Asian power, itself an uncertain prospect) might sometime in the future become that counterweight that the American Right might deem particularly useful. The essential nature of the US–China relationship through the nineties has been (a) one of considerable mutual benefit and importance to both countries, and certainly much more important than bilateral US–India relations; (b) one in which it is the Chinese that have been much more on the defensive politically, yet it is Beijing that is desperate to sustain and not allow its relations with Washington to deteriorate, if it can at all help it. For both Russia and China, regardless of their overtures to each other or their improved economic and military exchanges, it is their respective and separate relations with the US that each considers paramount. And the US is fully aware of this. For all the political self-advertisement of India to the US about its value as a counterweight to China, it is India that needs the US much more than vice versa, and it is the US therefore that sets the basic framework for any enduring relationship between the two.

Between 1991 and May 1998 (Pokharan II), for all the talk of a new era in US–India relations, there was little to show on the ground. In its own way, this reflected precisely the point made earlier—the reduced salience, geo-strategically, of South Asia after the end of the Cold War. The nuclear tests of 1998 changed this by introducing a new, but still essentially negative political sailence to the region. If the initial US response to the tests was one of anger and opposition, this quickly (within a few months) shifted to acceptance of India's (and Pakistan's) *de facto* nuclear status. The new US concern was to ensure that Indian ambitions would remain at the level of being a small nuclear power (SNP), thereby not complicating its own much wider geopolitical perspectives, and that nuclear rivalries and tensions between India and

Pakistan would be adequately contained.[13] The India–Pakistan nuclear face-off now obviously made Kashmir a potential nuclear flashpoint.

Hence the several and repeated rounds of high-level discussions between New Delhi and the Clinton administration in Washington, in which the Indian government sought to reassure the US that it could be its most faithful ally in the region and that its nuclear status could be of wider benefit to the US, even as New Delhi repeatedly skirted all efforts to be pinned down on the question of how minimum its declared position of seeking only a 'minimum credible deterrent' would be. For all the hoopla about President Clinton's visit to India in 2000 (made much more of in India than in the US—Clinton had been the most internationally peripatetic President to ever occupy the White House), in geo-strategic terms it is really the developments unleashed by 11 September 2001, that have for the first time introduced a new and 'positive' salience to South Asia for the US whose ramifications and implications will be more systematically explored in the following sections. But before that, a brief commentary on the US's nuclear weapons policies and perspectives in the post-Cold War era is in order.

The US and Nuclear Weapons

The one area where, initially, the end of the Cold War had an undisputedly positive impact unlike its more contradictory implications for the general geopolitical environment, was in respect of nuclear disarmament.[14] Once the Cold War ended, it became obvious to even the most intransigent of Cold Warriors and to the most dedicated of nuclear weapons advocates, that there was no escape from very significant reductions in nuclear arms. American nuclear policy now had to decide between two possible strategies. Only a small minority of 'experts' were advocating anything as radical as proceeding systematically towards global nuclear disarmament. True, their numbers had grown and now included prominent former nuclearists of considerable stature from Robert McNamara to George Lee Butler to Paul Nitze. But the main divide having a bearing on post-Cold War nuclear policy formation was between those advocating doing 'less with less' and those advocating doing 'more with less'.

In the first group were certainly not arms-eliminators but they were arms-moderators. They argued as follows: the US had won the Cold War. The time had come to systematically reduce the nuclear arsenals of the US and Russia and to wind down the qualitative arms race between the two. Even so, the premier nuclear status of the US was assured. It was also time to put various non-proliferation measures on the agenda such as making the NPT permanent in 1995. Going in for a Comprehensive Test Ban Treaty or CTBT would make it very difficult for newcomers to develop their nuclear arsenals even if new entry to the nuclear club was not, strictly speaking, prevented. The CTBT would put a genuine cap preventing qualitatively significant further development of nuclear weaponry by the existing nuclear weapons states (NWSs), including the US. But this was a price worth paying since its uniform application worldwide would still leave the US pre-eminent on the nuclear front since this would be a collective sacrifice. Besides, what need was there to explore or develop new nuclear weapons or pursue new nuclear pathways?

Those in the second group were the arms-racers and developers, loath to acknowledge any diminished role for nuclear weapons and keen to find new purposes and goals for these weapons in order to justify and promote further nuclear weapons development and extended reliance on them. Obviously there was a strong supply-side constituency (the military–industrial complex) favouring such an approach. The story of the 1990s is the story of how the first group, temporarily ascendant in the immediate aftermath of the end of the Cold War, would slowly but surely lose ground to the latter. Before 1995, those advocating an abrogation of the ABM Treaty or even a limited 'Star Wars' programme were a small minority even within the Republican Party. In the latter half of the 1990s, the Democratic Party had itself come around to endorsing a limited 'Star Wars' programme. By the end of the millennium, the Republicans had ensconced themselves in Congress and in the White House. The US refused to ratify the CTBT. Instead of the world getting a powerful and permanent restraint measure as a step towards greater nuclear sanity, the CTBT was effectively scuppered. Soon after, the Bush administration withdrew from the ABM Treaty and announced its plans to develop a full-fledged NMD.

In short, the US declared its intent to not simply maintain its current nuclear eminence but to further deepen and develop it. It was also a declaration of the US intent to militarily dominate space through the unbridled development of all kinds of 'frontier' technologies. This is aggressive American unilateralism at its most brazen. Russia under Putin has decided it has no option but to go along with such American behaviour, and rather than risk creating tensions with the US through forthright opposition, settle for whatever sops it can get through greater economic aid, minor political concessions, and military-technological subcontracts (spin-offs of the NMD project) for its arms industry. Besides, the specifically 'nuclear shield' dimension of the project might well fail to overcome the immense technological problems besetting such a grandiose venture.

The latest arms agreement between the US and Russia in May 2002, to reduce each side's deployed (but not stored) missile strength to between 1,700 and 2,200 by the year 2012 is a farce. One of the key gains of earlier START treaties—preventing MIRVing of missiles—is now rescinded, while the NMD plans have been endorsed. Russia, for economic and technical reasons (the impossibility of its maintaining more than a much smaller arsenal) would have had to reduce its missile strength to around 1,500 regardless of any treaty. As deeply disgruntled but weakened sections within the Russian establishment understand only too well, this is capitulation being disguised as a 'new era of cooperation and friendship'.

After 11 September 2001: Extending American Dominance

11 September 2001 did not mark the beginning of some remarkable new phase in global politics. Homeland USA was attacked and suffered civilian casualties in a way that it had not suffered since its Civil War of the nineteenth century. But this in itself would not justify the event's classification as the harbinger of a new era. Even the American state's reaction did not represent a divergence from pre-existing patterns of behaviour. Indeed, the purpose and thrust of America's subsequent behaviour can only be grasped properly if it is situated within the framework of its already established global perspectives.

Let us start by taking up the issue of terrorism. International political terrorism did not begin with 11 September. Nor will it end with the capture and punishment of those responsible for the deeds of that day. Such terrorism is carried out, sponsored, and supported not only by individuals or groups but by states themselves. These include, to name but a few states, Pakistan, India, China, Russia, Israel, and the USA itself. In declaring a war on global terrorism, the US was merely rationalizing its own well-established predilections to continue its selective war on selected opponents justified through selective definition of terrorism and terrorist agencies, hiding its own terrorist culpabilities. This is not to say that it was not deeply disturbed by the threat now posed by Al Qaeda and similar terrorist groups, and therefore determined to do everything possible to prevent future attacks of a similar kind. It obviously was and is. But this was, and is, only a part of the story and not even the most important part.

To understand that much more was involved in the US reaction against the Taliban regime of Afghanistan than just the determination to prevent such attacks in the future we need to cut through the mystifications and obfuscations that cloaked the purposes and meaning of the US military assault on Afghanistan. Was this a terrorist war of revenge and imperial expansion as many a long-standing critic of US foreign policy would aver, or was it a just war? In India, the US, and elsewhere, there have been many who have argued that this is a just war. Certainly, the Western and Japanese media (and most of the media in India) has treated it as such. If this is accepted then it does not mean the US was not guilty of terrorist acts in Afghanistan. But the nature of its culpability would be qualitatively diminished as compared to a situation where its claim of waging a just war is itself deemed false and unacceptable.

In the first case, the focus would shift to the issue of whether the US, in waging this just war, was using just means, i.e. taking sufficient care not to cause suffering to 'innocents' (civilians but not Taliban soldiers even if they had no connection whatsoever to the events of 11 September). We have no consensually accepted account of casualties, civilian or military. But the use of 'daisy cutters' (the most indiscriminate bombs in the conventional, non-nuclear arsenal) and cluster bombs, the fact that there were considerable civilian casualties, and hardship to hundreds of thousands (if not millions) of refugees already in a pitiful economic condition, would provide ammunition to those who believe there was misuse of means, and that persistent aerial bombing in a country with no capacity whatsoever to resist such action, is hardly the exercise of minimal, reasonable, or proportionate force.

There would, however, also be others who argue that in such a full-scale and justified war, civilian casualties were sufficiently restricted to warrant an overall balance sheet assessment quite favourable to the US even with regard to the means used in pursuit of the war. The fact that a repressive Taliban regime was overthrown to the approval of many or most Afghans is a consequence that was seen as having reinforced the US case. Indeed, since Osama bin Laden has apparently escaped capture in spite of the US war on Afghanistan, the primary justification given to the public for having dealt retributive justice for 11 September in this manner now rests on the fact that the Taliban has been overthrown and that Al Qaeda cells in Afghanistan have been eliminated or have shifted elsewhere. Others, of course, would see this outcome as the replacement of one ruthless and authoritarian regime by another regime (comprising the forces of the Northern Alliance and others) also ruthless and authoritarian, whose past record is both better and worse than that of the Taliban.[17] They would also point out that the failure to capture the presumed perpetrator-in-chief, Osama bin Laden, despite the military assault, gravely weakens the consequentialist argument in favour of the war.

The nature of this discourse—whether or not the war on Afghanistan was a just form of retribution for 11 September should not be allowed to obscure a crucial fact. Discussions endorsing the justice of the US war on Afghanistan are simply a form of special pleading on behalf of a US administration not itself engaged in such pleading! Within 48 hours of 11 September, the US government made the following public declarations. It cited Article 51 of the UN Charter claiming the right to act in 'self-defence' although the Article in question does not allow for war to be waged against an individual or a group, and demands regular reporting to the UN Security Council, use of force after all other steps have been taken, and so on. Although the US cited Article 51, it had no intention of obeying its provisions and channelling its retaliatory actions through the UN Security Council.

The US declared it would make no distinction between suspected terrorist culprits and the country that harbours them—an extraordinary claim not warranted by international law. It also declared that the US was henceforth engaged in a 'war against global terrorism' that would take a long time. The US, therefore, talked of an '8 to 10 year program' of combat. In short, the US disregarded all existing international laws and norms. It declared what was, in effect, a unilateral right to define who 'global terrorists' were or are, and to pursue them wherever they may be and in whatever manner the US saw fit.[18] The US gave itself the right to attack any deemed 'enemy', which could be countries and regimes as well as groups or individuals since no distinction was to be made between terrorists and countries/governments harbouring them. Being a war, any US action in the future does not have to await the actual perpetration of a terrorist act, but can as in any war, take the form of surprise and pre-emptive attacks on a continuous and repeated basis against any perceived enemy.

In short, the US has not so much demanded that its war on

Afghanistan be considered a just war but that its declared 'war on global terrorism', whose goals, forms, methods, targets, scale, and length of time are all to be decided by the US itself, be seen and endorsed as a just war. The war on Afghanistan is thus *automatically* a just war because it is simply one part of this all-encompassing just war project! The political scope of this US claim is nothing short of breathtaking, and all in the name of fighting a selectively defined terrorism. Both intellectual and moral scrupulousness demand opposition to the US effort to legitimize in this manner a global political project whose purposes go well beyond the issue of how best to cope with the problem of terrorism. But then when has there ever been much evidence of the existence of such intellectual and moral scrupulousness amongst Realists, be they from the US, India, or anywhere else?

There were two fundamental gains for the US from its actions in Afghanistan going well beyond the issue of 'fighting terrorism'. First, the widespread endorsement of the US action, including the subordination of the UN, and even the creation of an 'international coalition' of states, many of which are themselves guilty of practicing terrorism, was a profound ideological–political–diplomatic gain.[19] What the US had now achieved, which it did not possess before 11 September 2001, was a new *legitimization* of its specifically military conduct abroad. Its second great and new gain was its military–political entry into Central Asia on a depth and scale that it had never before had. The one weak spot in its post-Cold War effort to dominate the Eurasian landmass was Central Asia and the Caspian region. This area is not just the 'backyard' of Russia but abuts Iran and China, which along with Russia are considered by imperial America's most determined protagonists as its most serious potential rivals. As if this was not enough to make the area of vital geopolitical relevance to the US, the Central Asian and Caspian region, which along with Afghanistan and other states also includes Kazakhstan, Turkmenistan, Azerbaijan, and Uzbekistan, is also the largest untapped source of oil and gas in the world.[20]

Throughout the 1990s, the US actually increased the number of its military operational bases worldwide as compared to their spread in the Cold War era. The US now has 'status of forces' agreements with ninety-three countries. For the first time ever it has militarily implanted itself in Afghanistan and in the various Central Asian Republics, especially in the strongest and most regionally ambitious country of Uzbekistan. Even in Pakistan, it is only after 11 September that it has been able to establish the kind of full-scale, heavily-manned, and widespread military bases in the northern provinces (Jacobabad and elsewhere) that it never ever had before during the whole Cold War period when Pakistan was considered its most 'allied ally' in South Asia. In the immediate aftermath of 11 September, the Russians protested about US efforts to establish military pacts and bases in agreement with the various Central Asian regimes in what, after all, was their 'backyard'. However, Moscow shifted to glum acceptance of the new reality when the US simply disregarded these Russian protests and went ahead anyway.

The US is now ensconced in Central Asia for the very long term. It has no intention of leaving and the reason is only peripherally the war on terrorism and the chasing up of the remaining cells of Al Qaeda or other similar groups. On the oil-gas front, it is only after 11 September, in June 2002, that the US was successful in brokering an agreement between a Western consortium of oil companies and the three regimes of Turkmenistan, Afghanistan and Pakistan to construct what the US has long wanted—a pipeline running from Turkmenistan through Afghanistan and Pakistan, thereby skirting Russia and Iran. Other connections from other Central Asian countries can then be made when and where necessary.

The Fateful Triangle: US, India, Pakistan

For Indian Realists, 11 September and its aftermath provided both good news and bad news. The bad news was that the importance of Pakistan to the US was dramatically reasserted. The good news was that the US's war against terrorism promised opportunities that could be exploited by an India keen to get American support in combating Pakistan-sponsored terrorism in Jammu & Kashmir. The key to understanding the deeper and wider ramifications of the now qualitatively greater political investment by the US in South Asia depends on how one evaluates the overall situation. Does the good news outweigh the bad, or vice versa? This is indeed a question that needs to be accurately answered.

The large majority of Indian Realists have inclined towards the former position. This is why they have essentially welcomed and backed the US assault on Afghanistan, and the US's new and stronger implantation in Central Asia. This has been the analytical prism (reinforced by various claims about the new-found importance of India after Pokharan II and supposedly acknowledged as such by the US) through which subsequent developments have been interpreted. Hence, Indian military-political brinkmanship against Pakistan, both after the 13 December 2001 terrorist attack on the Indian Parliament, and after the 14 May 2002 attack in Kaluchak, Jammu, when this brinkmanship was ratcheted up a few more notches, are deemed to have created a stronger tilt of the US towards India. Wasn't even more pressure put on the Musharraf regime by the US than ever before? Weren't there clear statements from Western capitals about how terrorism in J&K would not be tolerated and that Musharraf had to prevent such actions in the future? Wasn't this a tribute to the success of India's 'coercive diplomacy' including its component of calculated if implicit nuclear brinkmanship? Pakistan's 'nuclear bluff' had finally been called. Such at least were the representative views of most of the Indian 'strategic community'.

Of course, from across the border, interpretations could be, and were, different. It was Pakistan's 'coercive diplomacy' that was widely deemed successful. Ultimately, when Islamabad upped the ante, threatening a possible nuclear response to even a 'limited' conventional military incursion by India into Pakistan territory or into Pakistan controlled Kashmir, the US and the West took most serious note of this. So much so, that they went to the extent of depleting their Embassy staff and warning Western/US nationals to leave the region. And this essentially American pressure, both in visible and not-so-visible forms, dissuaded India from making such an incursion or attack. It even led to a measure of de-escalation by India, simply on the basis of a reiteration of promises (which had also been made months earlier) by the Musharraf regime that his government was not responsible for the December or May attacks, condemned them, and would do everything in its power to prevent them in the future. It was India that had resiled from its earlier insistence that this time promises would not do, and New Delhi would *first* have to see tangible action on the ground, not just publicly voiced reassurances.

The truth of the matter is that it was possible for each side to claim a diplomatic–political victory because, unlike Kargil, this time there could not be a clear or obvious verdict of political success for one side or the other. The 'coercive diplomacy' that really worked was neither India's nor Pakistan's but that of the US! The US, at least, was sufficiently alarmed at the prospect of a conventional conflict breaking out between the official armies of the two countries, and of the possibility that this could lead to a nuclear exchange in unforeseen and unforeseeable circumstances (no matter how remote these might be deemed), to exercise a decisive mediating and curbing role. It has its own interests to consider and pursue, which clearly could not be helped by any 'diversionary' war in South Asia. Though American interests in the region are long term, this is no guarantee that the next time there is a crisis situation between India and Pakistan, or the time after that (or after that, and so on) it can always prevent a conventional conflict from breaking out with all its escalatory potential.

It is an obvious given that the US enjoys all the benefits (and burdens) of playing a balancing role between India and Pakistan. This is another way of saying that it occupies the advantageous apex point in the fateful triangle between the three countries. The central thrust of the foreign policies of India and Pakistan respectively is to woo the US and seek to use its support against the other. This situation can only be altered if India and Pakistan were to move towards each other independently, relatively speaking, of the US and its concerns. Of this there is virtually no chance, not at least in the foreseeable future. So we come back to the crucial task of properly evaluating the deeper implications and consequences of the new and stronger US presence and preoccupation with South Asia. Here the most intelligent method of analysis, even in Realist terms, is not to look at how the US fits into the foreign policy perspectives of India or Pakistan, but at how India and Pakistan fit into the geo-strategic perspectives of the US.

The metaphor that best describes the system of nation states today and for at least the next decade, if not more, is not multipolarity, polycentrism or even simple unipolarity, the kind of terms most favoured by Realism. For the logic of Realism is that any attempt at single-state hegemony will quickly bring about countervailing forces and alliances and is, barring the very short term, untenable. Unipolarity is but a brief transit point towards multipolarity or polycentrism. It has to be, since the principal mechanism shaping international politics is, and has to be, the 'balance of power'. However, once one recognizes that Realism was never an adequate framework for understanding the *systemic* rivalry of the Cold War era (never a simple bipolarity) nor for grasping the post-Cold War situation, then one can find more easily the appropriate metaphor to describe the world order It is a hub-and-spokes arrangement with the US at the hub and connected to various states by separate spokes.

Geo-strategically, South Asia is important to the US for two reasons, one 'northwards', the other 'southwards'. In regard to the latter, it is the South Asian littoral state of India that is important. India must be brought in as a junior and obedient ally into the framework of American efforts to dominate the Indian Ocean region. Beginnings in this direction have already been made. Quite obviously, Pakistan cannot here replace India and the interests it serves for the US. In regard to the former, South Asia, post-11 September, derives its new importance in relation to the new possibilities and prospects that the US now has in Central Asia. Here the important South Asian state is not India but Pakistan. And contrary to many illusions currently entertained in India, it cannot replace Pakistan and the distinctive interests that a pliant Pakistan serves for the US.

As long as Indian Realists delude themselves into believing that the primary strategic concern of the US in Pakistan is to combat terrorism, they will continue to hold the illusion that the US can, and probably will, shift decisively towards India and against Pakistan in the not-too-distant future. It is only by recognizing the more strategic and longer-term functions that Pakistan fulfils or can fulfil for the US, that India can move towards disabusing itself of illusions. It is only if the most unlikeliest of scenarios were to emerge—the complete break up of Pakistan into different territorial entities—that would then allow or enable India to extend its de facto control (through puppet regimes or the like) into much of what is today territorial Pakistan, that India could replace Pakistan as the US's favoured South Asian base for its Central Asian concerns.[21]

Pakistan then is important to the US for four main reasons: (a) The Pakistan connection to the Middle East via Saudi Arabia remains useful, (b) Pakistan's role as a major staging-post for US involvement in Central Asia has now become even more important, (c) Of all the fifty-four Muslim majority states in the world, it is Pakistan that has the most developed elite, the largest and most skilled pool of scientific-technical personnel, the most sophisticated and battle-hardened army, and nuclear weapons, and (d) Pakistan has been a very long-term and generally reliable client state of the US.

The nature of contemporary American dominance, or American imperialism as it should more bluntly be called if one is not into Realist soft-soaping or hypocrisy, is different in one key respect from nineteenth or early twentieth century imperialisms. The US cannot and will not undertake direct control of the populations of client states. The governments of such states must fulfil three functions for the US. They must pursue and sustain neo-liberal economic policies. They must support and endorse the essential contours and thrusts of US foreign policies, especially in their own geographical regions. They must maintain control of their own populations. That is to say, the US does not just need client regimes but *stable* client regimes. How that stability is to be established is very much a secondary and pragmatic issue. If today in Pakistan this requires defeat of Islamic fundamentalist forces and a movement towards secularism and democracy within the internal body politic, then fine. Alternatively, the US will happily reconcile itself to a more authoritarian and communalized India ruled by the BJP and the Sangh Parivar (whose economic and foreign policies it is largely delighted with, provided this is compatible with the maintenance of internal political stability.[22]

This American need for a stable client regime in Pakistan carries serious implications in respect of an issue that is at the heart of India–Pakistan relations, namely Kashmir. It is, again, widely assumed in India that US involvement here can be beneficial to the Indian position on Kashmir. That both the 'logic of existing circumstances' and the reality of Indian power will eventually push the US towards supporting the dominant view within the Indian elite (barring the yearning for *Akhand Bharat* and therefore the recapture of Pakistan controlled Kashmir in some circles of the Hindutva right) that the Line of Control (LoC) be made into an international border. Of course, the Indian elite has travelled some way from 1998. Few of those who supported Pokharan II even realized that from then on Kashmir would inevitably become internationalized, or at least Americanized. As such, India's basic, and effective, diplomatic stance between 1964–98 that this was a bilateral issue, which should be of no concern to anyone else, was now rendered nugatory. It did not take long for adjustments to be made by a steadily increasing number of Indian strategists. The Kashmir issue, they said, was now internationalized (actually Americanized) even if the play of words by the government continues—the US is 'facilitator', not 'mediator'. India needed to recognize this new reality as also the fact that there could be real benefits in this situation, given the trajectory of US–India ties.

There is much wishful thinking here. There is no obvious 'logic of evolving circumstances' at work in favour of India. Pakistan will not accept the LoC as an international border. No government in Islamabad can afford to do so without destroying its internal credibility, American pressure or no pressure. Indeed, the best way for the US to destroy the prospect of having a stable client regime in Pakistan, or indeed one in India, is for it to take political sides with one against the other on such an issue. In fact, its own strategic perspectives will push it to explore possibilities outside of the inflexible positions of the two governments.

The crucial question that the US must now address is what eventual political outcome in Kashmir will best suit its own evolving perspectives in Central Asia. So far, there has been no real reason why the US government had to seriously think along such lines though outside lobbies in Washington have been exploring this issue.

Now that must and will change. Among the options the US will begin considering is whether a Bosnia-like resolution, namely Kashmir as a 'US protectorate' in all but name, whatever its formal or legal status might be, is most advantageous to it. Perhaps a soft-border and partial sovereignty/independence 'solution' with formal security guarantees provided by India and Pakistan might be the best option assuming this is the most effective way to institutionalize American influence in Kashmir? Nothing is certain. The Kashmir issue is not about to be solved readily or easily. But possible outcomes have become more open-ended than ever before. There are now four actors—the Indian and Pakistan governments, the US, and the people of Kashmir on both sides of the border. It must be the hope of those who seek justice that the voices of the last named will become ever stronger. But we will just have to wait and see.

Meanwhile, the choices open to a thinking public remain what they have always been when faced with the ambitions of empires and empire-builders. There have always been those inside and outside the imperial core who would rationalize, justify, serve, collude with, and apologize for empires, colonialism, slavery, usually in the name of 'reasons of state'. Today, in the face of the American empire and its builders, it is no different. We have the same category of colluders with rationalizers, justifiers, and apologizers for empire, nuclearism, neo-liberal economic exploitation. But the more modern category label under which they are likely to be found is Realists, who in South Asia ironically, suffer from being both too Realist, and not Realist enough! Their principal term of justification is also a more modern version of the older notion of 'reasons of state', today called protecting or serving the 'national interest'—a more problematic and useless analytical or explanatory principle in international relations it is almost impossible to find.

Fortunately, there have also always been, now and in the past, those who would refuse such postures in the effort to create a better and more humane world order. In our present, that struggle is simply inseparable from the stance of utmost moral, political and intellectual intransigence against American imperialism. The choice, as always, is for each of us to make.

NOTES

1. If air, land, and sea were the earlier battlegrounds where military supremacy had to be pursued, the US now believes it is space. Control of space is deemed vital on two fronts: for information and surveillance domination, and direct military control through its militarization–nuclearization so that not just space but earth can also be dominated. The key avenue to be followed for achieving this is the constructing of the National Missile Defence (NMD) system, or what the US government prefers to call the Ballistic Missile Defence (BMD) system, with its exploration, development, and testing of 'frontier' technologies. The aim is to eventually put in place a new generatoin of weapons like lasers, particle beam weapons, etc., as well as erecting a missile defence shield that then immensely strengthens the nuclear offensive system. The purpose of the NMD is to establish a twofold unilateral global dominance of the US—both in nuclear and in conventional military terms—over all other states, particularly over nuclear weapons powers. That these are indeed the central aims and purposes of the NMD is not just conjecture or interpretive judgement by anti-nuclear disarmament advocates but what the pro-NMD military establishment itself says. See *United States Space Command: Vision For 2020*, US Space Command, Director of Plans, Peterson AFB, Co 80914–3110, DSN 692–3498, 1997.
2. Zbigniew Brzezinski, *The Grand Chessboard: American Primacy and its Geostrategic Imperatives*, New York: Basic Books, 1997, p. 23.
3. A Brzezinski quote: 'Russia is viable as a nation state. I don't think however, it has much future as an empire. If they are stupid enough to try, they'll get themselves into conflicts that'll make Chechnya and Afghanistan look like a picnic'. See Tariq Ali, *The Clash of Fundamentalism*, London: Verso, 2002, pp. 278–9.
4. Ibid., p. 40. Brzezinski seeks to divide Russia from China but is perfectly willing to offer vassal status to either of the two or even to Iran if any of them are willing to accept such ranking in a US dominated world order.
5. Foreign Direct Investment constitutes only 5 per cent of total world investment—95 per cent of total capitalist investment takes place within the industrialized countries. Of this 95 per cent, 72 per cent flows from one industrialized country to another. Only 2 per cent of total global investment flows from the 'north' to the 'south' of the world economy. 75 per cent of FDI, especially investment in Africa, Asia, and Latin America is mergers and acquisitions or the purchase of recently privatized public enterprises. Only 25 per cent is 'greenfield' investment, i.e. the setting up of new plants. See, *International Viewpoint*, Manchester (UK), June 2002, p. 33.
6. Peter Gowan, *The Global Gamble: Washington's Faustian Bid for World Dominance*, London: Verso, 1999.

7. In 1995, the US dollar comprised 61.5 per cent of all central bank foreign exchange reserves in the world. It was the currency in which 76.8 per cent of all international bank loans were denominated; in which 39.5 per cent of all international bond issues were denominated, as well as 44.3 per cent of all Euro deposits. The dollar was the invoicing currency for 47.6 per cent of world trade. Ibid., pp. 35–6.
8. TNCs have worldwide operations and get an increasing portion of their profits from overseas activity. But their control is centralized–nationalised, with over 80 per cent of major TNCs controlling their investment, research, and technology decisions from their home offices in the US, Germany, and Japan. Through the 1990s, among the top 500 companies of the world (calculated on the basis of market capitalization), there was a very substantial shift from Japanese capital (losing ground) to the US (gaining ground) with Europe as a whole barely holding its own. According to the *Financial Times* (London), 28 January 1999, US companies in the top 500 rose from 222 to 244 with Japanese controlled companies falling from 71 to 46 and European ones (of which Germany had 23) at 173. If one looks at the top 100 companies, 61 per cent are American, 33 per cent European, and 2 per cent Japanese. Of the top 25 companies whose capitalization exceeds US $86 billion, over 70 per cent are US, 26 per cent are European, and 4 per cent are Japanese. See James Petras and Henry Veltmeyer, *Globalization Unmasked*, Delhi: Madhyam Books, 2001, pp. 62–6.
9. SAPs aimed at domestic deflation, currency devaluations, export drives, reduced budget deficits, emphasis on earning foreign exchange on capital accounts through privatization with the help of foreign companies, and liberalization of capital accounts. So US rentiers get their debts paid off, more export competition worldwide between third world countries in agriculture, textiles, etc., means cheaper US imports, and US capital can acquire more easily foreign assets and exploit, in pursuit of short-term gains, local financial markets.
10. While the overwhelming majority of the members of the UN were in favour of proceeding in line with the UN Charter calling for exploration of all peaceful methods for resolving the conflict before the launching of armed hostilities, the US acted systematically to prevent the Security Council from accepting any such process. A Russian peace plan accepted by Baghdad before the ground war started was rejected by the US because that would have, among other things, also raised the stature and importance of Russia in the Middle East. Iraq also called for the two occupations of Kuwait and Palestine to be treated according to common principles (which was perfectly correct) and offered to withdraw from Kuwait in return for the establishment of an international conference to discuss Palestine along these lines. But accepting such an end to the crisis would have raised enormously the prestige of Iraq

in the Middle East among the Arab populations and countries. This, again, was utterly unacceptable to the US, running counter to its basic strategic aims.

11. The third *Intifada* or Uprising (the first was the struggle of 1935–8, the second in 1987) was sparked by the visit on 28 September 2000, of Ariel Sharon accompanied by hundreds of armed bodyguards to the holiest Al Aqsa shrine of Muslims in Jerusalem in an act that was deliberately intended to humiliate and provoke Palestinians, the message being that Israel could do as it pleased over a people subordinated and subservient to its overwhelming political and military power. Since then the number of Israeli and Palestinian civilians killed are over 2,000 in the ratio of around three Palestinians to every Israeli, and over 20,000 injured in a ratio of around twelve Palestinians to every Israeli. Over a fifth of Palestinian casualties are aged 18 or younger. Israel's presence in the occupied territories is not only illegal, it represents the longest and most sustained military occupation (35 years) in modern history. It is a colonial occupation maintained by regularized and institutionalized violence and the threat of violence. On one side, there are tanks, aircraft bombings, helicopter gunships and strafings, heavy artillery, the most sophisticated of surveillance systems, the most powerful military force in the Middle East with nuclear bombs in the basement, backed by the most powerful state in the world constantly supplying Israel with military equipment, economic aid, and political–diplomatic support. On the other, there has been one crude home-made missile, home-made bombs, rifles, bazookas and stones. Yet the dominant form of media portrayal in the West of this situation and the dominant form of response of most governments (including an Indian government that sees its close relations with Israel as one of its great success stories) is that there are 'two sides to the story'; of Israeli 'violence' being a 'reaction' to Palestinian 'terrorism'; of calling on both sides to respond to US mediated efforts at bringing about 'peace' and a 'reasonable settlement' where reasonableness means nothing less than the acquiescence of the Palestinian people to some form of their own permanent submission to Israel. Neither today's Indian ministers nor most of their accompanying Realist cheerleaders who make up the unofficial 'security establishment' have either the integrity or the interest in pointing out that the violence of colonizer and colonized cannot be equated, and that Israel should not be allowed to get away with its brutal colonization behind the pretence of its 'perpetual victimhood'.
12. The Indo–Sri Lanka Accord, in effect, authorized an external power, India, to be the principal arbiter in a civil war through the intervention of the absurdly named Indian Peace Keeping Force (IPKF). Moreover, the Accord was recognized and supported by all the major world powers and not a few middling ones. However, this newly consecrated

status for India was contingent on it militarily overcoming or defeating the LTTE in Jaffna. Its inability to do so made its continued presence in Sri Lanka such a political liability that Colombo, which had agreed to the Accord, eventually had to demand the removal of the IPKF and effectively shelved the agreement. Since then successive governments in New Delhi have been careful never to get as involved in the Sri Lanka–Jaffna imbroglio.

13. For a clear statement of such US strategic perspectives, wherein the US is both willing to accept a nuclear India, yet also expects and insists that India must remain no more than an SNP, see Ashley Tellis, *India's Emerging Nuclear Posture*, New Delhi: Oxford University Press, 2001.
14. From 1987 onwards, there was the Intermediate Nuclear Forces or INF Treaty, the first such treaty to eliminate a whole class of nuclear weapons before their 'modernization/replacement'. In 1991 the US and Russia informally agreed to remove all tactical nuclear missiles from their surface ships. A serious beginning was made to substantially reduce not just weapons deployed but stored. Nuclear risk reduction measures and centres were established and alert levels substantially lowered. Three nuclear weapons states—Ukraine (most importantly), Belarus, and Kazakhstan—were denuclearized. Three threshold states—Brazil, Argentina, and South Africa—gave up this status. Two new Nuclear Weapons Free Zones covering Africa (Treaty of Pelindaba) and South-east Asia (Bangkok Treaty) were established. Serious efforts were being made to establish a Comprehensive Test Ban Treaty (CTBT) and a Fissile Materials Treaty (FMT) to prevent more production and stock-piling of weapons grade fuel for bombs.
15. Particularly shameful, yet typical of the Indian 'security establishment' is the unwillingness of most of its members to publicly point out that the NMD takes global nuclearization to newer and unnecessary, indeed insane levels; that it cannot prevent nuclear terrorism against the US; that it expresses an aggressive and unilateral attempt (the militarization–nuclearization of space) to dominate the world order in the future; that it pushes away dramatically the future prospects of global nuclear disarmament that everybody pays lip service to. Instead, the Indian security establishment is primarily preoccupied with regurgitating American deceits about how necessary for US and global security the NMD is, and in conjecturing about how India can 'benefit' from endorsing and supporting the NMD project.
16. There is, however, an independent and carefully 'conservative' estimate by Marc Herold, a university professor of economics at New Hampshire University, that estimates 3,767 civilian deaths in Afghanistan between 7 October and 10 December 2001. This is cited in Seumas Milne, 'the innocent dead in a coward's war', *The Guardian* (UK), 20 December 2001. Regarding the number who died in the 11 September attacks,

the roster of dead and missing isued by companies involved, including the airline companies and the New York Fire Department, is 2,405. Estimates from the *New York Times, Associated Press*, and *USA Today* range from 2,600 to 2,950, cited in M. Mann, 'Globalization and 11 September', *New Left Review*, Nov./Dec. 2001, issue (new) no. 12. The article by Milne in *The Guardian* cites a figure of 3,234 for 11 September.

17. Since the assault on Afghanistan has not secured the primary suspect or culprit, the justification for this 'humanitarian' intervention through arms becomes similar to the claims that the US and its supporters presented for Bosnia, Serbia, the 1991 Gulf War against Saddam Hussein, and so on. It becomes part of that larger issue of whether and under what circumstances is a military intervention to overthrow a tyrannical, undemocratic or oppressive regime by an outside power or powers justified? My own view on this tricky moral issue as it pertains to international relations is to be found in A. Vanaik, *India in a Changing World*, New Delhi: 1995. It is broadly similar to the view of Carol Gould on 'Cosmopolitical Democracy', in *Rethinking Democracy*, Cambridge, 1990. Briefly stated, this perspective argues that claims of national sovereignty and self-determination cannot in principle be allowed to override universal human rights, which by virtue of being universal, take precedence over nationalist claims. This justifies various forms of external intervention to promote human rights in other countries. But the question of *military* intervention does not fall straightforwardly at all into this permit. Thus one cannot simply militarily intervene to overthrow apartheid, Stalin's Russia, the Shah of Iran, etc., no matter how brutal these dictatorships. This is because a fundamental democratic right that must also be respected is the right of a people to overthrow *their own* tyrant where people (as they are in our world) are constituted politically in nation states. Therefore, one must oppose the military interventions in Afghanistan, Bosnia, Serbia, etc. However, this too is not an absolute, and the conditions in which external military intervention become acceptable, indeed necessary, is when the very category of the 'people' is threatened by genocide on a huge scale. The 'hugeness' is relative to the size of the population in question. This would apply to the conditions in East Timor in 1975, when one-third of the population was being massacred by Indonesia and to the recent massacre in Rwanda and to the Pol Pot regime in Kampuchea where, proportionately speaking, more people were killed than in Hitler's concentration camps. Fortunately the Pol Pot regime was overthrown by a Vietnamese military invasion in 1979. Preventing or ending a real genocide threatening the very existence of a population, not mass expulsions ('ethnic cleansing') nor even simply massacres or 'mass killings', horrific as they are, is the crucial consideration here. So genocide should not be defined or cited as casually as it so often is.

18. The US certainly made no bones about their larger ambitions. The US Ambassador to the UN, John Negroponte, informed the Security Council that this was a limitless war: 'We may find that our self-defence requires further action with respect to other organizations and other states.' See, T. Ali, op. cit., p. 300, as is often the case, the hard right in the US can be refreshingly honest about the government's intentions in Afghanistan. In his 12 October 2001 *Washington Post* column, the influential journalist, Charles Krauthammer, bluntly declared: 'We are fighting because the bastards killed 5,000 of our people, and if we do not kill them, they are going to kill us again. This is a war of revenge and deterrence. . . . The liberationist talk must therefore be for foreign consumption.'
19. After the end of the Cold War, the US has succeeded in suborning the UN to an extent inconceivable during the whole period between 1945–91. This is so in regard to the UN's legitimization of Operation Desert Storm against Iraq in 1991, and with respect to the shameful history of murderous sanctions imposed afterwards, which have caused suffering on a scale no country defeated in war has ever experienced in the whole of the twentieth century. The UN's 'inspection missions' against Iraq have been openly colonized by the CIA. It is true of the wars in the Balkans where NATO became the UN's main sub-contractor. The UN Secretary-General holds office only at the pleasure of the US. Boutros-Ghali was denied a second term on the basis of the US's sole vote while Kofi Annan, who has imbibed well the lesson of how to kowtow to the US yet maintain the illusion of self-dignity, has been rewarded with not just a second term but the Nobel Peace Prize. The US has set up, under the label of the UN, a War Crimes Tribunal for the Balkans to punish its enemies and protect its friends, but refuses to sign up to the International Criminal Court (ICC) on the grounds that members of its own armed services might be charged under it. It is, again, so obviously true with respect to UN endorsement of US behaviour in Afghanistan.
20. Earlier estimates of total oil reserves between 100 to 150 billion barrels (bb) have now been scaled down to around 50 bb or slightly more. The Caspian region's proven oil reserves are between 16 to 32 bb, which compares to the 22 bb of the USA, and the proven oil reserves of the Middle East, which is nearly 15 times as much. Kazakhstan has the largest oil reserves (proven) at between 10 to 16 bb, Azerbaijan between 4 to 1 bb, Turkmenistan at around 1.5 bb, and Uzbekistan at around 1 bb. Proven gas reserves in the Caspian region are between 236 and 337 trillion cubic feet (tcf) compared to the USA's proven reserves of around 300 tcf. Turkmenistan has around 159 tcf of possible (not proven) gas reserves, Uzbekistan around 110 tcf, Kazakhstan around 88 tcf, and Azerbaijan around 35 tcf. See, Ahmed Rashid, *Taliban: Islam, Oil and the*

New Great Game in Central Asia, London: I.B. Taurus, 2001, p. 144. It is not so much the size as the untapped character of these oil and gas reserves that is most seductive to the US, whose own reserves of both approximate to those in the Caspian region. The US is consciously following an energy policy of exploiting as far as possible and for as long as possible the outside world's reserves before having to depend primarily on its own.

21. There has been much talk of Pakistan being a 'failed state'. This is acceptable as a description of Pakistan's internal plight on the political, social, and economic levels provided matters are also kept in perspective. Even far weaker and far more 'failed' African states have rarely broken up over the last decades. This is testimony to the fact that even one major centre of power like the army can usually keep some kind of territorial–political control. In Pakistan the sources of unity provided by the army, the bureaucracy, a substantially integrated economy, and by the presence of a genuine 'Pakistan' nationalism among the public, even if this nationalism is searching for stronger roots than Islam, the 'two-nation theory' or opposition to India, should not be underestimated. Even the earlier tensions related to the 'Nationalities Question' have considerably receded.
22. The US government has offically declared as its policy the necessity to consider intervening militarily and politically in the name of protecting humanitarian principles, i.e. when violations of human rights are being carried out or condoned by governments. Of course, this is to be selectively and arbitrarily applied. So a possible future intervention in Iraq (as indeed was the intervention in Afghanistan) is also to be justified in the name of protecting the Iraqi people from Hussein's domestic brutalities. The official US response to the atrocities in Gujarat, however, were of a very different register, even though the culpability of the Narendra Modi state government was undeniable and the BJP at the Centre openly justified and rationalized this anti-Muslim pogrom. Washington declared that the events in Gujarat had no foreign policy implications and were a domestic issue for New Delhi that would not affect its relations with the BJP-led central government.

Russia and Central Asia in the US Coalition against Terrorism

ANURADHA M. CHENOY

The American involvement in Afghanistan has not been restricted to Afghanistan alone but is an involvement in the region. This was clear before the events of 11 September 2001 (9/11) and has become more evident with time. The map of US involvement covers the Central Asian States (CAS), the Trans Caucasian States of Azerbaijan, Georgia, and Armenia, as also Russia and South Asia. This paper looks at the extent and reasons for involvement. US presence in the region, as recent political history has shown, starts much before 9/11. But there are marked changes and continuities in their approach and strategy. While US interest in Afghanistan and their relationship with Osama bin Laden has been retold many times, it is their changing relationship in the former Soviet space that needs to be watched as the main area of geopolitics.

The Oil Beneath: Terrorism or the Oil Connection?

US geopolitics in the post-Soviet space has a history linked to the proven Central Asian and Caspian Sea oil and gas reserves that initiated a new and complex Great Game in the region. The Caspian is said to be the last great oil rush holding up to 200 billion barrels (bb), 10 per cent of the earth's potential oil reserves, as well as trillions of cubic metres of gas. This makes it the most promising petroleum region for the next twenty years. Turkmenistan is ranked the fourth largest natural gas reserve in the world. Azerbaijan and Kazakhstan's Tenghiz oilfields are potentially major producers. Governments and businesses are focusing on this region with the hope of major gains.

Pipelines that transport this oil and gas to markets provide revenue and give strategic importance to regions they cross. In exchange for allowing pipelines across their territory, countries negotiate cash payments or a share of the gas or oil transiting through. This brings both revenue and a sense of strategic importance. The routes for pipelines have led to competition amongst the big players and instability in smaller regimes that became subject to rivalries and intrigues. The issue behind pipelines is not just the costs involved which are one-fourth of the investments in extraction, but security for pipelines and the regimes that safeguard them. As Howard Chase, Director of International Affairs for BP Amoco, said: 'The basic question is not about investment in the pipeline, but rather about identifying the most timely and secure route for getting the oil to the market.'[1]

American oil analysts believe that by 2050, Central Asia is to account for up to 80 per cent of US oil imports.[2] The American Vice-President, Dick Cheney, has continuously spoken of the need for unimpeded access to this region for American geologists and pipelines so as to ensure a conservation-free fossil fuel base for the future for US needs. In fact, Dick Cheney kept repeating the importance of oil supplies flowing to the US throughout the presidential campaigns of 2000. At this stage, Afghanistan's situation in the middle of the vital region with abundant oil that forms the base of US national interests caused it to be the focus of the Great Game.

A number of pipeline projects underway pass through Russia and the troubled Caucasus and go westwards to Europe. Other alternate routes are planned to cross Turkey and Iran that could feed South and South-East Asian economies. However, a route through Afghanistan would be cheaper and more viable for the east. The US was clear that the end of Taliban control would greatly help US access to pipelines across Afghanistan. A 'friendly' regime in Afghanistan could provide alternate routes to those from Russia and Iran. Big oil is the biggest beneficiary from the post 9/11 American attacks that led to the fall of the Taliban regime and put the lid on other anti-American elements in the Central Asian region. Washington wants the Caspian Sea natural resources to flow through many pipelines and via different routes to avoid a shutdown by any one country or conflict. The Afghan oil route has been of special interest to Dick Cheney and recently he remarked: 'I cannot think of a time when we had a region emerge as suddenly to become strategically significant as the Caspian'.[3] But as analysts have shown, the oil here is useless until it is moved, and the only route that makes economic sense is through Afghanistan. Removal of the Taliban and Al Qaeda networks are thus not the only US interest in the region. A 'friendly' Afghan regime will be able to assist the oil companies to considerable lengths. The costs of the Afghan war would be covered in the post-war clean-up operations and the oil pipeline profits.

The Construction of the Anti-Terrorist Coalition: Mutually Assured Benefits?

The US has moved systematically to ensure its interests in the region. The first step after 9/11 was constructing the anti-terrorist international coalition. Russia, the CAS and all others in the post-Soviet space became allies in this coalition. The Russians needed this alliance because of their own ethnic secessionist problem in Chechnya that they labelled as one of terrorism. Clearly, Chechen rebels were assisted by Islamic fundamentalist groups, but the root of the problem is much deeper than terrorism. Chechen–Russian distrust goes back into history. While it may be redundant to recall Stalin's deportation of Chechens in the 1940s, it is worth recalling that Chechnya has not signed the Federal Treaty that constituted the Russian Federation in 1993 and that this region has been in the throes of a civil war since 1992. Whilst the Russians have accused the Chechens of terrorism, the Chechens backed by Western States have recorded human rights violations and excessive use of force by the Russians. The Russian leadership under President Vladmir Putin looked for an opening whereby they could re-assert their legitimacy over Chechnya and suppress this civil war. The international coalition after 9/11 gave them this opportunity.

The CAS needed the international coalition to offset the weaknesses of their own authoritarian regimes. They felt they could use the threat of terrorism and fundamentalism to curb anti-government movements, both from Islamic and other groups. With this coalition they could move out of the Russian orbit and get space to manoeuvre between Russia and the USA. They hoped for assistance against secessionist movements, whilst their own human right abuses could get condoned and they could get a better deal for extracting and transporting their oil and gas reserves.

The US on its part used these very weaknesses to get a greater foothold in the region as the following examples show. After 9/11, the US offer to both Russia and CAS assured these countries that the US use of former Soviet bases in CIS was only 'temporary'. They said CAS was part of Russian national interest. Uzbekistan, Kyrgyzstan and Tajikistan bases were needed for US operations in the Afghan war. As the outcome of the war became clear and the Taliban regime fell, the US Secretary of State said in December 2001 that the US did not intend to withdraw from CAS even after the war in Afghanistan since America had long-term interests in the region. US Assistant Secretary of State to CAS,

Elizabeth Jones, explained this further, stating that US wanted to support the CAS in their reforms and more aid would come depending on the direction of their reforms. Amongst the US interests she cited was 'the transparent development of Caspian energy resources'.[4] The transparency US wanted obviously does not go beyond oil profits.

By January 2002, the Uzbek and Kyrgyz Presidents entered into agreements with the US to upgrade and extend the lease of some of the bases. So, for instance, the Khanabad base was leased out to the US for twenty-five years. It already had 50–60 fighter jets stationed there. The Kyrgyz President with support from the Parliament declared that they were prepared to place Kyrgyz territory at US disposal. By February 2002, the US contingent at Manas airfield in Kyrgyzstan increased to accommodate F-15 fighters that had a range up to China, Russia, all of CIS, and the Indo-Pakistan border. The airport was set up as a staging ground for a long-term US presence.[5] Kyrgyzstan and Tajikistan being part of CIS collective security had violated its norms for these agreements. With this move, the US wiped out a decade of Russian effort in the CIS for collective security and the existing regional alliances.

All the CAS regimes (except Kyrgyzstan) have authoritarian regimes and Presidents that have arbitrarily extended their regimes. The growing opposition movements have been suppressed on all kinds of pretexts, the most favoured one being that they were extremist or fundamentalist. As de-industrialization and economic decline have led to an increase in unemployment and poverty, opposition movements have gained strength. Since centrist groups have also been disallowed, Islamic forces have gained since they have used their traditional networks of *madrassas* and mosques for mobilizing opinion. In Uzbekistan, the Islamic movement of Uzbekistan has functioned as the opposition in the Ferghana and Osh Valley, the most populated region in all CAS. The permission to the US for bases has increased the support for these Islamic movements that have accused the US of 'tormenting Muslims'.[6]

After granting US military bases on a long-term basis, the Uzbek President and Parliament decided in December 2001 to hold a national referendum on parliamentary reform, to make it possible for President Islam Karimov to remain in power for yet another five years. (Karimov has been in power since 1992 and had extended his term in 1995 and again in 2000 after a rigged election.) The Parliament declared that there was a need 'for unity in the war against international extremism'.[7] They stated that since terrorism was not a 'one day affair' it was necessary for Karimov to continue as President. The Constitution was thus appropriately changed. In Kazhakstan, President Nursultan Nazarbayev did the same thing, while in Turkmenistan S. Niyazov had already made himself President-for-life. Since the US government was arguing for transparency in oil deals, they certainly have been overlooking democracy.

Kyrgyzstan lacks the oil and gas reserves of other CAS and hence became most vulnerable. The US General Commander stated that the bases here were the key to the Afghan war. The Kyrgyz Parliament in December 2001 declared that the US military would not affect the geopolitical situation, but would help the aviation industry. They settled for accepting US $7000 for each take-off.[8] Since Kyrgyzstan shares a long border with China, US bases here threaten regional security.

Geopolitics and Conflicts in Trans Caucasia

That US interests go far beyond the Afghan war is further demonstrated in their military ties in Trans Caucasia, specifically Georgia. The US is supporting the construction of a pipeline via Turkey to the Mediterranean Sea so as to minimize Russian influence. Turkey is a member of NATO, but on the other hand, this pipeline has to go through Kurd areas where ethnic conflicts are ongoing. A protocol was signed between the Turkey, Georgia, and Azerbaijan Presidents in November 1998, for transferring Azerbaijan crude through Turkey. The main interest was independence from Russian pipelines. Though oil companies like Unocal have long advocated the Afghanistan route, plans for a Western consortium to open a pipeline from Baku to the Turkish oil terminal of Ceyhan in 2004 are in the offing. The Clinton administration was a key supporter of the Baku–Tbilisi–Ceyhan (BTC) pipeline. This BTC pipeline received a further boost in March 2001 when the Kazakh President pledged that oil from the East Kashagan field, expected from 2005, would be exported via this line. BP Amoco is the lead partner in this project.

Once the first stage of the Afghan war ended, the US Defense Secretary announced lifting of military aid and sanctions [US amendment 907] in the Azerbaijan, Armenia, and Georgia regions. This ban had been placed earlier because of the conflict between Armenia and Azerbaijan (on the Nagorno Karabakh autonomous enclave) and the ethnic conflicts in Georgia. In Georgia, two autonomous republics of Abkhazia and South Ossetia have initiated secessionist movements against Georgia and these two republics have also proposed that they re-join

Russia. Russia has shown open sympathies towards these two provinces, much to Georgia's concern. Georgia, on its part, has been sheltering Chechen rebels and has waged war in the Kedori Gorge with Abkhazia.[9] Despite the fact that there has been no change in these conflicts, the US has initiated a process of selected aid and military support. Defense Secretary Donald Rumsfeld initiated military co-operation with Azerbaijan and Georgia and even sent American troops to assist the Azerbaijan border troops. The US has proposed military contacts between Azerbaijan and Turkey. Given the fact that relations have long been strained between Armenia and Azerbaijan, the US has also promised some peacekeepers to Armenia, as part of the 'battle against terrorism'.[10] The US has declared this area a concern of their national security, thus ensuring their long term and unilateral interests here.

Russian bases from this region are thus being gradually removed and replaced by the US. President Putin initially reacted to this expansionism by stating that if they could accept US bases in Central Asia then why not in Georgia? Clearly the Russians know that they are not in a position to counter US moves either economically or politically. They believe, however, that they can intervene and influence the Trans Caucasian and the CAS by non-military means. The Russians have linkages with ethnic groups and ethnic Russians settled in these regions. They continue to share and control river communications and power grids. There are thus many ways that Russia can ensure their interests in these regions. Russian foreign policy makers believe that given their own current economic weaknesses, they are willing to play 'junior partners' with the USA and its allies in the region and in return have received some privileges. The Russians in June 2002 declared that they respected the territorial integrity of Georgia, and would not recognize the independence movements of autonomous republics. But they have also accused Georgia of shielding Chechen terrorists and threatened them with military intervention. Given Russian leverage, they were assured some control of the pipelines that would go through Georgia.

Flag or Trade in Central Asia?

An analysis of US involvement with pipeline deals reveals the extent of US interests in CAS. Turkmenistan, with the world's fifth largest proven gas reserves, has been part of US interest for several years. It has only two outlets for gas—one from northern Iran and the other through Kazakhstan that connects with the Russian grids. Saudi Arabia, Pakistan, and US have been interested in an alternate route, away from Russia. In 1996, an inter-governmental agreement was made between Turkmenistan, Kazakhstan, Pakistan, and Centgas oil consortium led by the Texan oil company Unocal to build 1,440 km. of pipeline across Afghanistan from Turkmenistan, following the road from Herat to Kandahar. Unocal also proposed that the pipeline cross the Pakistan border to terminate in Multan. It was believed that later another 500 miles of gas-lines would connect pipelines from Pakistan to India.

In 1995–6, the Afghans believed that this would help develop Afghanistan. But this proposed pipeline increased the competition between Afghanistan's neighbours, especially Pakistan, Saudi Arabia and Iran, and regional competition over the control of the pipeline fuelled the civil war and enhanced inter-ethnic rivalries, changing the power balance in Afghanistan. In fact, in 1995, when Unocal started negotiating the Turkmenistan to Pakistan pipeline through Afghanistan, both the US and Pakistani governments supported the Taliban, with the hopes of a deal. Sections of the Taliban leadership were even invited to Houston in 1997, to work out a deal. The Taliban was promised US $50–100 million a year as transit fees if the pipeline was built. But the Taliban at this stage favoured the company Bridas from Argentina because Unocal had links with the Russian Gazprom. Bridas on the other hand was closely linked to the Saudi company Ningharco, whose shareholder was Prince Turki al-Faisal Saud, head of the Saudi General Intelligence, who had been backing the Taliban since 1995. Unocal and the Centgas consortium (which includes Delta, Crescent, and others) continued to try to get the pipeline going. Unocal sponsored the Afghan studies departments and students for technical training for the pipeline. Gazprom dropped out of Centgas in October 1997. Unocal head of international affairs, John Maresca, has continued to argue for the Afghanistan route, and it was only in 1998 that these plans were stopped after US bombing of Al Qaeda bases and protests by feminists. This project was revived again in April–May 2002 once the Karzai government was installed and received international legitimacy.

Analysts believe that given the new relations between the Bush and Putin regimes, Bush would support the pipelines that go through Russia and break with the earlier policies of the Clinton administration. Unocal, however, continues to lobby for the Caspian/Central Asian oil export corridor from Turkmenistan south through Afghanistan to Pakistan. In fact the proposals of 'partnership for peace' that have been dangled to the CAS link military alliances with NATO to oil and pipeline routes.

Russia, who had vigorously opposed proposals for the security of CAS by NATO, has now accepted this prospect also.

US access to energy and natural resources forms the basic element of their national security. Control of oil pipelines is the basis of their strategic interests. Foreign policy aims thus coincide with their gas and oil companies' interests and key public figures and politicians double as advisors and stakeholders of oil companies. A lead in this combination of oil politics and foreign policy is Vice-President Dick Cheney himself. After his retirement from George Bush Senior's government, Cheney became President and CEO of Halliburton Company (HAL) in Dallas. HAL is a leader of the world's diversified energy services companies and is listed in oil and gas journals as such. It provides equipment and services to oil and natural gas companies and has been accused of human rights violations in places like Nigeria and Burma, where its partners were involved in using forced labour. Cheney is the company's biggest stockholder. This company got the clean-up contract for Kuwait after the Gulf War. HAL works with Unocal and Total, and others involved with current business deals including with Azerbaijan, Iran, Indonesia, and Libya. Cheney has emerged as a champion of oil interests in the government and his statement: 'You've got to go where the oil is. I don't think about it (political volatility) very much' characterizes his stand.[11]

Under Cheney, during the past five years, HAL emerged as a corporate hog. It got US government contracts mostly linked with US army engineering works in hot spots like Kosovo, Bosnia, and Albania. HAL also benefited from at least US $3.8 billion in federal contracts and taxpayers uninsured loans. One of these loans approved in April 2002, by the US Export–Import Bank, guarantees US $489 million in credit to a Russian oil company, the Tyumen Oil Company, owned by the Conglomerate Alfa. The aggrieved firm in this contract was BP Amoco that commissioned a report on Tyumen and Alfa. This report, given to the CIA, said that Tyumen had virtually 'stolen' the Siberian oilfield through fraud. Further, public reports from Moscow showed that Tyumen was involved with drugs and crime deals.

HAL has got a US $160 million contract for oil drilling in Oman. In 1998, HAL acquired the Dresser Company. This company had helped rebuild Iraq's petroleum industry that was decimated during the Bush (Senior) and Cheney regime during the Desert Storm operations in the Gulf War. A report from the *Washington Post* stated: 'Cheney delivered fast, embarking on months of globe trotting and got HAL top level attention from prime ministers and oil sheikhs from Riyadh and Baku to Lagos.'[12]

It is not only Cheney who is directly linked with oil interests. To take some other current examples, Bush's father, former President and ex-CIA Director, is currently a member of Washington's Carlyle Group, a US $12 billion private equity firm that employs a number of Republicans. Bush (Senior) specializes in Asia and is in and out of countries like Arabia and Kuwait (given his key role in the Gulf War).[13] The bin Laden group has invested in the Carlyle group. Their portfolio includes defense, telecommunications, etc. Many of the business deals are linked to oil by players with powerful connections to the Bush administration. Other important Republicans like John Sununu and Lloyd Bentsen uphold oil company interests. Former Ambassador to Pakistan Robert Oakley has also been hired by Unocal, as also Henry Kissinger, who has been consultant to Unocal, and Z. Brzezinski who is consultant to Amoco and has attempted to lobby for US foreign policy to pay more attention towards the Caspian Sea and the CAS. Clearly, then, it is more than just terrorism that interests the US in this region, and their involvement in the Great Game is going to last till the oil does.

Russian Concerns

Russia wants to use their own grid and pipelines for transporting Central Asian oil and gas as they did traditionally. They have often stated that there was not so much need for new pipes since existing pipelines should be used and Russia could meet the transportation needs for Caspian Sea oil and gas.[14] At the CIS Summit in June 2001, President Putin created the permanent body for security and cooperation known as the 'Caucasus Four', consisting of Georgia, Armenia, Azerbaijan, and Russia, with the latter as the driving force. All these States need Russia to ensure their stability and Russia needs them for economic and energy reasons as well as markets. But at the same time, these States would also like to exercise some independence and have tried to set up their own alternate groups. US interest in this region has given them this new space.

Russia sees the US as a competitor in Central Asia, the Caspian region, and in Afghanistan. Witness for instance their national security document of January 2001 and their military document of 29 September

2001. These documents list seven threats. While the first threat is international terrorism as in Chechnya and Dagestan, the next most important threats are the struggle for spheres of influence in the former Soviet Republics and US and NATO assertiveness.

At the same time, the Russians would like to engage with the US and do business with them, as Putin's November 2001 visit to the US shows. L. Katsnelson, Director of Volgotanker, Russia's main oil shipping company, which along with Azerbaijan Tanker dominates oil transportation in the Caspian, stated that 'the convergence of American, Russian, and Iranian interest in the Afghan conflict is laying the foundation for a big boost in Caspian oil transportation'. At the same time Russia is tying up with competing partners. They are working out a tie-up between German capital with Russian and CAS energy resources, which implies that Western Europe would no longer have to buy oil from US firms.

Russia is keen to boost the deep-sea harbour prospects of Murmansk on the Barents Sea as a major gateway for Central Asian oil flows to the West. It appears that US resistance to Central Asian oil passing through Russia is weakening because of Russian pressure and the new strategic partnership evolving between the two. Further, both these countries believe that they will get some share of the proposed pipelines through Afghanistan now that a 'friendly government' is installed here. In fact, Russian analyst Leonid Smirnyagin argues that this arrangement would provide a good basis for Russian–US friendship.[15] Russia will, however, continue to assert itself in this region, which it sees as an area of its 'strategic interest'.

Central Asian States: Subjects or Activists?

States like Kyrgyzstan, Tajikistan, and Armenia need Moscow for economic and security reasons. Kazakhstan, with a Russian population of 43 per cent, cannot afford to alienate Moscow, and has continued the closest partnership with it. Even if they are confident of US bases, they know that they cannot afford to alienate Moscow in the long run.

In Kazakhstan, Chevron Oil Company is managing oilfields in Tenghiz. Chevron, the Russian Lukoil, and Rosneft are building a pipeline from Tenghiz to Novorossiyisk on the Black Sea. Here, Russia has been the biggest shareholder with a stake of 24 per cent, though this stake is being constantly diluted. The development of Tenghiz and

Chevron's entry was put in place while George Bush (Senior) was President. Kazakhstan is also linked to the Caspian Consortium pipeline that is examining the various routes we have mentioned earlier.

Uzbekistan had evolved an independent policy towards Afghanistan and the various factions in the power struggle. Their policy saw several zigzags and inconsistencies. For instance, in 1996, Uzbekistan backed General Dostum, an ethnic Uzbek who controlled the area adjacent to Uzbekistan. In 1996, when Dostum launched a campaign against President Rabbani and Ahmed Shah Masood, the then Defence Minister, the hand of Tashkent in this internecine conflict was clearly visible.[16] Before this, Rabbani (an ethnic Tajik) and Tajikistan's President Emomali Rakhmonov had signed a treaty of friendship and cooperation that took no account of Uzbek interests. This led to insecurity for the Uzbek leadership who then went in for some accords with their neighbours. In 1999, when Dostum's troops were routed, Uzbekistan's President Karimov held talks with Ahmed Shah Masood and Moscow to patch up relations between Dostum and Masood. However, during the civil war, Masood backed the Tajik opposition, whose forces included Islamic insurgents from Uzbekistan who opposed the Karimov regime. The Northern Alliance had thus collaborated with forces who were against the Uzbek and Tajik regimes at different points of time, linked up with Islamic insurgents and the Russian military. Since factions of the Northern Alliance are in power behind the Karzai regime, these contradictions can be a source of rivalry again.

Uzbek forces have in the past tried bombing alleged Islamic bases in the Tajik mountains and have mined their borders with Tajikistan and Kyrgyzstan. Both these governments have protested against these moves. The Uzbeks have officially complained that the Tajiks have not been able to control the rebels in the Ferghana Valley that is the stronghold of the IMU. But Dushanbe does not control this territory, even though they signed a peace treaty with the rebels in 1999.[17] The Uzbeks tried again in May 2000 with the Northern Alliance Foreign Minister to work out a strategy against the IMU. It is in both Russian and American interest to stay in the region that they believe would fall prey to local ethnic conflicts. Since in the past Taliban victories in the northern province of Kunduz against Masood's forces were considered a serious threat to CIS borders and had led to serious contemplation of their fortification, Russia will want to safeguard its interests here. At the same time, the CAS and especially President Karimov's radical measures against the clergy have radicalized the opposition and forced it to adopt subtler methods. The suppression of Islamic activity has been accompanied by a wholesale clampdown on public and political life in general.

In Tajikistan, the Islamic rebels continue to be in control of the mountain regions, and are based in Ferghana Valley. President Rakhmonov stated that some of his officials supported them. These rebels have raided Kyrgyzstan and Uzbekistan. The CAS and Russia's years of struggle against their militants have not succeeded in wiping these out, but actually compounded the problem. The CAS States have now used more muscle to curb dissent since they believe they have the backing of the US. Since the US is interested in their own war against terrorism, they overlook the excesses of these regimes.

Turkmenistan has stayed out of collective security arrangements with Russia, even though they had some bilateral arrangements for guarding their borders with the Russian military. They had refused to sign half the inter-governmental agreements of the CIS and did not implement those that they had signed. Turkmenistan even had some independent relations with the Taliban regime, to whom they provided gas supplies.[18] Once they joined the US coalition, they crossed sides and all kinds of anti-democratic measures were justified as the cult of its leader Turkmenbashi grew. There is even a loyal opposition led by the former Foreign Minister, Boris Shikmuradov. Other opposition movements like the Agzybirlik were destroyed and dissidents imprisoned. Turkmenistan has thus been given a free hand to do what it pleases.

The Trail and the Conclusion

US policy in the CAS, Trans Caucasia and the region has become more proactive and interventionist after 9/11. Before 9/11 it was trade before flag. For this they were willing to accommodate Russian and other powers as their oil companies pushed into CAS. They did not want to get directly involved with ethnic conflicts and disputes in the region. Despite their theory that there was a power vacuum in the region, they had proposed the Turkish model for these States. After 9/11 they want to be independent and assertive actors in the region. Their hope is to safeguard their oil and hegemonic interests in the entire region. The nature of their expansionism has been through military bases and engagements. With this they have managed to encircle both Russia and China as well as isolate the CAS from each other and from Russia. Russia, because of its lack of resources and ethnic problems, especially in Chechnya, has agreed to become a junior partner in this exercise and has been systematically giving up on many of its interests. The US policy has changed from flag following trade to trade following flag. Even the oil companies are not happy with this approach, as ethnic conflicts are only likely to increase with such blatant interference.

The Central Asian oil and gas producers like Turkmenistan and Azerbaijan have taken positions independent of Russia and asserted their independence of choice. Turkmenistan has stayed out of collective security arrangements with Russia, even though they had some bilateral arrangements for guarding their borders with the Russian military. Uzbekistan, Kyrgyzstan and Tajikistan have initiated independent ties with the US. They guarantee stronger support, free of Islamic opposition. Given the American penchant for establishing bases where there are authoritarian regimes, they will excuse excesses against opposition groups to protest or mobilize. Azerbaijan is directly linked with US oil interests and US will to freeze the conflicts here and in Georgia until it serves their purpose.

The point now is how and in what form is this hegemonic politics going to unfold. Beneath the ethnic rivalries, religious conflicts, and bloodshed, oil and gas routes clearly fit into the New World order. It is hegemonic politics and not geopolitics that will characterize the post-11 September era.

NOTES

1. Howard Chase, Interview with *Eurasianet*, 15 March 2001.
2. *Oil and Gas Journal*, 10 September 2001.
3. *Guardian*, 23 October 2001.
4. *Current Digest of Post Soviet Press (CDSD)*, vol. 54, no. 1, 30 January 2002, p. 1.
5. *Izvestia*, 16 January 2002, p. 2; *CDSP*, vol. 54, no. 3, 13 February 2002, p. 2.
6. *Nezavisimaya Gazeta*, 9 October 2001, p. 1; *CDSP*, vol. 53, no. 4, 7 November 2001.
7. *Kommersant*, 7 December 2001, p. 3; *CDSP*, vol. 53, no. 49, 2 January 2002.
8. *Vremya MN*, no. 1, January 30, 2002, p. 5; *CDSP*, vol. 54, no. 1, 30 January 2002, p. 3.

9. *Kommersant*, 1 March 2002, p. 1; *CDSP*, vol. 54, no. 9, 27 March 2002, pp. 2–3.
10. *Nezavisimaya Gazeta*, 19 December 2001, p. 5; *CDSP*, vol. 53, no. 51, 16 January 2002, p. 2.
11. Nina Burleigh, *Washington Post*, October 2001.
12. Ibid.
13. Ibid.
14. *Eurasianet*, 22 May 2002.
15. *AFX News*, 29 October 2001, p. 1.
16. *Moscow News*, 2002, pp 2–3.
17. Ibid., 14–20 March 2001, p. 2.
18. Oleg Panfilov, 'Turkmenistan and Turkmenbashi', *The Moscow Times*, 14 August 2002, p. 1.

US Interests in Central Asia

NIMMI KURIAN

Three important dimensions, each representing vital national interests, are coalescing to form a single US policy towards Central Asia and the Caucasus. The lure of potentially vast energy reserves provides the primary interest and the region is fast emerging as a focal point of US energy security considerations. It is the crucial energy dimension that provides the context within which US policy to the region is crafted, and the prism through which the US predominantly views the region. Underpinning this are the strategic and military dimensions that support and reinforce the all-important energy interest. Economic and strategic considerations have tended to move in tandem with the core quest of seeking energy resources, each subserving the other. The paper begins by looking at the emerging patterns in US energy policy and Central Asia's role and importance within this rubric. It then explores the interplay of the three key US interests as well as the likely implications that ensue from these policy initiatives.

Growing Energy Needs

Increasing the nation's energy supplies is fast emerging as a major US policy concern. The report of the National Energy Policy Development Group released by President George W. Bush on 17 May 2001 addressed itself to the task of formulating a prioritized action agenda for securing the country's energy requirements over the next quarter century. The *Cheney Report*, known after Vice-President, Dick Cheney, who was its principal author, notes the increasing US dependence on imported oil. As per the findings of the report, this dependence was likely to rise despite optional exploitation of domestic resources such as those in the Arctic National Wildlife Refuge (ANWR) and other prospective areas.

The report is unambiguous in the implications this holds for national security and future economic growth. The report underlines the need to 'make energy security a priority of our trade and foreign policy.'[1] Domestic energy production presently accounts for 73 per cent of total US energy consumption and will rise from 72.8 quadrillion btu in 2002 to 90.7 quadrillion btu in 2020.[2] However, this will prove to be increasingly inadequate to meet energy needs since consumption is set to outstrip production. This will result in an increasing dependence on imports to meet the energy demand–supply gap. Imported oil currently accounts for 52 per cent of its petroleum needs. This is slated to rise to 66 per cent by 2020.[3] Consequently, US oil imports will have to increase from 10.4 million barrels (mb) per day to 16.7 mb per day during this period.[4]

The *Cheney Report* recommends a twin strategy to deal with the task of securing the energy flows. While on the one hand it recommends an increase in US imports from the Persian Gulf countries, on the other it calls for a policy of diversification of oil supplies aimed precisely at reducing the dependence on the Middle East. The Gulf currently accounts for 18 per cent of US petroleum imports. This relatively modest level of dependence on the Gulf is, however, set to rise in the future as US energy needs rise. The countries of the Persian Gulf boast of the largest reservoir of oil with proven crude reserves accounting for 65 per cent of total global reserves. It also contains the world's second largest reserves of natural gas, estimated to be around 1,918 tcf.[5] This fact, combined with the fact that the Gulf region possesses substantial 'spare' or 'idle' capacity, makes the Gulf undeniably a critical region in US foreign policy considerations.

While increasing dependence on the Middle East becomes a reality, the US is set to pursue strategies aimed at also reducing this dependence. The strategy of diversification of sources of supply is considered essential since overdependence on any one source could leave the US economy vulnerable to supply disruptions and inflict considerable economic damage. The *Cheney Report* urges the government to actively seek and promote other sources of supply, especially the Caspian Sea Basin, Sub-Sahara Africa, and Latin America. Bush reiterated the importance of this strategy thus: 'Diversity is important not only for energy security but also for national security.'[6] Pursuit of the goal of diversification was also essential since it would stave off the adverse effects of price volatility and instability. As a fungible commodity, increasing sources of supply of oil translates to lower prices and increased energy security.

Energy Potential of the Caspian Sea Basin

The US directed increased attention to the Caspian Sea Basin that lies landlocked between Kazakhstan, Uzbekistan, Turkmenistan, Azerbaijan, Iran, and Russia. The 700-mile long Caspian Sea, which contains six separate hydrocarbon basins, is the focal point of global attention on account of considerable reserves of oil and gas that are yet to be fully developed. There is, however, considerable disagreement on how much the Sea can yield. Estimates of proven oil reserves range between 18–34 billion barrels with 235 bb in possible reserves.[7] Estimates of proven gas reserves range from 236–337 bb and 328 bb in possible reserves.[8] While the bulk of the oil in the region is located in Kazakhstan and Azerbaijan, Turkmenistan is the leading gas producer, with the world's fourth largest reserves, followed by Uzbekistan and Kazakhstan, which also have substantial reserves of their own.

For development and full utilization of the resources, the legal status of the Caspian Sea needs to be delineated among the members, which remains an issue of contention between littoral states. Prior to 1991, ownership and development rights in the Sea had involved only Iran and the Soviet Union, governed by the 1921 and 1940 bilateral treaties between them. Following the emergence of the new states, there is no agreement on the sharing of the resources of the Caspian. The differences over the legal status have resulted in a criss-cross of claims and counterclaims by the states. Any decision to develop the resources will have to depend on an agreement among all the littoral states. Russia takes the position that the Caspian is an inland lake and is, therefore, not subject to the United Nations Convention on the Law of the Seas. The US supports the position held by Azerbaijan and Kazakhstan that the Caspian Sea is a sea and, therefore, should be divided into national sectors.

With no natural outlet to the sea, the landlocked Caspian needs an extensive network of pipelines to transport the oil gas resources from the resource-holders to the resource-utilizers. While in theory, oil could travel by pipelines in almost any direction, the choice of export routes has often been influenced by larger geopolitical and security factors and seldom by economic considerations. The selection of one pipeline route over another involves high stakes as it confers several attendant benefits to a host of players in the form of transit fees, jobs, and development of infrastructure, besides critical access to oil and natural gas. While a particular route might make eminent economic sense, it may run aground on political and security considerations. Powerful factors influencing the choice of any route would include, for instance, the degree of control that it would bestow on the countries through which the pipeline passes and the vulnerability this would generate for importers. The US has high stakes in the selection of pipelines since it is seen as vital to ensure control over the flow of oil to the international markets. The imprint of geopolitical considerations is all too evident in the words of a US official who noted: 'the stakes in the Caspian and Central Asia are simply too high to base the decision on its commercial interests alone.'

US interests in the Caspian Sea basin rise from a confluence of factors. The primary attraction is the existence of potentially large reserves of oil and gas still waiting to be tapped. A considerable portion of these reserves is likely to be earmarked for exports since levels of domestic consumption within these countries remain relatively modest. The development of the region's oil and gas fields would also represent commercial opportunities for US companies. As new oil and gas exporters join the market, the additional volumes of oil will provide more freedom of choice to oil-importing countries, besides keeping oil prices down. The allure of the Caspian reserves also arises from the additions these would make to the pool of reserves outside the OPEC and hence very valuable from a strategic point of view.

US oil companies have been actively engaged in the oil and gas sector in the region. Major US energy giants such as Chevron, Texaco, Exxon, Mobil, and Halliburton have invested substantial sums in the region. Kazakhstan, with proven oil reserves of 16 bb, has attracted the largest share of US investments. Chevron has acquired a 45 per cent stake in the Tengizchevroil (TCO) venture to develop the giant Tengiz oilfield in Kazakhstan. Since the Caspian's oil-bearing formations are at a depth of 15,000 feet, offshore oil production and operations have opened opportunities for US firms with special drilling and processing equipment. US firms like Bechtel are also actively involved in providing the construction, financial, and allied services. Owing to its state-of-the-art technology, the US is also a leading supplier of oil and gas services and equipment.

The US government has also extended strong support to US companies and businesses operating in Central Asia and the Caspian and Caucasus regions. It facilitates commerical projects through a host of bodies such as the Export-Import Bank (Exim Bank), the Overseas Private Investment Corporation (OPIC), and the US Trade and Development Agency (TDA). Together, these focus on maximizing US commerical interests in the region and provide wide-ranging assistance to US companies. The OPIC provides insurance cover to US investors as well as financing for energy and non-related projects. While the TDA provides funding for conducting feasibility studies and technical assistance to the governments in the region, the OPIC offers trade and export finance to companies.

Strategic Interests

The Great Game being played out in Central Asia marks a two-fold quest, namely control over the oil and gas production and, just as importantly, control over the piplelines that will transport this to energy-hungry markets of the world. The issue of pipeline selection has assumed a great deal of geopolitical significance and has resulted in an intense political and commerical competition among players, each vying for control and to outbid one another. The existing network of pipelines from Azerbaijan and Kazakhstan run through Russia to the port of Novorossisk in the Black Sea. This has given Russia considerable leverage over the flow of oil and over the Central Asian economies. It has also used this leverage wantonly by arbitrarily raising tariffs and placing limits on the volume of oil to be transported.

The pursuit of US commercial interests is underpinned by a set of geopolitical interests. Primarily, the US is interested in preventing the emergence of a major power in the region. These interests thus include ensuring an erosion of Russia's influence and dominance in the region and excluding Iran through a policy of containment and isolation. Undertaking the task of safeguarding access to oil resources serves another US strategic goal, namely preventing the rise of potential new powers in the international system. The US thus commits itself to ensuring the safety of energy flows to its allies and thus removes any incentive on their part to develop capacities to secure these on their own. By providing for the security of its allies and by '. . . enmeshing their foreign and military policies in alliances that America dominated, Washington prevented these former and potential great powers from embarking on independent, and from the US perspective, possibly destabilizing foreign policies.'[9]

Pipeline Politics

The geo-strategic imperatives are vindicated by an examination of the maze of oil and gas export routes catering to various energy-hungry destinations. Each route has its powerful backers and sponsors, underscoring the intense competition both between companies to gain lucrative contracts and between countries to wrest control over main export routes. The Northern route backed by Russia proposes the use of Russia's extensive pipeline network in the region to transport Caspian energy to the world market. This route would clearly bestow a considerable degree of Russian control over the flows. The Southern route would run through Iran, which already has in place a pipeline network and a ready outlet to the Gulf. This would also be ideally suited to serve the Asian markets. This too would be unacceptable to the US for the leverage it would afford Iran. Investments in Iran would also be problematic since Iran is subjected to economic sanctions under the Helms–Burton legislation and the Iran–Libya Sanctions Act, for its alleged role in supporting international terrorism. US companies are barred from conducting basiness with Iran, and under the ILSA, US sanctions apply to non-US companies investing more than US $20 million in the energy sector.

The US favours an East–West transport corridor to enable the flow of oil from the Caspian to markets in the West. Development of energy infrastructure and a complementary distribution system thus become an imperative. The US has supported the Baku–Tbilisi–Ceyhan (BTC) route that will transport oil from Baku in Azerbaijan to Turkey's Mediterranean port of Ceyhan through Tbilisi in Georgia. The BTC pipeline bypasses both Russia and Iran as export routes. The project entails considerable construction and transport costs and is estimated to cost nearly US $2.9 billion and cover a distance of 1,090 miles. It is a consortium led by British Petroleum and includes Unocal, Eni Spa, Statoil, Itochu Corp, Turkish Petroleum, and the US–Saudi venture Delta Hess. Expected to have the capacity to ship one million barrels of oil a day, the consortium has set 2004 as the target for completing the construction of the pipeline. Senator Sam Brownback underlined the importance of the East–West pipeline through Turkey by terming it as 'one of the most important means of insuring the cementing of a Silk Road Corridor of Freedom' which was essential to prevent the countries in the region from becoming 'economic hostages to Iran, much in the same way that they were economic hostages to the former Soviet Union'.[10]

The BTC project, however, is not without its detractors who criticize it as being too politically motivated. Its political attractiveness has clearly been a deciding factor, as Stephen Mann, US Advisor on Energy Issues in the Caspian, admitted: 'We have never said it is just about business.'[11] This predominantly political logic motivating the project to the exclusion of other critical factors is criticized as being short-sighted and dangerous.

Its commercial viability is also seriously questioned and there is skepticism whether the Caspian has enough volume of oil to justify the huge construction cost of the BTC project.

Another alternative route proposed by the US was the south-eastern route from Turkmenistan through Afghanistan to Pakistan. In the mid-1990s, the US company Unocal along with Bridas of Argentina reached an agreement with the Taliban to build a gas pipeline from Turkmenistan to Pakistan. Despite not having any oil reserves of its own, Afghanistan's asset lay in its strategic location. As an alternative to shipping Caspian oil through Iran to the Gulf, the Afghan route held a strong attraction to the US. An attractive and logical economic rationale appeared to be the growing energy markets of India and Pakistan. The project was, however, abandoned in 1998 as talks with the Taliban floundered. Although in the post-Taliban Afghanistan the prospects of reviving the pipeline project are clouded with imponderables, Afghanistan will remain an integral and key element of US energy strategy in the region.

US–Russia Energy Cooperation

While on the one hand the US seeks to diminish Russian dominance in the region, on the other, it is also actively promoting cooperation with Russia as a means to diversify its own sources of energy supply. Russia is being seen as an alternative and reliable source of energy and its importance has greatly increased in US eyes in the aftermath of the WTC bombings. Given the continued instability in the Middle East, the US is promoting Russia's role as a prospective stabilizing force in the energy market. During their summit meeting in May 2002, Bush and Putin signed a joint declaration on enhancing cooperation in the energy sector. As part of the new US–Russian energy dialogue, both countries agreed to cooperate closely to reduce volatility and ensure reliability of global energy supply. They also agreed to facilitate commercial cooperation in the energy sector and to encourage companies from both countries to jointly undertake exploration, production and refining activities, besides taking up joint projects in third countries. Also on the anvil are plans for faster modernization of Russia's energy sector through increased foreign investments aimed specifically at boosting the production in Eastern Siberia, the Far East, and other prospective areas. Russia's keen desire to maximize market share coincides perfectly with US interests to ensure increased flow of Russian oil to markets in the West.

MILITARY DIMENSION

There is also a clear military dimension to US interests and activities in the region. The military dimension will move closely in tandem with its energy policies and work to reinforce US policy in the region. As it becomes more and more involved in the region, the US will actively pursue traditional instruments of power, including an enhanced capacity to project military power into the region. As its dependence on energy imports rises, the need to secure uninterrupted access to these flows will assume increased importance and will receive priority concern. This will translate to a commitment to seek comprehensive military superiority. Reiterating the need for enhancing US military preparedness, Bush said: 'Our forces must be agile, lethal, readily deployable, and require a minimum of logistical support. We must be able to project our power over long distances.' Bush laid great emphasis on designing 'a new architecture' for US defence forces to serve US interests more effectively and to meet emerging challenges. This finds reflection in the US Defence Department's *Quadrennial Defence Review* (*QDR*) of September 2001. The *QDR* underlines the need for the US to retain the capability to send well armed and logistically supported forces on critical missions around the globe, even in the face of opposition.

An examination of US grand strategy in the post-Cold War period reveals that it continues to be devoted to the pursuit of overwhelming geopolitical dominance. Maintaining preponderance has remained a foremost US foreign policy goal and is seen as being of critical importance for securing its vital national interests. A reiteration of this is provided in the US National Security Strategy released in October 2002. Included in this is the US resolve to strike pre-emptively against potential threats. The pre-emptive strategy is considered necessary so as to '. . . dissuade potential adversaries from pursuing a military buildup in hopes of surpassing, or equalling, the power of the United States'. The document also underlines the resolve to pursue 'full-spectrum dominance'.

The military component of the war on terrorism in Afghanistan is clearly not drawing to a close. Instead, the anti-terror campaign is proving to be a stepping-stone for an enhanced US military presence in Central Asia. Central Asian countries have become vital in US strategic calculations owing to their location as staging posts for military operations. The US has established a major operations base at Khanabad airbase outside Tashkent in Uzbekistan. The Khanabad airbase was critical for the US to launch air strikes over northern Afghanistan and for operations of the Special Forces. Uzbekistan boasts of the best transportation facilities, airbases and military capabilities in the region. The Manas airport in Bishkek, Kyrgyzstan, served as the principal transportation hub for supplies to the coalition forces in Afghanistan. The access to bases and transit rights in Central Asia also enabled the US to avoid an exclusive dependence on Pakistan. In return for their critical support, Washington has pledged US $160 million to Uzbekistan and US $125 million to Tajikistan.[12] Military aid and training programmes had already begun under the Clinton administration, which had established security ties with Georgia, Kazakhstan, Kyrgyzstan, and Uzbekistan. The US has been engaging the militaries of the region through programmes such as the International Military Exchanges and training, the Warsaw Initiative, and the Cooperative Threat Reduction, and at the multilateral level through the NATO's Partnership for Peace. The US combat forces have also been deployed in the Caucasus with the stationing of US military personnel in Tbilisi, Georgia. Its strategic significance to the US is evident as the Baku–Ceyhan route will pass through Tbilisi.

Post-11 September, the range of US involvement in the region has encompassed the entire spectrum of diplomatic, military and political levels. The temporary bases in Uzbekistan and Kyrgyzstan are in the process of being transformed into semi-permanent military bases. Additional military assistance is being channelized through the Foreign Military Sales Financing Programme and the International Military Education Programme. Direct aid has also started flowing to Azerbaijan, which until recently was barred under the US Freedom Support Act (Section 7, Article 907). As this also placed fetters on the operation of US oil companies and placed them at a disadvantage, the clause was amended in February 1996. The US military is directly assisting Azerbaijan to develop a strong maritime capability in the Caspian. The US military is also directly engaged in naval cooperation with Azerbaijan aimed at enhancing its naval capabilities vis-à-vis Iran. Azerbaijan has sought US assistance in the face of tensions with Iran over the issue of conducting exploration activities in the Caspian. The continuing lack of agreement among the Caspian countries on the delimitation of the waters has resulted in a deterioration of maritime security.

Implications

The increasing US involvement and presence in the region has far-reaching implications. The US campaign against terrorism is predominantly a military campaign, flowing from a belief that views Islamic fundamentalism as a military problem which requires a military solution. In the dominant US discourse, Islam and Islamic fudamentalism are often used interchangeably, with their meanings suffused and their distinctions blurred. Such a polarized view glosses over the reality that the Islamist phenomenon is anything but uniform. It also chooses to ignore the fact that a wide majority of Muslims in Central Asia and elsewhere subscribe to the traditional, mystical variant of Sufism, which is both tolerant and moderate in its dispensation.This is in sharp contrast to the Wahhabi and Deobandi schools of thought with their accent on a distinctly radical interpretation of Islam. The US has also repeatedly invoked the spectre of a monolithic, militant Islam inexorably on the march. This conception has served US interests by providing it with the rationale for fighting the perceived threat on a war footing. This has also enabled the US to gain at first a foothold and later a greatly expanded presence in the region. Instability in Central Asia is also attributed to Islamic fundamentalism which is not seen as the very product of this instability. Such a view ignores that it has local taproots, emerging as a product of a widespread socio-economic destabilization. Societal discontent has been on the rise in the region in the face of stagnant economic growth, growing unemployment, rising crime levels and endemic corruption. Several militant Islamic movements in the region have effectively tapped this vein of domestic turmoil and are generating popular support for an agenda of change and reform.

Regimes in Central Asia have also further componded the crisis by placing severe curbs on channels of expression and opposition, thus there is outlet for societal anger. The development of multiple forms of political opposition was nipped in the bud quite early when most regimes in the region intensified crackdowns on all opposition parties. This has proven to be a vicious, self-fulfilling prophecy. As corrupt and unstable regimes launch fresh offensives and as the domain of civil society has shrunk, this has further fuelled disenchantment. Opposition leaders have been driven into exile, secular democratic political parties banned, and local media operates under tight state controls, while the authoritarian regimes seek out new means to consolidate power. As Boris Shikhmuradov, Turkmenistan's exiled former Foreign Minister observed: 'The more opposition there is, the better, but we are all in exile because there is no legal environment to operate it, and that is true for all Central Asia.'[13] There has been no change of leadership in Central Asia since 1991 and the trend is clearly towards perpetuation and consolidation of power. The environment of repression and socio-economic instability has proved to be a fertile breeding ground for militant groups. As Graham Fuller observes: 'If a society and its politics are violent and unhappy, its mode of religious expression is likely to be just the same.'[14]

Islam is also seen as being inherently incapable of democratic impulses and the two are considered incompatible. Islam is seen as 'an aggressive revolutionary movement, as militant and violent as the Bolshevik, Fascist, and Nazi movements of the past' and one that needed to be 'stifled at birth'.[15] The confrontation with Islam also assumes religious, cultural and civilizational overtones. Thus, Islam is seen as being irreconcilable with the 'Christian, secular West' and the interaction between Islam and the West is perceived by many as a 'clash of civilisations' á la Samuel Huntington. Seen thus, Islam becomes the new enemy of the West, replete with imageries of what the West stands for its value system.

Closely tied to the way the US perceives Islam, and as important, is the way in which the region in general and the Muslim world in particular perceives the US and its role in the region. It must be stressed that the region and its inhabitants are not passive entities and their perceptions form a very important and decisive component in the evolving dynamics. As Fuller notes, '. . . even as Westerners feel threatened by Islam, most in the Muslim world feel besieged by the West, a reality only dimly grasped in the United States.'[16] US troop presence across the region is a highly emotive issue and Osama bin Laden has led the call for the removal of non-Muslim forces from the region. Of the more than 25,000 US military personnel stationed in the Gulf, 10,000 are in Kuwait, 4,200 in Bahrain, 3,300 in Qatar, 6,000 in Saudi Arabia, 2,400 in Oman and nearly 500 in the United Arab Emirates.[17] Anti-Americanism has been fuelled by rising hostility towards US policies, especially the perceived bias against the Palestinians and the unconditional support to Israel. American troops stationed in the Gulf are also coming under attack, with the most recent being the shooting of two US Marines by two Kuwaitis described as Islamic activists. The incident in Kuwait is clearly no isolated incident and is symptomatic of a recognizable pattern across the region.

Resentment has been simmering in Central Asia also at US support and backing of authoritarian regimes. As participants in the war on terror, the Central Asian regimes have utilized the opportunity to fight their own local wars on political oppositions at home. In the name of stability, there have been intensified crackdowns on all forms of opposition, without inviting any censure from the US. As Mohamed Solih, leader of Uzbekistan's banned Erk party laments: 'Karimov shows it is possible to gain prestige and money and extend your rule on a whim and still gain American support in the post-terrorism world.'[18]

Conclusion

As it takes on ever-increasing commitments across the globe as part of the war on terrorism, the US treads a dangerous course. The campaign is fraught with dangers precisely because it sets itself no conceivable limits or parameters within which it could be confined. The pursuit of global pre-eminence will thus entail mounting costs in terms of both resources and personnel. Such a strategy will also carry huge burdens and immense risks, and will, ironically, further stoke the very instability that the US is attempting to remove.

The stationing of US troops in Central Asia and Caucasus and the participation of these countries in the war on terror also exposes them to considerable dangers. The use of their territory and their support to the US makes them potential targets and victims of terrorism. Given the porous nature of the borders, terrorist groups fleeing Afghanistan have sought new havens in Central Asia, exposing the entire neighbourhood to increased instability. Armed insurgents from Afghanistan have made incursions into Tajikistan, Kyrgyzstan, and Uzbekistan. This has prompted desperate measures, which have often worsened the existing situation. Uzbekistan, for instance, has attempted to reinforce its borders with Kyrgyzstan by building fences and laying landmines. Besides resulting in loss of human lives and injuries, such measures have also crippled local economies, which depended on a thriving cross-border trade. The geographical proximity and the permeability of borders have also turned Central Asia into a thoroughfare for drugs, arms, refugees and militants.

US presence in the region also has significant strategic implications for regional powers such as Russia, Iran, and China who have been warily watching the increasing US build-up. Iran has railed against US efforts to isolate it and identify it as a potential target in the war on terrorism. In his State of the Union address in January 2002, Bush had termed Iraq, Iran, and North Korea as constituting an 'axis of evil, arming to threaten the peace of the world'.[19] China too has found the enhanced and immediate presence of US forces so near its borders very disconcerting. It has resulted in angry outbursts from China, with Jiang Zemin bluntly remarking: 'China opposes US presence in Central Asia and the Middle East.'[20] While it publicly supports the war against terrorism, China has serious concerns on the impact this has on its own strategic interests in the region as well as on its relationships with Pakistan, India, Russia, as well as the US in the altered scenario. It also has been strongly urging a greater role for the United Nations and has strong reservations on the issue of intervention. The issue of US presence has also generated a great deal of criticism in Russia. Opposition parties have decried the Russian government's policies vis-à-vis the US and have interpreted the US presence as a threat to Russian national security. Dismissing such critics, Putin remarked: 'Decisions are taken on the basis of what we need in reality, not on the moon.'[21] And, he has decisively opted for enhanced cooperation with the United States, particularly in the energy field.

The prospect of developing potentially enormous reserves in the Caspian Sea basin has generated considerable hype and resulted in a 'Caspian frenzy' of huge proportions. Overoptimistic scenarios and inflated estimates have helped to drive this ever higher and higher. Seen through a rosy prism, the oil and gas reserves have appeared to the Central Asian countries as providing a short cut to instant prosperity. This misconception has had grievous effects, generating great expectations and likely to bring greater disenchantment in the face of the challenges that remain to be met. The enthusiasm and optimism of the previous decade is giving way to a more sobering assessment of the region's potential and of the daunting obstacles that remain.

NOTES

1. 'National Energy Policy', *The Report of the National Energy Policy Development Group*, Washington, DC, May 2001, www.whitehouse.gov/energy.
2. US Department of Energy, *Annual Energy Outlook 2002*, www.eia.doe.gov/oiaf/aeo.
3. 'National Energy Policy', op. cit.
4. US Department of Energy, Energy Information Administration (DOE/EIA), *International Energy Outlook 2002*, www.eia.doe.gov/oiaf/ieo/oil.html.
5. *Persian Gulf Oil and Gas Exports Fact Sheet*, March 2002, accessed at http://www.eia.doe.gov/emeu/cabs/pgulf.html.

6. US Department of Energy, *Caspian Sea Region*, July 2002, www.eia.doe.gov/cabs/caspian.html.
7. Ibid.
8. Ibid.
9. Benjamin Schwartz and Christopher Layne, 'A New Grand Strategy', *The Altantic Monthly*, vol. 289, no. 1, January 2002, p. 37.
10. Sam Brownback, 'Pursuing a Silk Road Strategy', speech at the Asia Society, 19 March 1998, www.asiasociety.og/speeches/brownback.html.
11. Cited in Mark Bermiker, *As Baku–Ceyhan Construction Date Nears, Debate Continues Over Project's Viability*, accessed at www.eurasianet.org.
12. Ahmed Rashid, *Central Asia Elites Suddenly Shift into Revolt*, 2 May 2002, www.eurasianet.org/departments/insight/articles/eav050202.shtml.
13. Ibid.
14. Graham Fuller, 'The Future of Policial Islam', *Foreign Affairs*, vol. 81, no. 2, March–April 2002, p. 60.
15. Amos Perlmutter, 'Wishful Thinking About Islamic Fundamentalism', *Washington Post*, 19 January 2002.
16. Graham Fuller, n. 14, p. 54.
17. Rajiv Chandrasekaran, 'Perceived Bias Against Palestinians Fuels Anti-Americanism in Gulf', *International Herald Tribune*, 12–13 October 2002.
18. Ahmed Rashid, n. 12.
19. www.whitehouse.gov/news/releases/2002/01/20020129.html.
20. Ariel Cohen, *Does China Want to Build an Anti-American Alliance Across Asia?*, www.eurasianet.org/departments/insight/articles/eav050402.shtml.
21. Cited in Igor Torbakov, *Putin Faces Domestic Criticism Over Russia's Central Asia Policy*, www.eurasianet.org/departments/insight/articles/eav021202.shtml.

USA's Involvement in Afghanistan: Third World Perceptions with Special Reference to South Asian Countries and Implications for the Future

SHRI PRAKASH

Range of US Military Interventions in the Twentieth Century

The history of US involvement and intervention in the management of the politics of the decolonized world is almost as old as its birth and creation. With reference to Asia, one remembers the US expeditions to 'open up' Japan and China. In the twentieth century, from being a welcome supporter as well as a spokesperson for the self-determination of colonial peoples in the days of President Woodrow Wilson, USA has become the self-appointed director and arbitrator of a 'unipolar' world. The change in Third World perceptions regarding the nature and purpose of USA's foreign policy started during the period of the 'Cold War' when the Western bloc countries allied to USA identified the Soviet Union and its supporters to be the principal source of authoritarian state systems not only within their own territories but also in those parts of the world that saw themselves as opposing any pro-American political or economic system, ranging from those run by military dictators or feudal chieftains or religious extremists and fundamentalists. As several expert analyses have pointed out, often from within the ambit of the academia in the US itself, ultimately, national, economic, or strategic interests as perceived by the public or the establishment predominated over principled support for democracy, human rights, or national liberation.[1]

The watershed that divides Third World perceptions about US foreign policy ventures in the post Second World War period is provided by the Vietnam War. After growing domestic opposition in USA and sustained successes scored by the Vietcong, it is now argued by several American analysts that it was a 'national' mistake for the US to have been involved in the Vietnam War. John Hellman in his book on the Vietnam War has pointed out that in the beginning of John F. Kennedy's term as the US President, the increase in counterinsurgency efforts made for a greatly expanded American commitment to Vietnam that would later confront President Johnson. Mike Mansfield, majority leader of the Senate, and Kenneth O'Donnell, Kennedy's assistant, both later reported that Kennedy had expressed to them during 1963 his profound dismay at his previous actions in Vietnam and his determination to extricate American forces after the 1964 election.[2]

Kennedy's assassination prevented him from implementing any of his privately expressed intentions. Instead, Johnson as President also greatly expanded the conventional war in Vietnam and resorted to conscription.[3] All that USA could do could not prevent it, under tremendous international pressure, from having to withdraw its forces and thereby allow the process of reunification of North and South Vietnam to be brought to a fruitful conclusion.

The Third World countries, most of them included in the Non-Aligned Movement (NAM), regularly passed resolutions at their summit meetings and put up similar statements in various fora of the United Nations asking for USA to withdraw from Vietnam. In India, governments constituted by different political parties ranging from the Congress, the Janata Dal, and the Bharatiya Janata Party have on various occasions and from a variety of platforms described the war being fought by North Vietnam against 'the US occupation forces' as a War of National Liberation. They saw in it the continuance of the same wave of decolonization that had brought independence to many countries of Asia and Africa in the twentieth century.[4]

A similar view was adopted by the Non-Aligned Movement of the US blockade of Communist Cuba and the Western, including indirect US, support to the apartheid regime in South Africa that later resulted in the imposition of comprehensive United Nations backed sanctions that ultimately crippled and undermined South Africa's apartheid government in the 1990s. Most of the newly independent countries backed the claims of Communist or mainland China for a permanent seat in the Security Council, which was not agreed to by USA for many years, the seat being occupied at first by Republican China or Taiwan. However, ultimately on this issue also the pressure from the Non-Aligned and Soviet bloc countries in particular made USA back down. In fact during the 1970s, USA agreed not to recognize Taiwan as any 'independent' country, accepted the 'one China' policy, and became one of Communist China's leading trade partners and sources of investment. The turnabout in USA's China policy showed how international pressure could impact on USA if it coincided with the latter's view of 'strategic engagement' with another country having not only a different political and economic system but also an opposing ideology. Again, such a change was seen to be in USA's 'national interest' since China could provide a large market in the Third World, a source of cheaper manufactured goods and other imports for the developed countries, and strategic support against the Soviet *bloc*.

USA's renewal of China's 'most favoured nation' status has always been accompanied by a debate about its poor human rights record but eventually commercial considerations have overridden any moral compunctions about not adhering to USA's declared goal of persuading or even pressurizing other countries to always improve their performance on the human rights front. When agreement has existed on the fact that international norms or rules have been contravened by a Third World country, often there have been differences among nations on how to deal with the matter. To cite just two examples—(a) The fight against international terrorism has been going on for a long time. In 1992, the United Nations Security Council voted to impose a ban on air travel and arms sales (as well as other sanctions) against Libya, because it refused to surrender agents implicated in the bombing of a Pan Am flight over Scotland in 1988 and a French airliner over West Africa the next year. The vote was ten in favour of the air embargo with five abstentions, but of the six temporary Third World members on the Security Council, four (Morocco, India, Cape Verde, and Zimbabwe) abstained. These four, joined by China, preferred an approach relying more on negotiation and less on ultimatum. (b) Similarly, in 1989, the first Bush administration proposed stationing the US navy off the coast of Colombia in order to interdict the transportation of cocaine from that country to the United States. When the leaders of several Latin American nations, including Colombia, protested that this action would violate their sovereignty, President Bush promised that no such steps would be taken without the prior agreement of all governments affected. Yet, apprehending General Noriega so that he could be tried in the United States on drug-related charges was one of the reasons President Bush gave for the military intervention into Panama in 1990, proving that the threat of intervention to capture drug lords is real, not empty.[5] One of the characteristic features of the end of the Cold War and the disintegration of the Soviet Union has been the termination of the duopoly that had become a constant feature of international relations during the post Second World War period.

A balance of power within the notion of Mutually Assured Destruction (MAD) was a publicly accepted construct of power relations between the USA-led and Soviet-led blocs. It implied then, as it does now, that there was an ever present fear of escalation to global nuclear war. Paradoxically, such a situation also created the background in which numerous 'proxy' wars were fought with the two superpowers supporting opposing countries from behind.[6] Vietnam, Korea, Israel–Palestine, India–Pakistan et al., the list of semi or fully 'proxy' wars after 1945 is a long one.

Sometimes the supporters of the superpowers played an autonomous role in these 'proxy wars'. A specific confluence of separate factors could lead, as it did in the case of US and Chinese support to Pakistan, in mutually opposed states siding with one country for reasons of strategic self-interest.[7]

Not all US interventions in other countries have been seen as arbitrary or unilateral. When the US forces took the lead in fighting against the German armies during the first and the second world wars they won almost universal support from existing or aspiring democratic countries and forces. The Indian National Congress opposed the onset of fascism, but it abstained from actively mobilizing for the Allied powers because they said that they were themselves subject to British oppression and that war had been declared without consulting them. The Congress said clearly that if Britain granted freedom to India, it would as a free country join the Allied Powers in their war against fascism. Similarly, the Chinese Communist Party, while campaigning for the ouster of all colonial powers from China, especially identified the invading Japanese armies as the main enemy of their National Liberation Movement. There is no permanent cause why Third World countries should always be anti-USA or anti-Britain. This has historically depended on how the developing Third World countries have perceived their self-interest in given situations.

Afghanistan as a Neutral and Non-Aligned Country and US Policy Towards Afghanistan

The long term dynamics of US foreign policy had not led it until the last few decades to pay any special attention to Central Asian countries beyond Iran and Pakistan. Indeed, even during the 1970s, the primary perception of the main threat to the 'free' Western-supported or recognized countries was said to be due to the persistent strengthening of Soviet military forces in Asia, but this did not include Afghanistan at that time.

Ramon H. Myers in his well known book, *A US Foreign Policy for Asia*, has pointed out that during the 1970s, US concerns regarding Soviet moves in the Cold War game were centred on the Asia-Pacific and not the Central Asian region. According to Myers, in those days the USSR was adopting low key postures in the Indian Ocean region.

> In addition to stationing 45 ground divisions on the Sino–Soviet border, the USSR has recently deployed surface combatants as well as ballistic missile submarines to its already large Pacific fleet, occupied former air bases at Da Nang and former naval facilities at Cam Ranh Bay in Vietnam, garrisoned division size ground forces on the islands of Japan's Northern Territories, and introduced SS-20 intermediate range missiles and long range bombers to the Asia-Pacific basin. This regional Soviet military might marks the beginning of a new strategic era. Soviet activities and manoeuvres with increasing number of ships and aircraft have a direct effect on the US–USSR military balance of power in the western Pacific and worldwide, particularly in view of the reduction of US naval and air units for operations in the Indian Ocean.[8]

Also, until the 1970s, Afghanistan a relatively small landlocked country, had striven hard to maintain its policy of neutrality and a status of being non-aligned with any of the two power blocs between whom the Cold War was being waged. As a country, Afghanistan had begun to develop its diplomatic skills at staying neutral during the Great Game between the Big Powers, Russia and Great Britain, in the nineteenth century, trying to secure their influence in the Central Asian region. Even during the reign of King Abdur Rahman who used a centrally defined concept of Islam, close to the Sunni orthodoxy of the Hanafi School, to undermine divergent local traditions and unify Afghanistan in the late nineteenth century, the country stayed independent by promising not to allow either the British or the Russians to have a predominant position within Afghan territory.[9]

The strategy of having an even-handed relationship with all the notable powers of the days was further extended in the 1920s to try and establish regular diplomatic ties between Afghanistan and the United States. The 1920s in Afghanistan were the days when King Amanullah, who had won the throne with the help of young modernizers, promulgated the country's first formal constitution, along with a range of liberal reforms. While formal correspondence was being exchanged between USA and Afghanistan for the initiation of diplomatic relations, King Amanullah was overthrown in April 1929 by more conservative forces who enthroned Nadir Shah as King. However, the moderate forces again reasserted themselves and Nadir Shah, whose regime was formally recognized by the Soviet Union in November 1933, was succeeded by Zahir Shah. In order to enhance its international status, Afghanistan joined the League of Nations in September 1934.[10]

An example of the balanced relations Afghanistan had succeeded in establishing with other countries, especially the big powers, was to be had when USA in its draft agreement for establishing diplomatic relations wanted the 'most favoured nation treatment' clause to be included as Article IV. Afghanistan objected to Article IV since it had not included such a clause in its consular treaties with other countries like Russia, Great Britain, and France. The US State Department concurred and the agreement to establish full diplomatic relations between Kabul and Washington was signed at Paris on 26 March 1936. A US consular mission was established in Kabul on 6 June 1942. Afghanistan continued to pursue a policy of strict neutrality during the Second World War and Kabul did not align either with the Allied or the Axis Powers. The German embassy continued to function in Kabul throughout the Second World War, although with a reduced staff at the insistence of Russia and Great Britain.

In the post Second World War period, too, Afghanistan continued to enjoy good relations both with USA and the Soviet Union while remaining reutral and later joining the Non-Aligned Movement. In 1946, USA supported Afghanistan's admission as a member of the United Nations, which took place without any opposition from any country. On 5 June and 23 November 1948, USA and Afghanistan respectively promoted their chancelleries to the ambassador's level. An agreement for USA to provide technical assistance to Afghanistan was signed in 1951.[11]

With the formation of the independent state of Pakistan in 1947, a new situation arose in Afghanistan's neighbourhood. Pakistan was opposed to the formation of an independent Pakhtoonistan while Afghanistan supported it. Further, US military aid to Pakistan once it joined SEATO and CENTO made Afghanistan take steps to get close to the Soviet Union. Top Soviet leaders visited Kabul in December 1955 and substantially increased Soviet economic as well as military aid to Afghanistan. In turn, USA sought to keep Afghanistan non-aligned by also increasing its aid by supplying food grains and developing the airport facilities in Kabul in 1957. USA again provided aid worth US $15 million to Afghanistan, which, however, declined an offer to join the military alliances being formed by USA against the Soviet Union. In June 1958, the Afghan Prime Minister Daud visited USA for a fortnight and received praise for his policy of neutrality. The US President, Dwight D. Eisenhower, paid a short visit to Kabul in December 1959 and gave an assurance of continuing aid to Afghanistan. These pledges were repeated when the Afghan King Zahir Shah visited USA in 1963. In 1967, under a new agreement, USA supplied large grain shipments and renewed the 1953 agreement concerning technical assistance to Afghanistan.

Friendly relations between USA and Afghanistan continued after the monarchy was overthrown in a coup in 1973 led by the King's cousin, Sardar Mohammad Daud, who also established the first Afghan republic. The US Secretary of State, Henry A. Kissinger, paid an official visit to Afghanistan in November 1974 at the invitation of the Afghan government. US assistance in the fields of economic, technical, and educational expansion was continued. Kissinger again visited Kabul in August 1976 and extended support to Afghanistan's policy of positive neutrality. This did not prevent the leaders of Afghanistan from infusing the country's fourth constitution in 1976 with strong socialist elements that further secularized the state, installed a one party regime and reformed the composition of the *Loya Jirga*, or the traditional tribal assembly, to include mainly the followers of the government.[12]

However, Sardar Mohammad Daud's policies to keep Afghanistan on a moderate course had created enemies among the communists entrenched in the Afghanistan army in the form of the Khalq and the Parcham factions backed by the Soviet authorities. The US strategy had all along suffered from the fact that on the one hand US officials like Joseph Foam had written about the presence of rich deposits of minerals like chrome ore, manganese, zinc, lead, and silver, and of the geopolitical situation of Afghanistan that could supply vital routes for trade and the supply of gas and oil from Central Asia, a fact that became all the more true later on with the disintegration of the Soviet Union and the desire of the independent Central Asian republics to secure the shortest route for their pipelines to the Arabian Sea. At the same time, other officials and US agencies at first argued that Afghanistan had little strategic value for USA. In 1953, a secret study by the US Joint Chiefs of Staff concluded that 'Afghanistan is of little or no strategic importance to the United States. Its geographic location, coupled with the realization by Afghanistan leaders of Soviet capabilities, presages Soviet control of the country when the situation so dictates.'[13] Hence, it was the Russians who mainly helped to build the military infrastructure in Afghanistan.

Benefiting from the hold they had within the Afghan armed forces, the Peoples Democratic Party of Afghanistan carried out a Russian backed coup in April 1978. A revolutionary council with Noor Mohammed Taraki as Chairman was constituted and Afghanistan was declared a Democratic Republic. Soviet Russia was the first to recognize the new government of the Democratic Republic of Afghanistan, which decreed a further set of liberal reforms overnight instituting land reforms, giving free education to all, and freedom to women. The Khalq faction headed by Taraki and Amin had a predominant role in the new government. Kremlin signed a treaty of friendship with the Communist regime in Kabul on 5 December 1978 in which the latter was assured of Moscow's military help.

In a country of low literacy, feudal estates ruled by warlords, where the literati mainly consisted of the Sunni Muslim clergy who saw the liberation of women as entirely anti-Islamic and communism as a denial of Allah, the Communist government had support mainly among the urban elites. A civil war started brewing in 1978 itself. The situation was further exacerbated by the infighting among the Communists.

Hafizullah Amin replaced Noor Mohammed Taraki as Prime Minister of Afghanistan in March 1979. The emergence of the Babrak Karmal regime backed by Soviet troops pushed Afghanistan into the Russian orbit after 27 December 1979, when the Soviet army entered the country at the invitation of its government to help fight the West-backed rebels—Mujahideens. Further, the refusal to accept US aid and the murder of the US Ambassador, Dubs, in February 1979 completed Afghanistan's rupture with USA. The Russian military 'occupation', as it was called by the dominant western governments and media, was condemned and criticized by most governments, especially the US, the UN and the Organization of Islamic Countries (OIC).

Post Soviet Intervention

By January 1980, press reports indicated that there were 80,000 to 1,00,000 Soviet troops in Afghanistan. On 14 January 1980, just a few weeks after the Soviet invasion, the UN General Assembly passed by a margin of 104 in favour, 18 against and 10 abstaining, a resolution that 'strongly deplores the recent armed intervention in Afghanistan as inconsistent with the fundamental principles of the UN Charter, and calls for the immediate, unconditional withdrawal of the foreign troops from Afghanistan'. This and several other resolutions of the UN General Assembly show how most of the Third World countries, including the non-aligned ones, disapproved of Soviet intervention in Afghanistan under the purview of the Brezhnev doctrine.

The Soviet military venture in Afghanistan was seen by USA in larger-than-life terms. According to Washington, it put the Soviets 'within striking distance of the Indian Ocean and even the Persian Gulf', an area of vital strategic and economic significance to the survival of western Europe, the Far East and ultimately the United States. The western liberal democracies, led by the US, which were very critical of the Islamic revolution in Iran in 1979, joined hands with the Islamic groups called Mujahideen to force the Soviets to withdraw from Afghanistan. According to Abdus Sattar, a former Pakistan Foreign Secretary, the US 'raised covert allocations for supply of arms to the Mujahideens, from US $250 million in 1985, to US $470 million in 1986 and US $630 million in 1987. The American contribution was reportedly matched by Saudi Arabia—Pakistan calibrated the flow of assistance to the Mujahideen cautiously but it became bolder with time and experience.'[14]

In order to put further pressure on the Soviet Union, 'the Carter administration postponed the Senate vote on ratification of the SALT Treaty, blocked US $2 billion in grain sales to the USSR, prevented American athletes from participating in the 1980 Moscow Olympics, halted sales of advanced technology to the Soviet Union, increased military aid to Pakistan after earlier refusing to do so, and accelerated contacts with the People's Republic of China'.[15]

Historically, Afghanistan had never been a vital area of concern for China. Between 1949–78, China's relation with Afghanistan was essentially a factor of its relations with the Soviet Union, India, and Pakistan. In these three decades, China did not give much aid to Afghanistan, nor any weapons or training for the Afghan army, nor was it a major trading partner. As a logical consequence of the close political, military, and economic relations China had with Pakistan and later on with USA and its allies, it tended not to support Pushtunistan and keep a distance from Afghanistan because of its own conflictual relations with the Soviet Union. Since 1979 China started championing the cause of the Afghan Mujahideen as a 'national liberation struggle' against the Soviet Union. Along with USA, China, which had minimal relations with Afghanistan, in a few months became a major protagonist in the Afghan civil war. According to China's analysis and statements, the Soviet action in Afghanistan was a step towards a takeover of the Gulf oilfields, control of the Persian Gulf, and search for warm ports for its operations in the Indian Ocean. In essence, it was identical to the explanation being advanced by Brzezhinski and the Central Intelligence Agency in USA. Beijing's other charge was that the Soviet troop movement into Afghanistan and the almost simultaneous Vietnamese move into Kampuchea were an integral part of a grand design to encircle China and therefore posed a dangerous security threat to it. In reply, the Soviet Union pointed to the anti-Soviet global 'United Front' created by China, a quasi-alliance of the NATO powers, China, Japan, and a string of other pro-Western nations. The Soviets justified their intervention in Afghanistan on grounds of wanting to win friends to break the encirclement of the Soviet Union by China, USA, and their allies.[16]

Whatever the perceived justification for the Soviet Union to send in its troops into Afghanistan, their presence did not succeed in counteracting the civil unrest aroused by the actions of the government of the Peoples Democratic Party of Afghanistan (PDPA), at first under the leadership of Noor Muhammad Taraki and Hafizullah Amin. The PDPA misjudged the level of political consciousness of the Afghan people and attempted to force reforms in Afghan society for which it was not ready. The PDPA regime initiated land reforms for which adequate preparations had not been undertaken and this resulted in the landed aristocracy as well as the peasants and a section of the clergy joining the opposition. The conservative sections of the Afghan society were also incensed by the regime's introduction of social reforms relating to women. The Taraki and Amin regime increasingly resorted to coercive methods to implement its policies, alienating even the oppressed sections of society. Hostile propaganda by Pakistan and Iran only aggravated the crisis. Starting in the second half of 1979, increasing numbers of Afghans began to flee the country and take refuge in Pakistan and Iran, producing recruits for the Mujahideen fighters.

The situation prevailing at that time around and within Afghanistan created conditions for external intervention led by the United States. In February 1979, the Shah of Iran was overthrown and replaced by the anti-US fundamentalist Khomeini regime. The USA sent more naval ships to the area and created a Rapid Development Force in order to intervene at a short interval. The military dictatorship of General Zia-ul-Haq felt threatened by the economic and political reforms of the PDPA in Afghanistan. Were these to succeed, they would have widespread repercussions in Pakistan, particularly in the Baluch and Pakhtoon areas bordering Afghanistan. This was another reason for the Pakistani government to support the Mujahideen insurgency in Afghanistan. The coalescence of Pakistani and US interests produced unexpected benefits for Pakistan. It was now perceived as a frontline state in the fight against Soviet expansionism. USA gave Pakistan not only political importance, sending many high officials to visit Pakistan, but also a major package of military and economic assistance worth US $7.22 billion. The arms pipeline into Pakistan became bigger and bigger, funnelling weapons into the hands of the Afghan counter-revolution.

The growing pressure of the Mujahideen military campaign added to the concerns of the PDPA and the fissures in its ranks. In December 1979, the Hafizullah Amin leadership of the PDPA was replaced by that of Babrak Karmal. In turn, in 1986, Najibullah took over from Babrak Karmal. These quick changes further alienated the support base of the PDPA. Najibullah's efforts at national reconciliation came too late to stem the growing tide of Mujahideen resistance.

India's Perceptions of the Afghanistan Situation

India found itself in a difficult situation as regards the Soviet intervention in Afghanistan. It had enjoyed good relations with a non-aligned Afghanistan and together with it supported the idea of an independent Pakhtoonistan, if it were to happen because of a people's movement. As an independent non-aligned country, it had clearly opposed USA's military intervention in Vietnam, the setting of American military bases in and around the Indian Ocean region and US sanctions against Cuba. The few occasions when Indian troops after 1947 were in action abroad was on peacekeeping missions, e.g. in South Korea and Congo as a part of the UN peacekeeping missions. It had also kept away from openly supporting the Soviet army's intervention in Hungary and Czechoslovakia, although formally Soviet action was claimed to have been sanctioned by the terms of the Warsaw Pact.

Mrs Indira Gandhi, the Prime Minister of India, articulated a standpoint that was later justified by the Geneva Accord concerning

Afghanistan. According to her, in principle, India was opposed to the presence of any foreign troops on the soil of any country. At the same time, Soviet military intervention, although undesirable, came about due to a whole series of actions by the Shah of Iran, the USA, and others to wean away Afghanistan from its close relationship with the Soviet Union. She wanted all powers to jointly create political conditions for Afghanistan to be independent, non-aligned, and democratic. This, she felt, would ensure the early withdrawal of Soviet troops from Afghanistan. She was the only head of government who demanded the withdrawal of Soviet troops from Afghanistan from a public platform in Moscow.[17] This historical fact has often been forgotten by her critics.[18]

There are, of course, those who have argued that the Soviet intervention in Afghanistan should have been openly opposed by India, who could have joined hands with Pakistan and USA to take part in the campaign to force the Soviets out of Afghanistan.[19] This would have led to India doing a full circle or a U-turn like Pakistan later did once USA decided to attack the Taliban, although they might justifiably be called a logical product of the arming of tens of thousands of Mujahideen soldiers. Mrs Indira Gandhi's policy was based on the principled opposition to all religious fundamentalism, which was espoused by most of the Indian nationalist leaders. Some American analysts feel that India was watching and waiting in order to be sure that Soviet intervention in Afghanistan would be successful. Were that to happen, it could lead to the formation of an independent Pakhtoonistan or other pressures on Pakistan likely to change its policy towards India.[20]

The Taliban Takeover and its Aftermath

It is a fact that with the help of massive military aid from the west, the Mujahideen managed to prevail over the conservative local clerics and mobilized the rural population in Afghanistan in a costly campaign to resist the Soviet forces and the communist PDPA, which did not 'believe in God (Allah)'. Confronted with domestic civil war and widespread international criticism, the Soviet forces withdrew from Afghanistan in 1988. Contrary to expectations, the government of President Najibullah maintained effective power in the main urban centres, with significant external backing, for four more years. The disintegration of the Soviet Union, however, reduced the last support enjoyed by the Najibullah regime, and in 1992, 20,000 Mujahideen entered Kabul, establishing an Islamic State headed by an Islamic Jihad Council formed from the seven Pakistan-based opposition factions.

The first decrees of the new governing council foreshadowed the draconian social and political legislation later enforced by the Taliban. The Council's Islamic laws included the banning of music, closing of theatres, the enforcement of compulsory prayer, veiling of women, and denial to them of paid employment. It became obvious almost immediately that the proclamation of such 'Islamic' decrees could not hide for long the struggle for personal power that was taking place behind the scene. The Afghan President, Burhanuddin Rabbani, was challenged by his Prime Minister, Gulbuddin Hekmatyar, who wanted full authority for himself, resulting in serious fighting in Kabul and the effective disintegration of the new Islamic republic.[21]

The internecine fighting was expected as those knocking at the gates of the capital belonged to different tribal groups now armed during the Afghan jihad. Former allies had now become competitors for the prize of power in Kabul. Commander Ahmad Shah Masood (Jamiat-i-Islami) moved towards Kabul from the north. Engineer Gulbuddin Hekmatyar (Hizb-e-Islami) was advancing towards the same objective from the south. General Abdul Rashid Dostum (Jambish-e-Milli) flew 2,000 of his well-trained Uzbeks into Kabul.[22] After a head-on clash between all of them, it was Dostum's and Masood's forces that controlled Kabul. The constant and bloody power struggle between various groups calling themselves Islamic created the vacuum that the Pakistani-trained and mobilized Taliban later tried to fill.

There are several interpretations of how the Taliban originated. One account says that their roots lie in the uprising in Kandahar by a group of young men, formerly students of religious schools set up by the Jamiat-ul-Ulema-i-Islam led by Maulana Fazlur Rahman for Afghan refugees in various parts of the North West Frontier Province in Pakistan. The students drove away the local Mujahideen boss and established a 'pure Islamic rule' led by one Mullah Umar. He was a veteran of the fighting against the Soviet army. It was only later the Pakistani intelligence agency, the Inter Services Intelligence (ISI), took over their organization.

The second interpretation, which is closer to the facts, stipulates that the ISI mobilized the Taliban from the *madrassas* or Islamic schools, trained and armed them, and inducted them into Afghanistan. The military skills of the Taliban, their training in the use of sophisticated weapons and fighting tactics were due to the training provided by the Pakistani army, whose soldiers and commanders also sometimes fought alongside the Taliban to keep a watch on them.

The Taliban was overwhelmingly a Pakistan-sponsored Pushtun militia. Once they captured Kabul, the Taliban representative in Islamabad was allowed to function as the head of the Afghanistan mission, after the eviction of Rabbani. It was not surprising that Pakistan extended official recognition to the Taliban government the very next day after the Taliban entered Mazar-i-Sharif.

They were also allowed to open consulates in Karachi, Quetta, and Peshawar. Saudi Arabia and UAE recognized the Taliban government following Pakistan. They were the only three countries to do so.

The Taliban government was never really in control of Afghanistan. It tried to unify the country behind its programme of radical Wahabi Islam, which enforced a uniform dress code for men as well as made it mandatory for them to keep beards, thought of as being the Pathan tradition. Women were not to go to school, could go outside the home only accompanied by a close male relative, and were not to hold any employment. All music was banned and television sets destroyed. According to the law of ijtehad, all pronouncements of Mullah Omar were to be treated as Islamic injunctions and law. This life of pure Islam could not do away with the fact that once the Taliban had captured power, those countries financing the Taliban did try to end the civil war. After the fall of Kabul to the Taliban, Pakistan made relentless efforts on behalf of the Taliban on the one hand to bring about some agreement between Kabul and Dostam, who still controlled Mazar-i-Sharif, and Rabbani and Masood, who controlled the Panjsher Valley, and on the other hand to gain international acceptance for the Taliban, including their representation in the United Nations.

The rigid and draconian laws enacted by the Taliban were not acceptable to many sections of the population, especially the Tajiks and the Uzbek groups. Dostam was still in control of Mazar-i-Sharif. The Uzbek militia and the Hizb Wahdat of Karim Khalili inflicted a devastating blow on the Taliban. Very soon, both Abdullah Malik and Ahmed Shah Masood had driven the Taliban to the outskirts of Kabul. Far from being able to realize their version of an ideal Islamic society, being in dire economic straits, the Taliban regime further facilitated the extension of opium cultivation and the narcotics trade, especially heroin exports to UK and USA.

The Taliban also provided sanctuary to hundreds of Arab 'Afghanis' who were on the Federal Bureau of Investigation's wanted list for attacking American establishments. This got extended to include those like Osama bin Laden and the Al Qaeda who were intending to attack USA.

Although USA had never accorded diplomatic recognition to the Taliban government, for some time they had played around with the idea that the Taliban would strike at opium cultivation and the narcotics trade and support their plans to explore and transport oil and gas from Central Asia. With these aims in mind, Robin Raphel, the in-charge of this region in the US State Department, paid two visits to Kabul to meet the Taliban government functionaries. One of the US oil companies, Unocal, started planning for the construction of an oil pipeline through Afghanistan at a cost of about US $8 billion.

The US hopes were totally belied not only by the Taliban's Islamic fundamentalism but by the marriage of Mullah Omar's daughter to the son of Osama bin Laden, the Saudi billionaire sworn to evict US troops from Saudi Arabia. Being an ex-CIA trained engineer and intelligence agent, Osama was not suspected of masterminding the hijacking of planes and the attack by them on the World Trade Centre until it happened on the fateful day of 11 September 2001.

The attack was followed not only by worldwide criticism and condemnation but also by the tightening of UN sanctions against Afghanistan imposed in 1999, cancellation of all flights to and from Afghanistan, a demand by the USA to hand over Osama bin Laden and close down 'terrorist' camps in Afghanistan or be prepared to face a military reprisal. It is interesting to note that the Taliban officially denied the existence of any terrorist camps in Afghanistan, pleaded on behalf of Osama bin Laden that he had no resources to organize such an attack, and called an Assembly or Shura of tribal elders to ask Osama to leave the country, which he had reportedly done four days before the American air attacks.[23] The Taliban government even sent a formal condolence message to the US government and said that they were opposed to all forms of terrorism. The USA and its allies Britain, Australia, and the UN, however, proceeded on the basis of reports prepared by their own intelligence agencies mainly based on intercepts of conversations on cell phones, to blame Al Qaeda and the Taliban for giving them shelter.[24] The Pentagon pushed ahead with its plan for bombing out the Taliban from Kabul. With the deployment of a few ground troops and the help of the Northern Alliance, US forces had occupied Kabul within a few months. Mullah Omar and Osama bin Laden fled but it is noteworthy that to date they have not been found, dead or alive, despite huge rewards being offered by the US government.

The Bonn Agreement installed an interim government headed by Hamid Karzai, changed with convening a national assembly or *Loya Jirga*, which would have the right to confirm his appointment, set up a commission to frame a new constitution and decide on a schedule to hold fresh elections.

According to the Bonn Agreement, all parties not believing in democracy—the Taliban and the Communist Party—were to be banned from Afghan politics. Afghans with a criminal record were also banned. New parties were to be registered with the Ministry of Culture. Those who fought against the Soviet forces would be allowed to form a party only when the US $ 22 billion received at that time was returned and the sources of their funding clarified. Among these parties are those of former President Burhanuddin Rabbani, the Jamiat-i-Islami, and the Northern Alliance, which includes the interim Foreign Minister, Abdullah, interim Defense Minister, Qasim Fahim, and Interior Minister, Yunus Qanooni.

South Asian Perceptions of US Intervention in Afghanistan

A significant feature of the situation as it has developed in South Asia is that governments in general have welcomed USA's help in fighting terrorism and removing the Taliban from power in Afghanistan, and participating in the conclusion of the Bonn Agreement that paved the way for the restoration of constitutional democracy. In many ways it marked a turnaround for US policy in Afghanistan, because earlier on it had done much to install an Islamic dispensation there.

India had, from the outset when the Taliban took over Kabul in 1996, entirely disagreed with it. Not only did India not accord diplomatic recognition, it allowed the existing Afghanistan embassy to continue to function as the representatives of the government-in-exile. External Affairs Minister, Inder Kumar Gujral, who later became the Prime Minister, in identical statements to both Houses of Parliament said on 25 November 1996 that the Taliban were 'obscurantist' with little respect for human rights and are not the legitimate government, even if they rule Kabul. His observation that they posed a threat to Indian security was proved right later when an Indian Airlines plane was hijacked by Pakistan-based terrorists after it took off from Kathmandu. It was ultimately allowed to land in Kandahar and the Taliban backed the demand of the terrorists for the release of a Hizbul Mujahideen leader. Only when this demand was met was the aircraft released. Hence, it was only expected that India would support UN sanctions against the Taliban after the 11 September attack on the WTC and back US demands for the closure of terrorist camps in Afghanistan, some of which were suspected to be sending mercenary terrorists to Kashmir. The Bharatiya Janata Party-led government was quick to offer even military assistance, if the US government wanted it, only a few days after the incident. This was in marked contrast to the overall neutrality displayed by India during the Gulf War in 1990, although India did vote for the UN resolution asking Iraq to withdraw from Kuwait. When some US military aircraft were allowed to refuel in India during the Prime Ministership of Chandra Shekhar, this was done in secrecy and later described as an 'emergency measure'. At that time the Left parties and even the BJP had opposed this action. However, in the event of the US action against the Taliban, almost all parties had no objections, except that some of the Left parties felt that the military action should have been conducted by a UN peacekeeping force and no US military bases would be allowed on Indian soil. India and USA held joint naval exercises off the coast of Goa and restrictions on the supply of nuclear materials were waived for both India and Pakistan.[25] India having a perception about the antediluvian nature of the Taliban, moved quickly in the direction of welcoming the Bonn agreement and the interim government led by Hamid Karzai and offered immediately to cooperate in the immense task of reconstruction in Afghanistan.

For Pakistan, the attack on the WTC and the subsequent global reaction against the Taliban was a force majeure, which turned its Afghanistan policy upside down. Perhaps, more than anything else, it was India's quick positive response in offering help to USA against the Taliban, to which Russia unlike the earlier times had no objection, which compelled Pakistan to make an one hundred and eighty degree turn from being the principal sponsor and advocate of the Taliban to President Musharraf's declaration that it had now become USA's staunchest ally in its 'global war on terrorism'. On 13 September, after his meeting with the US Ambassador to Pakistan, President Pervez Musharraf offered his full cooperation 'to combat terrorism in the region'.[26] USA asked for and got the use of Pakistan's airspace and ground bases. These steps were taken not without USA providing financial and other rewards and General Musharraf facing internal opposition in Pakistan from the conservative hardcore Islamic jihadi elements. Towards the end of September 2001, Washington announced an outright cash grant of US $ 50 million for Pakistan, the first such move since sanctions were imposed on it eleven years ago. Restrictions on sales of military spares and nuclear-related materials were also lifted.[27]

That Pakistan's role in the war on terrorism could not be whole-hearted despite President Musharraf's promises may be seen from a number of factors. The press in Pakistan understood the compulsions under which President Musharraf, who, as the officer-in-charge of the commandos in the Pakistani army had in all probability directly participated in the training of Mujahideen and the Taliban, was now parading as their opponent.

Any refusal on the part of Pakistan to cooperate with USA would have had disastrous consequences as Pakistan's external debt is more than 100 per cent of its GDP. Several sections of the Pakistani political parties, the middle class, and the army understood this fact and backed Musharraf. The Chinese Ambassador to Pakistan, Lu Shulin, said the Chinese government and people fully understood the delicate situation and supported the Pakistani government in its new policy. According to the Chinese Ambassador, 'China is Pakistan's trustworthy friend whether the weather is good or bad.'[28]

General Musharraf on his part continued to make a clear distinction between Taliban 'terrorism' and the 'freedom struggle' in Kashmir. On the one hand, he did not ask for an end to American bombing in Afghanistan even during the holy month of Ramzan, saying the war against terrorism cannot end halfway; on the other, addressing troops and officers at the Sialkot and Khairan garrisons, he claimed that his government's decision to support the fight against terrorism had ensured the safety of Pakistan's nuclear assets and its case on Kashmir to support the struggle of the militants.[29] This double standard in defining terrorism was only a political concession to the continued existence of heavily armed jihadis backed by a section of the Pakistani army.

At the same time, Pakistan initiated steps to build good relations with the new government in Afghanistan. Even before the Taliban had been evicted from Kabul, Musharraf claimed on 26 November 2001, that 'all Northern Alliance groups were in contact with Pakistan'.[30] Even before the *Loya Jirga* had met in June 2002 and confirmed the continuance of Karzai's interim government, Musharraf visited Kabul. On this occasion, Mr Karzai said that the Taliban rule from 1996 to

2001 was just a short period in centuries of good Afghan–Pakistan relations. The Pakistan embassy in Kabul was reopened. A high level joint ministerial commission was set up. Pakistan gave US $ 100 million to help in women's education, the development of information systems, and the anti-narcotics campaign.[31] It must be remembered that Musharraf's visit to Kabul followed an earlier visit by Hamid Karzai to Islamabad for two days on 8–9 February 2002. A red carpet welcome was accorded to him and during the visit he also named Afghanistan's new Ambassador to Pakistan. Karzai also visited Tehran. Iran's Deputy Foreign Minister, Mohammad Hassan Addli, promised that Iran was committed to participating in the reconstruction of Afghanistan through the new central government especially in infrastructure projects about which the Afghan government was keen, such as electricity, potable water network, real estate development, substitute cultivation, health, etc. A fund of US $560 million was allocated by the Iranian government for this purpose and it also promised to encourage the Iranian private sector to help Afghanistan.[32]

After the 1,500 strong *Loya Jirga* drawn from all parts of Afghanistan and its society had met in June 2002 and asked the Karzai government to continue, further developments occurred portending better regional cooperation. Pakistan totally deregulated its trade with Afghanistan and abolished the permit and the quota system. Exports to Afghanistan could now be made in US dollars or rupees. Pakistan permitted Afghan exports to India through the Wagah border but only selected Indian aid was allowed at the request of the Afghanistan government. The Pakistan and Afghan governments agreed to revive the Economic Cooperation Organization, which in November 1992 had been expanded to include seven new members, viz., Afghanistan, Azerbaijan, Kazakhastan, Kyrgyz Republic, Tajikistan, Turkmenistan, and Uzbekistan, apart from the original members Iran, Pakistan and Turkey. Recently, Turkmenistan, Afghanistan, and Pakistan have signed an agreement to build a gas pipeline. Afghanistan has also signed a non-aggression declaration with six of its neighbours to ensure that their governments do not allow hostile military activities to take place from their territories. These are Iran, Pakistan, Turkmenistan, Uzbekistan, Tajikistan, and China. At the same time, the Afghan Defense Minister has turned down US advice to forge a security pact with Pakistan.[34] In pursuit of its promise to fight terrorism, the Karzai government has handed over thirty terrorists, including some Pakistani ones, to India.[35] Karzai has said that disarming the warlords and building a national army were the need of the hour in order to be able to hold free and fair elections. As reported by the UN, seizure of illegal weapons is still continuing in Northern Afghanistan.[36]

India has always wanted and supported a democratic Afghanistan. At the Tokyo Conference in January 2002 out of the total assistance of US $4.8 billion for the reconstruction of Afghanistan, India committed US $100 million—30 per cent of the pledged amount India has already given to Afghanistan. An additional 1 million tonnes of wheat was pledged by India but the Pakistan government refused to allow its transshipment to Afghanistan through its territory. The Indian IT industry has plans to help Afghanistan. Larsen and Toubro, India's biggest construction firm, has submitted proposals to rebuild schools and hospitals and set up power plants. Offers have been made for the supply of office furniture by Indian firms. India's police academies are helping to train the Afghan national police in the Afghan capital. A Confederation of Indian Industry (CII) delegation visited Kabul and opened an office there in March 2002.

As regards the response of other countries in South Asia, one can note two trends. All governments condemned the attack on WTC, accepted USA's claim that it had been done by the Al Qaeda based in Afghanistan and did not oppose US military intervention. However, most countries had their unique statements and reactions. In Bangladesh, the caretaker government agreed to provide its airfields, airspace, seaports, and refuelling facilities to Anglo–US coalition forces.[37] Bangladesh's Awami League fully supported the government's stand. In Sri Lanka, President Chandrika Kumaratunga, although she condemned the attacks in USA, asked the Western powers to include the LTTE among the terrorist organizations to be liquidated and wondered why they were being asked to negotiate with them.[38] The Iranian President, Syed Mohammad Khatami, too condemned the attacks and sympathized with the American people.[39] Iranian media said such attacks were completely forbidden in Islam.[40] It also reported that many Pakistani troops had been fighting alongside the Al Qaeda forces and their bodies had been brought back to Pakistan.[41] Iran favoured a UN led 'anti-terror coalition' in which President Rafsanjani was willing to participate.[42] It viewed USA's unilateral attacks on Afghanistan as a part of a long-term plan to dominate different regions of the world. USA, Iran said, was following double standards on terrorism as originally it was supporting the Taliban. Iran signed a Bilateral Pact with Russia to fight terrorism on 20 October 2001. Russia is building a nuclear power reactor in Iran.[43] While 47.6 per cent of Iranian people wanted neutrality, they also supported a UN supervised election and an Afghan national government comprising all ethnic groups.[44] In Nepal, Prime Minister Sher Bahadur Deuba condemned the attacks on the WTC and agreed to join USA's global war on terrorism.[45]

The oppositional trend was mainly provided by Muslim organizations in Bangladesh, Sri Lanka, Iran, and Pakistan. The Ameer of Jamaat Islami, Bangladesh, Motiur Rahman Nizami, said that the attack on innocent civilians in Afghanistan for punishing one individual without any concrete proof was a violation of Islamic, democratic, and humanist laws as well as the Charter of the United Nations. Demonstrations were held in different parts of Bangladesh opposing the American attacks.[46] In Iran, Syed Aytollah Mohajerani, the head of the International Centre for Dialogue among Civilizations, said that the whole course of events in Afghanistan was 'a play to project Muslims as supporters of terrorism and murder'.[47] One can see that perceptions were very different at the government level and amongst sections of the people in the Muslim countries.

Future Possibilities and Options

The fact that now there is an international consensus on the installation and support to a democratic political system in Afghanistan, which includes the neighbouring Muslim countries, is a long-term indicator of stability for the first time after thirty years of civil war in Afghanistan. However, there are many obstacles still to be overcome within Afghanistan before an optimistic scenario is realized.

Karzai's government has suffered two major political assassinations and an unsuccessful attempt on his own life. Even after winning the *Jirga's* mandate to be in power for eighteen months, Karzai continues to be protected by US security personnel. His hold over his country is tenuous. Warlords are calling the shots in their respective strongholds, collecting revenue, and providing safe passage, thus keeping the Kabul administration weak and impoverished.

Much of the aid promised at the Tokyo conference has yet to materialize. The return of refugees, some 9,20,000 from Pakistan, 75,000 from Iran, and 9,000 from the Central Asian States, has only increased the responsibilities of the Afghan central government.[48]

Even with a good harvest in 2001 of 3.56 million tonnes, it is a good 8,00,000 tonns lower than the 1999 harvest. Four million Afghans face starvation and cannot be supplied food because of lack of cooperation from the warlords.[49]

Pakistani propaganda continues to project the issue in Afghanistan as a tussle between the Pushtuns and the rest. The UN Global Illicit Drug Trends reports a return to opium growing and drug production, the size of the annual output being 2,000 tonnes in 2002.[50]

The differences on the ground between various groups persist. the ruling alliance favours liberal and secular values, whereas the Pakhtoon mindset favours tribal culture and adherence to Islam. Tajiks in Kabul hold sway over eastern Afghanistan and enjoy the blessings of Russia, India, and Tajikistan. Dostum's Uzbeks at Mazar-i-Sharif enjoy the patronage of USA, Russia, Turkey and Uzbekistan. Herat and Bamiyan under Ismail Khan and Khalili respectively are supported by Iran. Unless different groups are absorbed within a two-party system, a national army and police administration consolidated, agriculture restored, and revenue collections resumed, merely holding elections will not produce stability. Till then, Afghanis will suffer and Afghanistan will survive with question marks hanging over it.

NOTES

1. David Louis Cingranelli, *Ethics, American Foreign Policy, and the Third World*, New York: St. Martin's Press, 1993, p. 33. Cingranelli points out that there is abundance of examples of US support to authoritarian states in the twentieth century. He lists the governments of Spain, Portugal, Paraguay, Argentina, the Dominican Republic, Guatemala, Brazil, Haiti, Greece, Cuba, South Korea, Taiwan, Vietnam, Nicaragua, and the Philippines.
2. John Hellman, *American Myth and the Legacy of Vietnam*, New York: Columbia University Press, 1986, p. 67.
3. Ibid., loc. cit.
4. V.D. Chopra, ed., *Vietnam Today and Indo-Vietnam Relations*, Delhi: Gyan Publishing House, 2000, p. 213.
5. Robert L. Rothstein, *The Third World and US Foreign Policy: Cooperation and Conflict in the 1980s*, Colorado: West View Press, 1981, passim.
6. Richard N. Haass, *Intervention: The Use of American Military Force in the Post Cold War World*, Washington, DC: Carnegie Endowment for International Peace, 1994, p. 3.
7. Shri Prakash, 'Sino-Pakistan Relations in the 1960s and the 1990s: A Comparative Analysis', Key Issues, *The Journal of Parliamentary Studies and Contemporary Affairs*, New Delhi, September 1998, pp. 83–98.
8. Ramon H. Myers, ed., *A US Foreign Policy for Asia: The 1980s and Beyond*, Stanford University: Hoover Institution Press, 1982, p. 2.
9. Claude Bruderlein, 'The Role of Islam in Shaping the Future of Afghani-

stan', *Peace Initiatives, Special Issue*, vol. 3, no. 1, 3 Jan.–June 2002; *Afghanistan: Towards Reconciliation and Reconstruction*, New Delhi: Peace Publications, pp. 44–5.

10. Mohammad Khalid Maaroof, *Afghanistan in World Politics*, Delhi: Gyan Publishing House, 1987, pp. 29–31.
11. Ibid., p. 37.
12. Ibid., p. 65.
13. American Foreign Policy: Basic Documents 1977–80, quoted in Abdus Sattar, 'Afghanistan: Jihad to Civil War', *Regional Studies*, 1996.
14. Chintamani Mahapatra, 'American Role in Afghanistan', in *Afghanistan and Asian Stability*, ed. V.D. Chopra, New Delhi: Gyan Publishing House, 1998, p. 90.
15. Robert McNamara, *Out of the Cold: New Thinking for American Foreign and Defense Policy in the 21st Century*, London: Bloomsbury Publishing Ltd., 1990, pp. 82–3.
16. Sujit Dutta, 'China and the Afghan Conflict', in *Afghanistan: Geneva Accord and After*, ed. V.D. Chopra, New Delhi: Patriot Publishers, 1988, pp. 120–3.
17. Inder Malhotra, *Indira Gandhi: A Personal and Political Biography*, p. 218.
18. V.D. Chopra, 'India's Stand on Afghanistan Crisis', in *Afghanistan and Asian Stability*, op. cit., p. 214.
19. Jagat S. Mehta, *The March of Folly in Afghanistan*, Delhi: Manohar, 2002, passim.
20. Ramon H. Myers, 1978–2001, op. cit., pp. 25–6.
21. Claude Bruderlein, 'The Role of Islam in Shaping the Future of Afghanistan', op. cit., p. 50.
22. Kamal Matinuddin, *The Taliban Phenomenon: Afghanistan 1994–7*, Oxford University Press, 1999, p. 7.
23. 'No Terrorist Camp in Afghanistan', *NEWS*, Delhi: Public Opinion Trends (POT), March 2001, pp. 1–2.
24. 'US Security Officials see Osama's Hand', *NEWS*; POT, 15 September, p. 219.
25. 'Washington Announces US Dollars 50 Million Grant to Pakistan', *Dawn*, 30 August 2001; POT, op. cit., 3 October 2001, p. 233; 'Report on US–Indian Joint Naval Exercises', *Nation*, 13 December 2001; POT, 8 October, p. 299.
26. 'Musharraf Meets with US Ambassador', *NEWS*, 14 September 2001; POT, op. cit.
27. Loc. cit.
28. 'Chinese Ambassador's Statement on 50th Anniversary of Sino–Pak Diplomatic Relations, *NEWS*, POT, 5 October 2001, p. 235.
29. 'Musharraf Meets Troops', *NEWS*, POT, 8 October 2001, p. 289.
30. 'Pakistan in Contact with NA Groups', *NEWS*, 27 November 2001; POT, 8 October 2001, p. 281.

31. 'Pakistan and Afghanistan Pledge to Fight Terrorism', *NEWS*, 3 April 2002, POT, vol. XXVII, no. 42, 26 July 2002, p. 348.
32. 'Karzai' visit to Tehran', *Iran News*, 6 March 2002; POT, vol. XVII, no. 1.
33 'Finance Minister Shaukat Aziz Meets Afghan Vice-President Hidayat Amin Arsala', *Frontier Post*, POT, vol. 7, no. 56, 26 June 2002.
34. 'Afghanistan Defense Minister turns down US advice', *Daily Times*, 30 June 2002; POT, vol. XXVII, no. 54, 16 September 2002.
35. *Frontier Post*, 30 June 2002; POT, vol. XXVII, op. cit.
36. 'UNAMA: Disarmament in Northern Afghanistan Yields Nearly 200 Weapons', *UN Weekly Newsletter*, vol. 58, no. 1, 4–10 January 2003, p. 4, also see Report on 'Afghan Situation', in *Nation*, 4 July 2002; POT, vol. XXVII, no. 54, 16 September 2002, Dhaka.
37. *Independent*, 10 October 2001; POT, vol. XXVI, no. 268, 13 November 2001.
38. *Sunday Times*, Colombo; POT, vol. VII, no. 85, 28 November 2001.
39. *Iran News*, 13 September 2002; POT (Iran Series), vol. VI, no. 90, 12 October 2001, p. 653.
40. Editorial, *Tehran Times*, 15 September 2001, POT (Iran series), op. cit.
41. *Tehran Times*, 25 September 2001; POT (Iran Series), vol. VI, no. 85, 27 September 2001, p. 619.
42. *Kayhan International*, 26 October 2001, POT; vol. VI, no. 95, 29 October 2001, p. 693.
43. *Kayhan International*, 3 November 2001, POT, vol. VI, no. 98, 6 November 2001, p. 711.
44. 'Joint Statement by Rabbani, Patin and Rakhmanov', *Kayhan International*, 23 October 2001; POT, op. cit.
45. *Rising Nepal*, 13 September 2001; POT (Nepal Series), vol. VII, no. 100, 11 October 2001.
46. 'Jamaat, others protest US attack on Afghanistan', *Financial Express*, Dhaka, 9 October 2002, POT; vol. XXVI, no. 267, 12 November 2001.
47. *Iran News*, 16 September 2001; POT, vol. VI, no. 91, 16 October 2001.
48. *UN News*, Letter, vol. 57, no. 25, 22–8 June 2002, p. 1.
49. Mahendra Ved, 'Afghanistan in the Changing Context', *Bulletin-News from Non-Aligned World*, vol. 24, no. 5, 26 November 2002, Delhi: International Institute of Non-Aligned Studies.
50. Ibid., 3 December 2002.

Vladimir Putin's Course After 11/9: A 'Democrat's' View of Russian Interests in Central and South West Asia

HARI VASUDEVAN

After the events of 11 September 2001 and the US-led intervention in Afghanistan, the compliant attitude of the Russian government to US intervention in the region drew sharp criticism in the Federation itself, as did the marginal role left for the country in the overall anti-Taliban campaign. Such criticism increased in scale with the assumption of permanence by US bases in Central Asia and the Caucasus, and the expansion of NATO into Eastern Europe in 2002. Although following the events of 11 September 2001, the US-led campaign against terrorism commanded sympathy in the Federation, carte blanche to the US to intervene in a rgion in which Russia had major interests was considered impolitic.[1] A.A. Migranian, major publicist and presidential advisor under the Yeltsin regime, has written recently of what transpired as marking 'the end of Russia' as a subject in international affairs,[2] suggesting that the response was at variance even with much of the pro-West foreign policy of the Russian Federation that had gone before. The implication is that Russia's security has taken a downturn since the Yeltsin period, when Moscow often asserted a position sharply critical of US and NATO policy, despite Russia's initial interest in a US–Russia condominium in global affairs, the country's pro-Western tilt in foreign policy, and the regime's reliance on Europe and the US for formulation and implementation of economic reform. The Georgian crisis of 1993, the Tajik Civil War and the Kosovo conflict (1999) were the most remarkable instances of this independent stand in the past, but they were not exceptional. A rhetorical posture that put 'Russia first' was a hallmark of the administration, it is argued, and even if it did little to add a sharpness to such postures through military action, it utilized its authority in global forums to create outcomes that it favoured. The election of Vladimir Putin appeared to presage a strengthening of this trend—given the image of the President as a strong figure—but the position he took in 2001 went against the grain of practice and expectation.

In India, a 'realistic' perspective on Russian policy evolved in such circumstances; and it strengthened New Delhi's tilt towards Washington—the consequence of a sense that Russia had ceased to matter as a force of significance in the region, even if she had had some potential in this regard at the time of Soviet disintegration and the formation of the CIS. South Block's initiative followed from the notion that Russian policy post 11/9 was the consequence of economic and military weakness: that the US had decided to compensate for that weakness in a decisive manner and to intervene as a major actor in the South Asia neighbourhood. The guarded pursuit of such a line, though, indicated uncertainty among functionaries concerning their reading of what transpired as much as suspicion of US intent. The complexities of the region suggested other perspectives concerning Russia's decisions and the US presence.

In this brief paper, without passing verdict on the Putin Administration's course, and following a strict historical approach to the problem of Russian decisions that followed 11/9, I outline the way decisions came to be made, going beyond a straightforward association of what happened with the country's economic and military disabilities. The latter were undoubtedly significant for decision making but, since disabilities held good for the earlier administration as well, but seldom prevented it from an adventurous foreign policy, they cannot be held to be all there is at issue. The paper argues that Russia's position was taken with a sharp sense of its own interests and the merits of the case: following the conclusion that there was little to be gained from Central Asia in terms of active presence as far as any actor is concerned. Undoubtedly, it was assumed that when stakes were higher, and international support for an anti-US stand were greater, as in the case of the current Iraq crisis, alternative responses were possible; but in the case of the US's Afghan initiative, strident action was not considered worthwhile.

The argument is divided into three sections. Section 1 shows how foreign policy on 11/9 was Presidential policy: that despite many compulsions that determined the making of policy in the Federation, the nature of these compulsions and their inner contradictions allowed the President to assert his authority; that the pro-US lobbies of the time had little ascendancy in the way policy was made. The account then turns to Presidential response to 11/9 in Section 2,[3] indicating the context in which President Putin took his decisions to participate in the anti-Taliban coalition and permit the establishment of US bases in

Central Asia. Thereafter, the argument shows, in Section 3, the considerations that underpinned these decisions, where, with due attention to Russia's experience in Afghanistan and Central Asia in the decade following disintegration, the Russian President asserted his identity as a 'democrat' to work with the Western Alliance. 'Democrat' here signified sympathy with the views of Russia's first Foreign Minister, Andrei Kozyrev, and the many 'democrat' activists of the period prior to Soviet disintegration. Such views went along the lines that the Federation must follow its self-interest, defined in the most narrow terms, with an oblique eye only to broader formulations concerning geopolitics. The views were not necessarily associated with Russian parliamentary parties that trace their origins to the 'democratic' movements in the USSR of 1989–91—the most powerful of which follow a distinctly different line. Inevitably, the argument raises questions concerning how US intervention in the Central Asian region has been interpreted in India—issues that are dealt with in this Section.[4]

Russian Foreign Policy Post 11/9

In this course of events, crucial to the way Russian foreign policy was shaped after the events of September 2001 was Presidential authority in the Federation. True, the Ministry of Foreign Affairs had its own importance in the policy making set-up—as did a number of lobbies; but ultimately the President was the paramount figure to whom all referred. Specific pro-Euro/US interest groups, or ad hoc parliamentary coalitions, did not decide what was to happen. An explanation for this lies in the constitutional authority of the Presidential office, and the very character of Russian politics placed the President in an exceptional position. The former followed directly from Boris Yeltsin's reinforcement of the institution in 1991,[4] the exceptional powers given to the institution by Parliament following the August putsch of 1991 and the disintegration of the USSR in December 1991,[5] and the terms of the 1993 Constitution,[6] when the Russian Executive ceased to be responsible to Parliament in any serious manner. Russian politics, meanwhile, as most interpretations agree, involved deep centralization and the fragility of party politics, allowing the Presidency an unusual degree of authority in public life.[7]

Such aspects of the Federation's political system also partly determined the authority of the President with regard to the various deep structural factors that were crucial to Russian foreign policy and that took shape in the way Russian economic and political life developed. These were factors that generated compulsions which policy invariably recognizd, even if the public was primarily aware of oscillations in the policy-making establishment between 'Atlanticists' (who were pro-NATO) and 'Eurasianists' (who called for an independent Russian course in global affairs). Here, too, pulls and counter-pulls cancelled, leaving the Russian Presidency as the prime agent of manoeuvre; and where this was not the consequence of balance and counterbalance, it was the upshot of the uncontested authority of the Presidency that was less related to an ex-officio position and more linked to habit and practice. An examination of specific structures indicates this.

(i) *The network of factors that linked the Russian Federation with the superpower status of the Soviet Union.*

Here in the case of pacts, agreements, and a new international presence for the new Russian State—associated with START and SALT, the OSCE summits discussions at economic forums—the unusual role that President Yeltsin had come to play in presenting democratic Russia as the antithesis of the USSR gave the Presidency a special role in such interactions. With time, connections with the World Bank or the IMF came to be overseen by advisors to Yeltsin, such as Boris Fedorov or Anatolii Chubais. But the vicissitudes in the fortunes of such functionaries ensured that the President played the pivotal role in decision-making.[8]

(ii) *The energy complex and the system of exports of oil and natural gas*

Although the main source of official revenues was now dominated by major state corporations—Rosneft, Lukoil, Surguftneftgaz, and Gazprom—not only did the government own shares, but the Federation's executive (and specifically the Presidency) directed appointments and played an important role in further disinvestment. State patronage was required by companies that had serious foreign interests.

(iii) *The network of interests that handles the country's debt*

Crucial to a country with a debt of 144.4 billion Roubles (1 April 2001)—65 per cent of GNP—the issues are in name dealt with by the Cabinet, the Vneshkombank, the Ministry of Finances, the Committees of the Duma, and a number of lobbies and crucial intermediaries. However, as crucial periods, such as the 1992–3 inflationary period, the time around the Presidential election of 1996, and the crisis of August 1998 demonstrate, pending the upshot of the attempt by the President to create a decision-making apparatus centred on the Vneshkombank, pivotal authority lies with the President.

(iv) *The network of interests that handles Russia's dealings with the CIS*

A number of ministries and institutions have nominally been involved and all have signed agreements between the states concerning co-operation and trade. But it is accepted that of the 1,200 agreements signed between the CIS states, the overwhelming majority continue to remain on paper. Where crucial areas, i.e. fuel and debt, are involved, there is impromptu action that makes the relationship the domain of the President in the Russian case.

(v) *The interests that deal with the Federation's integration into the global market and into Europe*

The integration of the Russian Federation with the global economy revolves partly around the energy complex and partly around special regions and regional associations. In the latter case, *c.* 30 per cent of exports are said to come from ten Russian regions. This enables the presidency, through its supervisory organs, to maintain some grip on the economic relationship the country evolves with the outside world. Russia's links with NATO, with the IMF and the World Bank, with the World Trade Organization, and with the European Union have all been guided by the Presidential apparatus since the birth of the Federation. This was the consequence of Boris Yeltsin's exceptional position in the country's relations with the outside world from January 1992.

Presidential Response to 11/9

It was from a position of such authority in the making of foreign policy that Vladimir Putin, like President Yeltsin before him, came to deal with the fallout of the events of September 11, eventually taking a forceful position of cooperation with the US and NATO and expressing solidarity with the alliance. At other levels in Federation politics, a range of opinions were expressed at the time concerning Russia's stand—each representing powerful interests, from Rushailo of the Security Council[9] to Viktor Ozerov of the Federation Council's own Council for Defence and Security[10] and Rozogin of the Duma's Committee on Foreign Relations.[11] But it was clearly the President's authority that counted and determined Russia's course.

Here, President Putin moved towards a stand of collaboration and cooperation from a tense situation of tension where he had been following a position hostile to Washington in his approach to the abandonment of the ABM regime. Until the Trade Tower crisis, he had been fixed on critical approach to the position adopted by G.W. Bush's government that was clearly focused on an advancement of US hardware, abandoning an international regime for the control of missile development, at a time when Russia was unable to compete in the new line of weaponry without untoward burden on the Russian budget. The debate had thrust into the forefront of Russian public life one of the shibboleths that focused national pride—her nuclear and missile force, which, although ramshackle, buoyed up the aura of Russia's position as heir to a superpower. It had also raised uncomfortable questions concerning why the standard-bearers of Russia's democratic revolution against the Soviet State, who were committed to regimes of arms control, could countenance US refinement of weapons of mass destruction when the country had the legal means to create a nuisance about it. Putin had taken a strident position, refusing to underwrite the US initiative, bluntly calling it an abrogation of the ABM Treaty.

After the events of 11/9, Putin confined differences of opinion on these issues to the background of policy and took advantage of the situation to argue for US, NATO, and international cooperation with Russia in tackling terrorism, arguing that the US had underestimated the substance of this threat.[12] He argued that the US, in focusing on improvement in its hardware and developing strategies concerning NATO expansion, had failed to deal with more fundamental dangers to security—such as international terrorism.

The Russian President involved himself closely with the US and its allies in planning the anti-Taliban campaign of October 2001 and organizing the successor regime in Afghanistan. He was clear that the CIS could not, by itself, undertake coordinated military action against the Taliban regime, stating that neither he nor the other Presidents who had put together the Combined Rapid Reaction Force of the CIS (i.e. the leaders of Kazakhstan, Kyrgyzstan, and Tajikistan) had any such intention.[13] He also made it clear that Russia had her hands full in

Chechnya and was unwilling to undertake a war on two fronts. Reaction from the international community to the 'source' of the terrorist acts of 11/9, hence, according to Putin, would have to unfold within the framework of international law, but Russia was unwilling to place herself in the vanguard to the action. If, therefore, Foreign Minister Ivanov was correct that the US President did not want Russian participation in the planned action against terrorism nor Russia's approval for its use of Tajik bases for its anti-Taliban campaign,[14] it was equally true that the Russian government was not keen on this participation beyond the role of an 'also-ran'. President Putin made it clear that the Tajik government was at liberty to make its own decisions about the presence of foreign troops on its territory.[15]

Considerations Behind the Decisions

In thus taking this course, Putin was undoubtedly guided by Russia's impotence as a military power—her lack of capacity to drive any sort of bargain against the combined force of the US and its allies. This was the consequence of the degradation during the 1992–2002 period of the military industrial complex that the Federation inherited from the Soviet Union—a degradation that will leave Russia with only one weapon production system by 2014, and a supply over the next ten years to the navy of c. 250 warheads and to the airforce of *c.* 200 missiles at best. This is the equivalent of the nuclear arsenal of France, Britain, or China.[16]

Such 'decline', however, does not explain the utter lack of criticism or qualification on the part of the Putin administration concerning actions in its own neighbourhood: for it left the option of manoeuvre in international forums and polemical opposition—normal initiatives of the Yeltsin administration. Arguably, rather, President Putin took a line that came quickly to him as a 'democrat' in Russian politics—a position that, since the beginning of the Yeltsin era, had implied a close association with the US and the NATO powers generally. The President's credentials in this respect are clear. Deputy to the 'democratic' mayor of St. Petersburg, Anatolii Sobchak, in 1990–6, he was closely linked to the Democratic Russia movement that provided ideological input that underpinned the post 1991 regime in Russia. Personally, he had also been close to the Euro-American business lobby. In St. Petersburg, he was connected with names such as the BNP Dresdner Bank, Procter and Gamble, Coca-Cola, and Gillette, and when he came to prominence from 1997 in Moscow, as a member of Boris Yeltsin's entourage, his rise was connected with the recommendations of privatization chief Anatolii Chubais. Although, after the assumption of the Presidency, Putin reined in major oligarchs with Euro-American links—Gusinskii and Berezovskii—his proximity to other members of the fraternity is substantial—to Boris Fedorov of the United Finance Group, for instance and Valerii Yashin of Sviazinvest.[17]

Such a position, though, insufficiently stresses Putin's own special interpretation of the 'democrat' course—a distinction clear from the difference between this interpretation and that of the standard 'democrat' parties of the Federation—the Yabloko and the Union of Right Forces (SPS). Both the latter have argued for a position of neo-isolation on the basis that Russia is economically and militarily weak, and that issues that concern her lie strictly within her borders and, at most, the borders of the CIS. By this world-view, it is of no concern to Russia whether NATO expands or not, since the country's main concern is self-regeneration; and politics in Brussels and Washington must be focused on persuasion of Euro-American functionaries that they plough a dangerous course by assertions that a 'Russian threat' exists (since it excites rejection and alarm in Russia itself). These views have been articulated at different times by Vladimir Lukin and Grigorii Yavlinskii (of the Yabloko) and figures such as Boris Nemtsov (of the SPS)—all of whom subscribe in various ways to the notion that it has been precisely the adventurism of various elites in the past that has cost Russia and Russians their own interest. The stand is opposed to the ideas of the 'left and nationalist' parties in the Duma (the Communist Party of the Russian Federation and the Liberal Democratic Party of Russia) who contend that Russia's interests lie in a reconstitution of the 'Union' in some form.[18] Other parties are qualified about the 'democrat' position, though they do not oppose it (as is the case of the 'Unity' Party, and the Fatherland-All Russia formation).

Vladimir Putin, while at one with 'liberals' and 'democrats' regarding the necessity for policy to concern itself with the narrow interests of the Federation, follows a more complex perspective. For the Russian President, a canny use of international forums and regimes is not to be neglected in the achievement of Russia's interest—even if serious military or government initiative should be restricted to the confines of the Federation. Such manoeuvre can run to substantial support for Russian companies that have an international range and that have a serious link with the State—such as Lukoil. Again, Putin is not convinced of the innocence of Euro-American interests in and around Russia. Surrounded by secret-servicemen who have been trained with a deep sense of foreign threats to Soviet interests, and amicable as he is with businessmen and academics who have a raw impression of a US sense of fairplay,[19] Putin has seldom considered that it is safe to allow NATO to do as it wishes.[20] Whatever his sense that democratic Russia must find her friends in the West, the Russian President is well aware that many in the West consider the Federation to be an unstable source of political and nuclear infection in the world—a state to be contained, guarded and, if necessary, divided.

Crucial to the perspective also, though, is the sense that involvement in the internal affairs of the Central Asian states cannot help Russia—a position that marks off the 'democrat' Putin from Boris Yeltsin, who had grown up with a notion of Russia as a great power for the whole of his professional life. Yeltsin was criticized by 'democrats' for this. Hence Egor Gaidar argues that Yeltsin's character was used by CIS partners and 'on a number of occasions, this turned out to be to the detriment of Russian national interests'. Gaidar candidly states 'this often took place at a friendly chit-chat with leaders of the states of the CIS. . . . Knowing Boris Nikolaevich well, the leaders . . . more than once made use of his weakness, extracting one-sided, imbalanced concessions that hardly guaranteed the interests of Russia.'[21] The idea has been crucial to Putin's adoption of a nonchalant attitude towards the establishment of a US and NATO presence in Central Asia. While deeply aware of the close trade connections the Federation has with the region, and the interconnectedness of Russia and these States through their common energy arrangements and mutual concerns where internal security is concerned, the Russian President is well aware that further control is impossible. This is clearly indicated by Putin's attitude towards the Commonwealth of Independent States, where, while maintaining Russian interests and a Russian presence, the President has ceased to take a forward stance.

The position marks an important departure in the perceptions of Presidential officials and was a consequence of the state of affairs in Central Asia and the CIS by 1999, when Vladimir Putin became Russian Prime Minister. In the early years of the CIS's history, Boris Yeltsin attempted to take a series of initiatives to breathe life into the organization. His forays (partly to create a 'common economic space' of the type that had been formulated in November 1991, partly to establish common institutions to deal with banking and security matters) were systematically undermined by discouragement by international monetary agencies and internal interests in Russia that found the agenda insufficiently profitable. The work of figures such as Boris Berezovskii was crucial here. As Russia's main intermediary on CIS affairs for much of Yeltsin's Presidency, for Berezovskii the CIS projects required to be quantified in terms of profit and personal benefit—to be set against the effort, investment, and returns associated with privatization. The conclusions of his account-keeping weighed heavily against development of CIS links and against the Yeltsin programme (imperfect as it was in the chaotic situation of the time)—a picture to be repeated in the case of other leading 'oligarchs'[22] (i.e. those who benefited most from the Russian privatization of the 1990s).

In turn, Russia's pursuit of her own path of economic reforms required independent activity from the Central Asian States—who then devised their own strategies to offset the collapse of markets for their products in the Russian Federation. These were the circumstances in which Uzbekistan's independent programme of state control and limited privatization evolved—taking stock of how to deal with the sudden collapse in demand for local cotton in Russian factories. Benefits that Russia might have received from the connection in the way state and private companies negotiated export of oil from the Caspian region were undermined by the bitterness engendered by this 'parting of ways' on important issues, and the Central Asian States, as well as those of the Caucasus, became competitors with Russian companies such as Lukoil in the exploitation of Caspian Sea resources. In the course of this tussle, when Russia sought to establish a firm stake in the affairs of the Caspian shelf, it became clear that the CIS was of little use to the Federation as a forum for creating common ground. Russia was only able to establish a forceful presence through the manoeuvres of the Lukoil company and the Ministry of Foreign Economic Relations during international negotiations with major oil interests. This indicated what was important here, and official interests working with the clout of an old Soviet relationship were of little significance.

It is this situation that has led to Vladimir Putin's increasing nonchalance to CIS, especially Central Asian, affairs in the recent past. Like most functionaries, he has registered the emergence of other interests in the region, especially those that have revolved around the GUUAM Pact, supported by the United States and the European Union, which allows for coordination of economic and military interests between Georgia, Ukraine, Azerbaijan, Moldova, and Uzbekistan. He has also indicated his own attitude towards the CIS, with no exceptions made for Central Asia, through an important decree of 2000. Despite an absence of any call to re-assess the value of the Russian government's symbol of its special relationship with the CIS, i.e. a Ministry that existed for cooperation with the CIS since 1994, Putin abolished this at the inception of his Presidency, dividing the responsibilities (tellingly) between the Ministry of External Affairs and the Minsitry of Economic Cooperation and Trade.[23] To allow other powers to reinforce their position in the area comes as a short step, rather than as a 'defeat' or a concession. The Russian Presidency was already well on its way out of Central Asia in a substantial sense long before the events of 11 September 2001.

The subtext of Putin's choice, which has undoubtedly not been lost on Indian functionaries, is important. There is an implication that a substantial presence in Central Asia is not worth the effort—that any power that seeks to establish a major position is doomed to expense and disappointment, and that if profits are sought, they are best sought specifically, through the private sector, backed with goodwill. Given Russia's long links with the region, the position is a comment on the future of the US presence in the area. Unless backed up by a broader vision of control and back-up, any long-term intervention faces the prospect of turning into an ulcer. And even if that vision and back-up is there, it is questionable whether direct or substantial control is the best way to realize the desired ends.

NOTES

1. *RFE/RL Newsline*, 10 January 2002. Speaking at a press conference in Astana, State Duma speaker, Gennadii Seleznev, spoke against the long-term deployment of US forces in Central Asian States. He argued that decisions about permanent American bases in the region could only follow discussions between the Central Asian States and Russia. According to Seleznev, US use of airfields in Uzbekistan and Kyrgyzstan meant that the US would not only attempt to control the situation in Afghanistan, but also on the Indo–Pak border, the western areas of China, and Kazakhstan.
2. A.A. Migranian, 'Konets Rossii?', in *Svobodnaia Mysl*, vol. XXX, no. 7, 2002.

3. *FFE/RL Newsline*, 10 January 2002. This was put most bluntly by the President himself in a speech quoted in *Kommersant Daily*. Putin took the position that the 'presence of American partners in the region must be solved by Washington and the related countries on a bilateral basis'. The daily went on to argue that the presence of US troops can only help Russian efforts to protect its border from illegal immigration and the trafficking of drugs and weapons.
4. The country's Executive Presidency was created in 1991 and the first elections to the position took place in March 1991.
5. H.S. Vasudevan, 'Russia's Presidency', *Economic and Political Weekly*, 1994.
6. For the terms of the Constitution of 1993, see the official website of the Russian Government. When consulted on 16 March 2003, this dealt with the authority of the Presidency in Section 4 (on the Presidency itself) and also in Section 5 (on the Federal Assembly), Section 6 on the Government of the Russian Federation, which indicates clearly that the Cabinet is not responsible to Parliament strictly, and that the President has exceptional control over it), and Section 7 on the Judiciary (e.g. Art. 125–9 on the Constitutional Court indicates the dependency of the body on the Presidency).
7. Michael McFaul, *Russia's Revolution*, Cornell University Press, 2002; Archie Brown and Lilia Shevtsova, eds., *Gorbachev, Yeltsin, Putin, Political Leadership in Russia's Transition*, Party Formation and the Russian Political System, Washington, 2002; H.S. Vasudevan, in *Rethinking Russia*, eds. M.K. Palat and Geeta Sen, New Delhi, 1994 and the more recent work of Joel Ostrow on the character of the Russian political system.
8. See A.M. Salmin, 'Iznanaka Vneshnet Politiki', in *Rossiiskaia Politiia*, Moscow: Politeia, 2001. Undoubtedly the finest and most comprehensive essay on the Russian foreign policy establishment that has been written to date. Salmin, however, fails to see the exceptional authority that the Presidency has come to occupy in all the 'sub-systems' and institutions that make up the 'seamy side' of foreign policy. Like many scholars, he assumes that Presidential authority is temporary at best, failing to see its unusual force where many institutions run against each other. For the institutions of control that reinforce this authority under Vladimir Putin, see also A.A. Mukhin, *Kto est' Mister Putin I Kto s nim prishel*, Moscow: Gnom I D, 2002.
9. *REF/RL Newsline*, 9 November 2003. Rushailo, commenting after the Afghan operation, was strident that the conflict with terrorism did not justify NATO expansion.
10. *REF/RL Newsline*, 20 November 2003.
11. *RFE/RL Newsline*, 19 September 2003. Rogozin sharply called for adherence to international law in dealing with the terrorist problem.
12. *RFE/RL Newsline*, 12 November 2003, 14 September 2003 and 17 September 2003. Mention is made of Putin's sympathy for the US

after 11/9 and his public statements critical of the US neglect of terrorism in the past.

13. *RFE/RL Newsline*, 18 September 2003. These statements followed a discussion with the concerned Central Asian Presidents.
14. *RFE/RL Newsline*, 19 September 2003. Ivanov stated that G.W. Bush wanted Russian cooperation, not participation. Eventually, one led to the other. See *RFE/RL Newsline*, 1, 2 & 6 November 2003 and mention of Russia–US cooperation in the building of bases in Northern Afghanistan in *RFE/RL Newsline*, 6 November 2003. But the distinction should be borne in mind, and it is important that the US gave this impression at the very inception of its operations against the Taliban.
15. *RFE/RL Newsline*, 24 September 2003.
16. Madhavan K. Palat, 'Russia in the Twenty-First Century', unpublished paper presented at Rajiv Gandhi Trust, New Delhi, on 25 November 2002.
17. On Putin's views on Europe as an alternative power-source, see statements that he made during his visit to Germany in September 2001. Here, at a time when coordination with NATO was on the anvil, Putin argued that (i) NATO expansion was of little use in the prevailing situation, (ii) with due respect to the US, Europe should conceive of itself as a power-source, depending on Russian raw material and resources for this purpose. See *RFE/RL Newsline*, 26 September 2003, 27 September 2003.
18. N. Ziadullaev, 'SNG' *opyt I itogi desiatiletiia in Svobodnia Mysl'*, vol. XXI, no. 4, 2002, p. 51.
19. A.A. Mukhin, op. cit.
20. Various reports in *RFE/RL* concerning the expansion of NATO and Presidential views. These views were also expressed at the time of the Trade Tower Crisis.
21. E.T. Gaidar, *Dni porazheii I pobed*, Moscow, 1996, and N. Ziadullaev, op. cit.
22. Jaques Sapir, *Le Krach Russe*, Paris: La Decouverte, 1998, provides good summaries of attitudes of the 'oligarchs'. Also Myriam Desert and Gilles Favarel-Garrigues, 'Les Capitalistes Russes', *Documentation Francaise, Problems Politiques et Sociaux*, no. 789, Paris, 1997, Rose Brady, *Kapitalizm*, Yale University Press, 2000; Anders Aslund, *How Russia became a Market Economy*, Washington: Brookings, 1995, and Ruth Brady, *Kapitalizm*, New York, 1999.
23. A.M. Salmin, 'Iznanaka Vneshnei Politiki', in *Rossiiskaia politiia*, op. cit., pp. 120–2. The Ministry was formed on 10 January 1994, elevating the status of a State Committee of the Russian Federation for economic cooperation with the member States of the Commonwealth (formed on 15 January 1993). Yeltsin himself once decreed its abolition (30 April 1998), but was persuaded to restore it on 22 September 1998.

[illegible]

[illegible]

[illegible] with the [illegible]

[illegible] Both [illegible]

[illegible]

[illegible]

[illegible]

[illegible] the [illegible]

[illegible]

[illegible] and [illegible]

[illegible]

Contributors

KANTI BAJPAI is a former Professor at the School of International Studies, Jawaharlal Nehru University, New Delhi. Presently he is the Headmaster of Doon School, Dehra Doon.

ANURADHA M. CHENOY is a Professor at the School of International Studies, Jawaharlal Nehru University, New Delhi.

GULSHAN DIETL is a Professor in the School of International Studies, Jawaharlal Nehru University, New Delhi.

J.N. DIXIT is a retired Foreign Secretary and was India's Ambassador to Afghanistan. He is a well-known author and commentator.

V.P. DUTT is a former Professor of the University of Delhi and Member of Parliament. He is a prolific author and a pioneer of Chinese studies.

SALMAN HAIDAR is a former diplomat who retired from Indian Foreign Service in 1997 as Foreign Secretary. He is currently associated with the Academy of Third World Studies, Jamia Millia Islamia, and also with the Centre for Research in Rural and Industrial Development, Chandigarh.

NIMMI KURIAN is Associate Research Professor at the Centre for Policy Research, New Delhi.

JAGAT S. MEHTA is a doyen of former diplomats. Foreign Secretary. Since retirement as a Foreign Secretary in 1979 he has been active as a teacher, commentator and an author.

SHRI PRAKASH is a Professor at the Academy of Third World Studies, Jamia Millia Islamia, New Delhi.

ACHIN VANAIK is a Visiting Professor in the Department of Political Science, University of Delhi.

HARI VASUDEVAN is a Professor at the Academy of Third World Studies, Jamia Millia Islamia, New Delhi.